PRAISE FO
SPIRITUAL BUT NUT RELIGIUUS

It is important to have people that can dwell in the rich complexity of human life, and then guide with nuance to the heart of it. To simplicity. To spiritual path. To flow. Catherine and Gil do this — integrating tools, stories, dreams, orientations, theories, questions, and their lives. They guide and encourage life in the mystery — this is so needed today.

—*Tenneson Woolf, co-founder, Fire and Water Leadership & Rite of Passage Journey. Author of* Most Mornings *and* A Cadence of Despair.

* * *

In these days of spiritual awakening and decline in church attendance Catherine and Gil's book is an excellent resource for both spiritual seekers and faith communities searching for new ways to meeting spiritual needs. Their years of leading Wisdom's Way Interfaith School and pilgrimages to Ireland has given them authentic background material on which to draw.

—*Jeanette Renouf, PhD., D.Min., founder of three schools of spiritual direction as well as Tacheria Interfaith Spirituality Center, Tucson, AZ.*

* * *

Packed with stories of spiritual experiences and wisdom from people who have left religion behind in favor of a spirituality that defies labeling, *Walking with the Spiritual But Not Religious: Spiritual Companions for a Post-religious World* demonstrates how seriously spiritual guides and companions must take the spiritually independent. Each of Catherine and Gil Stafford's stories illustrates a sacred way of hearing, welcoming and responding to the Spirit as it shows up in people who have left traditional religions far behind. If your work involves holy listening, you need to encounter these stories. They will challenge you from the past and into the future.

—Teresa Blythe, founder of the Phoenix Center for Spiritual Direction and author of *Spiritual Direction 101* and *50 Ways to Pray*.

* * *

Catherine and Gil, "Pilgrims of the Spiritual Quest" who are spiritual and non-religious, have given us an exceptional book focused on healing the soul. Using the pilgrimage way as direction, they tell their own stories and the stories of others who have rejected contemporary religion, as they companion them in their spiritual quests. With (W)Holy Listening and The Circle Way as their ground, they explore spiritual practices that will enhance those companions on their quest. They write with deep clarity and understanding about practices they themselves have experienced, such as the Enneagram, dream work, creation of rituals, personal narrative writing, ally work. This is a fascinating and valuable book for all of us who are spiritual directors/companions in this "Post-Religious World."

—*The Rev. Dr. Frank R. Williams, Board President, Tacheria Interfaith Spirituality Center*

* * *

Catherine and Gil are master storytellers who have woven a unique and precious tapestry of wisdom and practices gleaned from the exquisite art of holy listening and full-hearted engagement in the mystery of life.

* * *

WALKING WITH THE SPIRITUAL BUT NOT RELIGIOUS

SPIRITUAL COMPANIONS FOR A POST-RELIGIOUS WORLD

CATHERINE A. STAFFORD

GIL W. STAFFORD

APOCRYPHILE
PRESS

Apocryphile Press
PO Box 255
Hannacroix, NY 12087
www.apocryphilepress.com

Copyright © 2022 by Catherine A. Stafford & Gil W. Stafford
Printed in the United States of America
ISBN 978-1-958061-09-1 | paper
ISBN 978-1-958061-10-7 | ePub

Please join our mailing list at www.apocryphilepress.com/free
We'll keep you uptodate on all our new releases,
and we'll also send you a FREE BOOK. Visit us today!

CONTENTS

For our spiritual directors:
Ruth Wiles, Elizabeth Cummins, Amanda Peterson,
Michael O'Grady, Scott Haasarud, Al Marcetti,
and all our many beloved companions.

ACKNOWLEDGMENTS

Our companioning journeys began with our families who sculpted within our hearts the beauty of storytelling and deep listening. For all those conversations around the dinner table where ideas were explored, and we were encouraged to keep pursuing more.

For the countless brave vulnerable conversations with so many companions who shared their hearts and souls searching for the deeper wisdom of their journeys.

Publisher John Mabry who put his trust in our proposal bringing our words and work to life. And Editor Janeen Jones who offered invaluable corrections, additions, and clarifications to hone the words into a cohesive offering.

The women who attended the Arizona Council of Grandmothers gatherings where ancient wisdom, compassionate listening, confidential circle agreements, asking for what you need and offering what you can were woven into tending for the well-being for all who came.

Christina Baldwin who creates the dance of teaching and storytelling with compassion, expertise, and wisdom.

The "Soul as the Source of Story Writer's Circle" who held non-judgmental learning space to support the writing process.

Tacheria Interfaith Spirituality Center Board who embraced the vision of Wisdom's Way Interfaith School providing opportunities for spiritual growth and companionship for those seeking wisdom in the world.

Wisdom's Way Interfaith School pilgrims who journeyed

together honoring The Circle Way practices and holding brave, safe space for each other.

Joanne Priest who created a soulful mandala spoken by Spirit into her imagination and drawn by her hands for our book. (wisdommandalawhispers.com)

For Cathy who had the courage to do what everyone warned against—writing a book together.

To Gil whose unwavering encouragement helped to reveal the writer within Catherine.

And we must never forget our muses, allies, and guides who spoke into our imagination, dreams, and words bringing new insights to our companioning work.

INTRODUCTION

Words are just words.
Beliefs are just beliefs.
At best, they are pointers to the real.
—Jeffrey J. Kripal

M ax's text read, "A mutual friend recommended you. I don't have any religious background, but I've had an experience I can't make sense of. Could we chat over text?"

I wrote. "Sure. Tell me about your experience."

"Paranormal, maybe? My mom died. Now she's talking to me."

"In your dreams? Or while you're awake?"

"Awake."

"What'd she say?"

"Be careful."

"What'd you think she meant?"

"Not sure."

"Is there something you should be wary of?"

"You mean like everything in the world?"

"Indeed. But more specific. Like your personal life?"

Walking with the Spiritual But Not Religious takes a fresh look at being a spiritual companion for those who self-identify as something other than religious—SBNR, Nones, not religious, agnostics, atheists—who have experienced something unexplainable, and those who have encountered the paranormal (religious or otherwise). Life is a pilgrimage and the two of us have walked mountainous trails with those who are rapidly becoming the most identifiable slice of Americana's spiritual landscape. We have sat in coffee shops, pubs, and in our living room providing a listening ear and open heart, the mutuality of (W)Holy wisdom listening. We have practiced being spiritual companions for years via text, phone, email, Skype, Zoom, FaceTime, and face-to-face. We have been wherever we are needed to hold safe and brave space.

Max's text led to multiple Skype conversations. After a year, Max suggested we meet for coffee and we continue to connect regularly. The topics roamed the kaleidoscope of spiritual companion relationships: walking foggy paths of uncertainty, climbing breath-sucking mountains, enduring cold rain and whipping wind, all the while trusting the intuition. Max never took a walking pilgrimage with us. In fact, most of our spiritual companions have never walked pilgrimage with us. We have, however, "walked the pilgrimage way" with those trying to navigate their spiritual path while dealing with life's everyday hills and valleys: choosing a career, changing careers, losing a job, looking for community, making decisions about whether you want a life partner or who will be your life partner, leaving your life partner, death of a life partner, parent issues, older parent issues, children, no children, the grief of not having the children you wanted but couldn't have, illness, the fear of death, dying. We've also walked with those who have experienced something that defies their worldview and their words to describe what happened—the mystical, paranormal, and weird.

We have walked many of these pilgrimages ourselves and with others.

Spirituality is itself a pilgrimage, a quest, to explore the mysteries of life. Who am I? What is reality? What is happiness? What is consciousness? Religion, on the other hand, is a transaction between the institution and its followers: keep the dogma, practice the rituals, and in turn the religion will guarantee a better life on earth that leads to a positive afterlife. As pilgrims of the spiritual quest, we did not set out to create rules, establish a specific practice, or create a community for the spiritual but not religious. We have simply lived the pilgrimage life— a long walk of companionship, mutually seeking wisdom, asking questions, listening soulfully, focusing on healing the soul.

Max, like many of our spiritual companions, could loosely be described as spiritual but not religious. A growing populace who "constitute a quiet but radical rejection of religion in all its dogmatic and dangerous forms"[1]—those who are not in search of "the" truth but who instead desire a reality of lived experiences with the divine, in whatever form the divine is experienced. Research continues to produce global evidence that increasing numbers of people self-identify as not spiritual but not religious. This growing phenomenon exists not only in Western culture, but broadly in the East as well.[2] Interestingly, the SBNR are often written about as if they are a recent phenomenon. They are not. For example, in early nineteenth-century America, the Transcendentalists began searching for the intersection of science, nature, and the spiritual experience— something American Protestantism could not or would not embrace. Influenced by Emanuel Swedenborg and Jacob Boehme, Transcendentalism brought together poetry, the art of the novel, and social justice under the umbrella of individual experience grounded in community. Ralph Waldo Emerson, Henry David Thoreau, Margaret Fuller, Louisa May Alcott, and George Ripley were early devotees of yet another experiment in being spiritual but not religious. The threads of their thought remain in the spiritual fabric.

Categories, though, can be off-putting, particularly for those intentionally choosing to live outside the religious marketplace. Self-identifying as not religious can be frightening for those who are questioning their religion, uncertain if they should or could walk away. From our experience, though, the not religious are:

- like Max, who have no religious background, are possibly agnostic, but have an interest in some form of spirituality;
- or were abandoned by their religion, because of gender, sexuality, divorce, political views, or a host of other differences (or "sins" as determined by their religion), but still hunger for the spiritual life;
- or have left their religion for any number of reasons (including those above), never to return, yet still long for a spiritual experience;
- or are agonistic, ambivalent about God, and uncertain about the spiritual;
- or are atheist, with or without a religious background, yet have had an experience, possibly through meditation or some paranormal experience, which eludes description;
- or some combination of the above;
- or some other reason, known or unknown, conscious, or unconscious.

Most of the self-declared SBNR we have met, regardless of why they have arrived at this conclusion, have each shared a desire to live a spiritually authentic life. "Religion is belief in someone else's experience, spirituality is having your own experience."[3] But we have also listened with open minds to those who are curious because they have had an experience that has eluded their explanation. We believe our role as spiritual companions is to offer a space safe for our companions to become "brave"[4] enough to explore the significance of their experiences, spiritual or otherwise. This is the reason we have included experiences with the paranormal into our definition of the spiritual. Safe space feels soft and is free of judgment and unwanted advice. Brave space is strong enough to preserve the circle when harsh truth is spoken. Together, safe space and brave space fan the flame of spiritual dynamics.

Such a spirituality can appear elusive in the contemporary world where bits and pieces of the truth can simultaneously be everywhere and nowhere—a world where religions are dialethic, both true and false at the same time. Though resisting an intellectual definition, an experience of the divine can be unearthed on the pilgrim's labyrinth, where the ground of indelible authenticity is experienced through an apprenticeship of poetic wisdom, a transmutation of personal reality that is spatial rather than temporal.

There is a plethora of books about the spiritual but not religious. There are few written while living among them, as do the authors of this book, who also see themselves as not religious. While we have spent most of our lives living in the religious world, after years of spiritual struggle and theological deconstruction we walked away from traditional religion. We have rewritten our personal spiritual narratives. While some of the stories of our religious past still inform our personal myth, the dogma of our past tradition no longer drowns out our voices. You'll hear more about our pilgrimage throughout this book. Our purpose in writing *Walking with the Spiritual But Not Religious* is fourfold.

- First, we acknowledge our subtitle as reality: we are spiritual companions in a post-religious world.

Religion is prevalent but has lost its relevance. It can no longer unite; it only divides.

- Second, we want to create a safe and brave place for the not religious to explore their path—from where they are to where they want to be.
- Third, we want to delve into what it means to accompany someone who is not religious and not confined by religious language.
- Fourth, we want to share what practices we've learned along the way of being spiritual companions and what we've needed in our "backpack" to accompany the not religious.

WHO'S WRITING THIS BOOK?

As spiritual companions, we have walked our separate pilgrimages through professional careers in education and organized religion. Catherine is a seeker of Wisdom and a pilgrim of compassionate presence. Her journey has included being an educator for over thirty-five years as an elementary teacher, college professor, and finally a public-school superintendent. All along this trail, (W)Holy listening has been her practice. In 2012, she stepped off the public-school trail onto a new path leading her into the forests, fields, waterways, and sometimes deserts of interfaith spiritual exploration and companioning. She's a graduate of Tacheria Interfaith School of Spiritual Direction in Tucson, Arizona. In September of 2014, Tacheria supported Catherine and Gil in beginning a sister interfaith school in Phoenix, Arizona named Wisdom's Way Interfaith School, of which Catherine was the director until retiring in 2022. Wisdom's Way Interfaith School continues to operate under the non-profit auspices of the Tacheria Interfaith Spirituality Center. She has also completed advanced coursework for The Circle Way. Remembering the ancient social process of the circle, we welcome everyone into safe space to explore and find their own authentic way in the world. Our wisdom school has followed the process and practices of The Circle Way, providing a map for the journey.

Gil has spent his life working among young adults and the spiritual but not religious. He has worked as a college baseball coach, university president, and an Episcopal priest on the campus of a public university. He's a writer and a spiritual alchemist. Life is a pilgrimage and he has taken many, including walking Ireland coast-to-coast.

We've also made this journey as a married couple. As parents. Now grandparents. We know the taste of success and the bitterness of failure. Experience has formed and matured us, yet it has not given us the permission to tell anyone how to live their life. We do not have all the answers—few, in fact. Our questions mount every day. While this book is not a memoir, we are storytellers. Some names have been changed and personas hidden. Other stories, with permission, are told as is. No matter which is which, all stories are true. The storyteller? Our voices are our own: I, we, she, her, his, him, they, theirs, ours, one, yet two identifiable souls in their singularity. Many personae, one soul, yet still, many souls in separate persona. The creators of the *Matrix Trilogy*, Lana and Lilly Wachowski, developed the Netflix Original Series *Sense8*, through which they have given us a visual artistic rendering of the imagination of eight separate souls as one, each one still having their own distinctive persona. (More about the LGBTQA mind-bender television series later in the book.) Imagination is a vital ingredient for walking as a spiritual pilgrim with a spiritual pilgrim. Walking together can also bring some interesting relationship-stretching opportunities.

For us, writing a book together has been exciting and overwhelming. We have worked at telling our stories in a way that flows from page to page as if written by one author—while, most importantly, ensuring that the other's voice is heard as distinctly our own. From the beginning, our primary goal in writing together has been to do whatever is necessary to allow both voices to be heard clearly—while at the same time not distracting you, the reader, from the point of our book. In order to accomplish our goal, we've incorporated three writing techniques we believe have enhanced our storytelling.

1. Both our fingerprints are on every page and some of the stories and chapters will appear seamless. Here, we've used the pronoun "we."
2. At other times, we will identify who the writer is, primarily because it is the storyteller's story to tell. We might use third person or subheadings in these situations. In other situations we will start a conversation and let the storyteller take over, using the pronoun "I."
3. There are times when we have not identified who is telling the story, or who is in conversation with whom. We have told these stories in this fashion because either anonymity is needed and/or because both Catherine and Gil have had these conversations separately with their own companions. In other words, we've blended several stories into one.

Primarily, we are storytellers that have woven together hundreds of experiences. Because of that, the outline of this book is not necessarily linear, nor is it a progressive process that leads to a clearly identified destination. We have not intended our book to be encyclopedic. And while we relied on a significant amount of research we definitely do not want it to read as academic. We're in conversation with each other and with you. Your input is longed for because we don't have all the answers—this is a story in process. Honestly, we hope you'll write your own personal narrative as the sequel to this book. Along the way, we'll ask questions as prompts to help you get the writing juices flowing. Our desire is to encourage and inspire you with the stories of other people just like you, who have made this journey and written their own personal pilgrimage. Some folks may be well-known and others not so much. With permission, we have written some stories and names as they were told to us. For other stories, we have been asked to change the name but not the story. In yet other circumstances, we have blended several persons' stories into one.

We tell stories because, when possible, it's always nice to be able to check out the pilgrimage path before beginning. What's the terrain we're hiking? Is it going to be hot, or cold, or both all in the same day? Could it rain or even snow? How much water do I need to carry? We thought we'd give you a little tour before you start.

WHAT WILL YOU FIND IN THIS BOOK?

This book can be something you can throw in a backpack. It's not intended to add additional weight; instead, the book itself can act as a spiritual companion. Your own personal wisdom guide filled with techniques for your personal spiritual care. The techniques are inclusive of the physical rituals, the pluriverse of spiritual practices, and the broad umbrella of the paranormal. Among other practices we'll explore are deep listening, The Circle Way, dream work, various forms of meditation, building rituals, and walking the labyrinth while incorporating the Enneagram. *Walking with the Spiritual But Not Religious* is based on our lives and work as spiritual companions. Everything we suggest, we have tried. The stories we tell have emerged from our experiences of going on pilgrimage, leading retreats, teaching in our wisdom school, and sitting face-to-face in (W)Holy wisdom listening sessions. Every story told was an actual event, though the names and circumstances may have been changed.

Pilgrimage is an important reality and metaphor for our life. We truly live our lives as a pilgrimage—one pilgrimage comprised of smaller pilgrimages, each interwoven into the next. And we have walked our pilgrimages alongside others. But the pilgrimage of life most often has nothing to do with walking. We've accompanied companions in finding their way through relationships, issues with parents, parenting struggles, career changes, job loss, illness, dying, and death. We have been spiritual companions for dozens and dozens of people suffering through the trials of life while living outside institutional religion. And we've learned countless lessons from their stories.

We've learned from the not religious by listening to them. What does it mean to be a (W)Holy integrated listener, a wisdom listener? We've included stories of the transformational power of the mutual relationship of being a spiritual companion. We will discuss how the spiritual companion listens with their mind, body, soul, and spirit. We'll cover the technique of asking open-ended questions. And the importance of only giving advice when it's asked for. We'll talk about how to model wisdom listening for use in everyday conversations with our family, friends, and colleagues.

Can the spiritual but not religious find a community to walk with them on their spiritual pilgrimage? And if they can't, how do they build their own? The Circle Way will be our guide for practicing life as a community. And we'll share real life examples of how The Circle Way has been implemented by us and some of our students in the formation of circles.

Many of the companions who are not religious are familiar with meditation, contemplation, and mindfulness. While similar, these are not identical practices. We will begin chapter six exploring the difference between these techniques and how and when to use them most effectively. We will then build upon meditation, contemplation, mindfulness, and Carl Jung's Active Imagination as the foundation for "Inspired Imagination," a trance experience that leads to an altered state of consciousness, whereby encouraging the inner artist to splash color, words, and images into the personal narrative. Inspired imagination is taken from the Celtic Bard's practice of *imbas forosna*, the artist's trance that connected them to the muse, the spirit. While you may not consider yourself an artist, writer, poet, or druidic bard, we all are the storyteller of our inspired life. The artist's trance can open the portal to discover our True Self, the protagonist of our personal narrative.

The Enneagram is an excellent personality discovery tool. But more than that, it is a model for understanding the ever-emerging world of higher consciousness. The Enneagram is not a flat one-dimensional nine-pointed star designed to pigeon-hole our personality into one particular "number." Instead, the Enneagram is a multidimensional sphere or series of spheres that encompasses the imagination to help reveal the past, present, and future as Now.

The ancient path of the labyrinth is a living laboratory for the spiritual growth process and a metaphor for our spiritual experience. Walking the labyrinth is an integrated practice, which incorporates the mind, body, soul, and spirit. The labyrinth is more than a serpentine path within a one-dimensional circle—it can also expand the imagination into a multi-dimensional, even spherical journey. We'll blend walking the labyrinth with our understanding of the Enneagram, Inspired Imagination and having conversations with those walking in the beyond.

Dreams are stories from our personal unconscious that can illuminate our waking world: the past, the present, and the future. We'll examine the dream life as a living narrative of our life. Our dreams are pages and chapters of our personal story. We will explore the realm of both sleeping and liminal dreams. We'll talk about the power of dream journaling. How to interpret dreams. And the personal work of wrestling with our meta-phoric demons who are often found in nightmares. Who are these images who arise in the night of the "Midnight Sun" and what story do they tell us about our unconscious life and the conscious world we live in?

Do you feel like you're alone on your spiritual journey? Or maybe you feel like someone is walking with you but you're afraid to talk about it. Who are your allies in this troubling world? Are they spirit animals? Angels? Ancient guides? Dead relatives? Who walks with you and who can be your Ally in the unseen world? Ally work is an ancient practice that can be incor-porated into our everyday lives.

Without a religion to rely upon, the not religious are often left trying to figure out how to create meaningful rituals for life in community: marriage and commitment ceremonies, open marriage ceremonies, naming ceremonies, healing work, transi-tion rituals, death, and burial rituals. And who will preside over these ceremonies? We'll discuss how to create rituals as well as provide examples from our involvement in helping the not reli-gious to create and put rituals into practice.

The not religious may have left behind a religious tradition. Maybe they were abused, shunned, disappointed, disillusioned, or simply bored. Still, they feel a longing for a spiritual path—not a new religion, nor the remake of an ancient one. They often seek a connection where the ancient and the future meet. We'll explore with our readers how to artistically process and create their personal narrative.

TIME TO BEGIN OUR WALK TOGETHER

We've led several walking pilgrimages through Ireland's Wicklow Mountains with the young, the not so young, the spiri-tual, the not so spiritual, the religious, the irreligious. A few of them knew each other before we began walking, most did not.

But there's a bond built when pilgrims share a challenge together. The Wicklow Way is one hundred miles of rugged yet sublime terrain. The combination of a physical test set against the backdrop of an ancient dark forest creates the potential for magic.

The spiritual companion is a living backpack. We've walked among the pilgrims, sharing stories that made us laugh, cry, sing, scream, and walk in profound silence. We "live each other's death and die each other's life."[5] These shared experiences are the rare opportunities for the simultaneous transmutation of the storyteller and the listener. These mutual moments have expanded the boundaries of our spirituality. And still, these glimpses of the mystical have often left us aching for a language to articulate what has happened to us. We have had to learn how to become at ease with our own discomfort so that we might hold safe space softly, lightly, for others while they spiritually thrash about trying to find their own way. And we've wrestled around with the imaginal daemons probably more than they have.

Max and I were sitting under an ash tree. "I was reading this book about John Dee," Max said. "Dee was trying to communicate with angels. My mom's an angel now, so I thought I'd check it out. The author suggested an inverse Kabbalistic name for ALLA would be ALLALA, God is not, not.[6] That took me down the Internet rabbit hole into Plato, Pythagoras, Neoplatonism, Gnosticism, Kabbalah, Hermeticism, alchemy. Crazy stuff?"

"It's called spiritual alchemy or negative theology. God is the absence. God is the silence."

"I've never heard God talk. Have you?"

"You've heard your mom speak from the dead."

Silence. Max stared into the tea leaves at the bottom of his cup.

After a bit, I continued. "Dinah has Prader-Willi Syndrome, she's neurodivergent. When I ask her a question, she says, 'I not, not know.' I used to think she didn't have an answer. But maybe she was talking about God? Maybe God is not, not. The absent God is where God is not seen, not heard, not felt, not experienced. God in the absence is maybe God's shadow? Or maybe the Presence of the Cosmos?"

"I not, not know," quipped Max.

Later that night, I blinked at Max's text. "Do you think I'm crazy?"

"No. But I see a therapist for my depression."

"I like what you said this afternoon about depression. What was it?"

"Inspired melancholy, a holy madness both Plato and Aristotle mused could lead to divinity."

"So, you think a therapist could help me become a god?" Max laughed.

"Probably not. But if they do, let me know. I might want to give them a try."

Spiritual companionship is a lifestyle of listening, holding in wonder—a way of being in the world, sometimes a mystery, other times a dream. Like seven spiraled pilgrimages, layers of process: mine, theirs, ours. Always asking what's next on the spiritual path?

CHAPTER ONE

WALKING WITH THE SPIRITUAL BUT NOT RELIGIOUS

Religion is for people scared to go to Hell.
Spirituality is for people who have already been there.
—Bonnie Raitt

"You ever thought about creating an app for the mystically curious? Like, if I wanted to text a mystic. Say, a question about something paranormal, something really weird. Otherworldly. What do you think?"

"Sounds cool."

"No. I meant you. Will you create an app for the mystically curious?"

"I don't know anything about creating apps."

"That's the easy part. That hard part is you being on the other end, or someone like you."

"I'm not a mystic."

"I'll ignore that."

YOUNG CONTEMPLATIVES

When a group of "Young Contemplatives" attending the Spiritual Directors International Conference were asked, "What do you consider to be the spiritual issues of our times?" None of the twelve mentioned anything about religion or church, temple, synagogue, or mosque. What they "craved" was a mystical experience, and a wise and well-prepared spiritual elder who could help them unpack the weird and the paranormal. The dozen millennials also agreed that capitalism and individualism are major issues in Western culture, as well as a lack of accessibility into the institutional circle of decision making. They said their own generation has a "total denial of limits," while paradoxically having an aversion to pain, grief, and discomfort. Their contemporaries, the contemplatives said, are searching for new ways to claim who they are as spiritual beings. When asked what spiritual practices they incorporate into their daily lives to support themselves through their challenges, their responses included empathy for others, self-care, music, meditation, the act of presence, being in conversation with the dying, embodied practices like yoga, social justice, deep listening, and "anything spiritual."

The Young Contemplatives may be yearning for what religious historian and philosopher Jeffrey Kripal calls a "new imaginaire," through which yet unseen spiritual worlds may emerge —spiritual concepts that are searching for a revisioning of the interpretations of evolution, the paranormal, the paraphysical, and the extraterrestrial. New ideas will emerge that Kripal says will yield a "deeper spirituality of transcendent consciousness" and the "enlightenment of the body."[1] The "imaginaire" of these realities is already emerging at the intersections of quantum biology and epigenetics:

Sophisticated revisioning of evolutionary theory in light of epigenetics (the study of how environmental factors, including presumably social and religious practice, can switch on and off particular gene expressions) and the quantum biology of extraordinary natural phenomena, like the eyes and beaks of migratory birds using quantum processes to "see" and "read" the geomagnetic field in order to navigate across the globe.[2]

Spirituality is the exploration of the mysteries of life, asking "big questions" without the expectations of pre-prescribed answers with the historical baggage of religion. Our examination of the ultimate questions of life posits the potential for what Kripal defines as "secular mysticism," which exists outside the confines of religion.[3] The practice of secular mysticism leads us into the new imaginaire where we might envision an inclusive panentheistic spirituality, one that might alter how we understand our relationship with the ecosystem. We ask ourselves: How do I claim who I am as a spiritual being? What is embodied integration? What is spiritual reality? What is consciousness? What is the presence of unconsciousness? No questions go unasked.

MYSTICS IN COMMUNITY

Marcus is tall and trim. He wears gold rim glasses that extenuate his silver glitter eye liner. He was wearing blue nail polish on that particular day. The tattoo on his right forearm represented his journey for inner peace. He has been on a spiritual quest from the days of his earliest memories. He tried hallucinogenics, chant, yoga, Eastern Orthodoxy, Christian liberalism, Wicca and Faery traditions, tarot, magic, and Druidry. The one constant has been his desire to find a community that will accept him for who he is as a spiritual being the wisdom of the amalgamation of his life experience.

"Do you know of any communities?"

"Like?"

"You know...the elusive collection of misfits who love ritual and liturgy and copious amounts of incense and singing bowls and chanting and laughing and storytelling and the orthodoxy of living. That community."

"Nothing comes to mind. Well, recently I did spend two awesome days with some Kabbalists—rabbis, cantors, and rabbinic pastors who are working for the transformation and renewal of Judaism. They've formed an organization they call OHALAH."

"What's OHALAH mean? Is that a Jewish word?"

"It's the Jewish acronym for the name of their association."

"Where did you meet them?"

"A mutual friend suggested to one of their organizers that they invite me to their annual conference to talk about pilgrimage. But after joining them at the morning prayer service and then a period of meditation, we started talking about what it means to be transformed, transmuted. The conversation turned into a series of meditation and contemplation sessions. I've sat with lots of people in silent group meditation, which has a nice vibe. But I had never experienced anything before like meditating with these folks. The energy was so intense I felt like I was levitating. I swear, I know this person across from me rose off the chair they were sitting on."

"Where do I sign up?"

"There was only one person at the conference who was from Arizona, and they've since moved out of state. I've looked around and I don't think there's a group like them here. I'm sure you could go to their annual conference. They were extremely hospitable."

"I've rarely seen you so animated," Marcus said.

"I've been thinking about going back next year. I have so

many questions. But simply being in meditation with them is a mystical experience sufficient to sustain me for a long time."

"Have you ever thought about creating an app for the mystically curious."

"No. And I don't want to."

"Hit a button, huh."

"No. I just keep getting asked that question."

"I just searched the App Store for the mystically curious and I got 'No Results'. Could be a wide-open field."

"No one's interested in such a thing—that's why it doesn't exist."

"Just saying."

The Kabbalists have a saying that if anyone declares themselves a mystic, then their parents should kill them.[4] While we wouldn't want to cause anyone to break the sixth commandment, we can understand the sincere admonition against the self-proclaimed mystic, prophet, guru, shaman, holy person, whatever. We've been witness to more than enough crime and abuse committed by religious leaders in God's name and that's not even considering cults. But when the Young Contemplatives who attended the Spiritual Directors Conference said they wanted "wise and well-prepared spiritual elders," what exactly did they mean?

FUELING YOUR SPIRITUAL EVOLUTION

Chiron appeared as wise as their name might connote a very fluid person in both appearance and speech. Very poignant in presence; maybe it was the wheelchair. Their words were delivered like an axe against an icy wall: intentional, precise, swift, and ironic.

"Have you read Maggie Nelson?[5] Doesn't matter. She uses the term 'spiritual cripple.' Not in defining her belief or disbelief in God, but her willingness to wrestle with the question of God.

I love Nelson's work. In the midst of her own depression, Maggie's mentor suffers a tragic bicycle accident, leaving her beloved friend a paraplegic. Like me, except mine was a misstep off a rock climb. Anyway, Maggie spends days, weeks, months helping nurse her mentor, her friend, back to life, a new normal. Reading Nelson strikes an obvious chord with me, forces me to revisit my musings about God. I wonder: If there is a God, that God must be sitting in a wheelchair, like me. The Disabled God.[6] I need a God who is embodied in this body. A posthuman body. Have you read Katherine Hayles? It doesn't matter.

"I don't have any use for religion. Not after my accident. The religious said trite and hurtful things. Always the dualistic motif: God equals good. Satan equals bad. But what about bad things happening to good people? Come on, God created the tree of knowledge of good and bad—both exist on God's behest. There's a balance, a yin and yang. Right? God perfectly disabled; the good suffered bad."

I half said to myself I'd have to wrestle with Chiron's convincing argument of God being both good and bad.

Chiron smirked and went on. "Been wondering a lot about artificial intelligence. There's a ton of research with implications for the disabled. It's one thing to imagine body part replacement, but what about placing my mind in a cyborg? Transformed from crippled life to an infinite life inside a machine. Heavy stuff. Have you read Philip K. Dick? He's your contemporary. Okay, boomer. No offense. Well maybe. Anyway, have you read the *Exegesis of Philip K. Dick*? It doesn't matter. Well, maybe it does? Have you?"

A thoughtful response is sometimes trapped in space yet absent of time. Chiron is not asking a yes or no question. Have we read Maggie Nelson, Katherine Hayles, Philip K. Dick, and *The Disabled* God by Nancy Eiesland?[7] Chiron is asking what fuels our spiritual evolution. Are we versed enough in queer theology, disabled studies, and posthumanism? Not to respond but to hear at the level of equals.

Chiron invoked a space of mutuality. Our internal work affected by their work. Chiron handed us some heavy stones for our pack. "Take nothing literal," George Gurdjieff advised. Much, if not all, is a metaphor. Literal or metaphoric, permanent or transient, everyone travels life's pilgrimage: walking, climbing a cliff, or rolling a chair. We want to ask the big questions, the questions that matter when nothing else does. Where's the community that will let me sit in circle with them: no judgment, no back talk, no correcting or fixing. Where's that community?

What is Chiron asking? Who are the people the young contemplatives are looking for? The well-prepared wise elders. In the twenty-first century, what does it mean to be well-prepared? And wise? For wisdom is earned the hard way and never self-proclaimed. True wisdom is only offered in small doses, and only given when asked for. Maybe the Mystic's App is not such a bad idea.

SPIRITUAL RADICALS

The Young Contemplatives at the SDI convention were brave to take questions from a room full of boomer spiritual directors. After the third question, I realized that the elder spiritual companions were only going to tell their own stories, regardless of the question. Their ramblings had little to do with millennials other than to suggest that the cravings of the "youngers" were perceived as no different than those of the "olders." None of the boomers who spoke made any suggestions about "new ways to claim who we are as spiritual beings." I wondered why not.

In an article entitled "Spiritual Radicals," published by *Spirituality and Health*,[8] a multi-generational group of diverse "spiritual trailblazers" were asked, "What's next in the future of spirituality?" Of the seven, three are Christians, one Jewish, and one Muslim. One is Interspiritual and uses yoga and self-aware-ness to help people step outside their own community to support others. And the sixth person is a scientist, Oxford-trained philosopher Emily Qureshi-Hurst, who said, "I'm not any closer to having a faith." Yet she was the only one of the six to provide "new ways to claim who we are as spiritual beings."

Qureshi-Hurst presents us with an intriguing allegory:

Imagine a glass bottle on the beach. It breaks into a few pieces and can easily be put back together. But then the pieces are swept up in the waves. Over time the pieces become smaller and smaller and distributed over a wider area.

The disciplines within academia are like the glass bottle that has been rolled in the tides.... Everything from mathematics to metaphysics stems from the same basic inquiry—the same orig-inal glass bottle.

As the edges of the sea glass become smooth... so too do the boundaries of theology and science. What once fit easily together now seems like it never could have been part of the same larger whole.

Qureshi-Hurst, who at one time was in the same camp as Richard Dawkins and Sam Harris, concludes her allegory by saying, "I hope there will always be those of us who walk along the beach picking up and reuniting that which the years have torn asunder. After all, how else could we come to know the rich and complex reality in which we live?" Her parting thought is, "There might be certain religious claims that don't fit with science, and there might be certain scientific theories that don't fit with particular interpretations of religion, but science and religion don't need to be in conflict."[9]

Qureshi-Hurst and physicist Anna Pearson collaborated on an article proposing the concept of "dependent salvation"—the notion that salvation occurs only in the human mind.[10] What they are exploring as the basis for this theology is an experiment supporting the quantum theory of indefinite causal order. In this experiment, "two operations A and B were shown to be in a superposition with regard to their causal order. Essentially, time, intuitively understood as fixed, flowing, and fundamental, becomes fuzzy."

In principle it is possible "for event 'A' to happen before event 'B' and for event 'B' to happen before event 'A'." Salvation is a future event that has already happened—it's a Philip K. Dick construct of anamnesis (sacred memory) of the future that is scrolling back toward the already present now.

Qureshi-Hurst and Pearson quote physicist and Anglican priest John Polkinghorne (1930-2021). Gil had the great fortune to spend some significant time with Polkinghorne, who in 2002 had just received the Templeton Prize. His book, *Quantum Physics and Theology*, would follow shortly thereafter. Polkinghorne often argued that in quantum mechanics, "an element of hand-waving cannot be avoided, but the key thing is to try to wave one's hands in a suitably promising direction."[11] Qureshi-Hurst and Pearson are exploring the intersection of quantum mechanics, time, and theology in imaginative ways that can lead us into new ways of living as spiritual beings—a waving of the hand in a "suitably promising direction."

Quantum theories should be reserved for the experts; however, having a well-informed lay person's understanding is critical for considering the emerging spirituality of the twenty-first century. The Copenhagen interpretation states that "a quantum state does not take on a distinct property until that property is measured and the probability wavefunction of the quantum collapses." This theory posits the potential that "physical reality depends on being observed or measured to take on any particular state." What that presents to us is the stunning idea that consciousness is at the center of quantum theory.[12] And Kripal says that quantum physics resonates with mystic aesthetics. Quantum theory, consciousness, and mysticism in the same sentence. Whew. With the new physics will arise "new metaphors, new images, and new comparatives...the impossible becomes possible."

One startling example is telepathy, which is often dismissed by the rational and the religious as well. Entanglement theory posits that once two particles have interacted they are "entangled" and will always be connected no matter where they are in the universe. "Space and time are both irrelevant, and communication is instant. Quantum reality, in a word, is nonlocal." Kripal imagines that entanglement theory presents the possibility that communication between "entangled loved ones is not only plausible but predictable."[13]

Catherine and Gil have been married over fifty years and have on rare occasion shared a dream. We've also shared thoughts and ideas without having previously discussed what we were working on. That has helped us a lot in writing this book. Gil's sister, who has Prader-Willi syndrome, still talks to her deceased mother who died in 2012: Telepathic experiences with the living and the dead. These are personal experiences; however, there is ongoing research on similar telepathic phenomena.[14] But what other big questions could quantum thinking present for the spiritually minded?

WHAT'S NEXT

The Young Contemplatives have already been entertaining these questions and are responding with answers that are informed by science they can readily access. Mayim Bialik, neuroscientist, author, and actress on *Blossom* and *The Big Bang Theory,* and Yuval Noah Harari, author of *Sapiens* and *Homo Deus* discussed the current state of the world, as well as the future. Their 2021 mediated conversation has been shown on YouTube, a video which has had over 200,000 views. The dialogue between the two was lively, while an example of civility and respect.

Bialik is a Modern Orthodox Jew and Harari is a secular Jew.

While neither finds much of a home in the academic world, they both exert significant influence, particularly among millennials. Both advocate for scientific ethics and its influence on the future of the technological world. Bialik and Harari both agreed that science is never enough as an influencer of how people live, move, and have their being in the world. They were divided, however, on whether religion should have a role in the global conversation. Their discussion about faith centered on the concept of free will and whether it exists or not.

In his books, Harari, a historian, dismisses free will. For him, our brain predetermines human behavior before our body acts. Our behavior, says Harari, is dependent on brain algorithms. Bialik, a neuroscientist, argued that the human is infinitely more complex—it is not just a brain in a body. We function, she insisted, as more than a rational brain. There is a distinction, she said, between the brain and the mind, which is the interplay of neurobiology, the environment, and cultural influence. She went on to say that there is always individual human variability that defies the predictability in human behavior, even in the intersection of the mind and faith.

The connections between Bialik and Harari are many, but what defines them both is that they are excellent storytellers. People think in narratives, not necessarily in pure data. As humans, we relate to stories, understand the world through stories, and make decisions based on the stories that influence us. Storytelling must be at the heart of every meaningful encounter we have with family, friends, neighbors, allies, and enemies, but especially with the spiritual but not religious. For the story we tell today must find its narrative in the post-religious world envisioned by both Bialik and Harari. And these new stories may well be found at the intersection of quantum physics and spirituality.

INTERSECTIONS

Our spirituality can be influenced by our understanding of quantum physics. And in turn, then, our practice of spiritual companionship will be equally nuanced. To be present to our companion, fully in the now, is to actively imagine that which is yet to exist, but already is taking place in the time we have not observed. We may say in accordance with the quantum model noted above, that there exists the potential of the future scrolling backwards into the present. While the spiritual companion maybe doing excellent work in the now, they will always be working to listen with ears of wisdom, to ask more vulnerable questions, and to seek ways to help their companion uncover the hidden secrets of their dreams. The spiritual companion will encourage the "techniques of selfcare," the gathering of new tools, and the discarding of those that no longer have meaning. The goal of the spiritual companion is to be fully present, a presence that encompasses the past, present, and the future.

The art of the spiritual companion, soul craft, is never at the beckon and call of the practitioner. It is an acquired skill. Like magic that appears effortless, it only works after years of toil, training, rehearsal, and refinement. But suppose that what we hope to achieve has already been manifested in our mind—that is, the potential of the future that already exists. Our mind entangled in the mind of those who already have the wisdom and those who will have the wisdom. The spiritual companion that the young contemplatives are yearning for, those wise souls who know they know nothing but know everything they need to know to be present for those who seek their wisdom. To recognize that what could be, already is—to imagine new ways of claiming our authenticity is to claim who we already are as spiritual beings. This is the work of tapping into the eternal wisdom so that we can release its healing energy into the world.

"You have Netflix, right?" Eve asked.

"Yeah."

"You like the Wachowskis?"

"*The Matrix?*"

"Yes. But what about *Sense8?*"

"Fascinating stuff. Kind of quantum physics meets post-human spirituality," I said.

"Really. That's what you think?" Eve shook her head in disappointment.

"What's your take on *Sense8?*" I asked.

"It's a story about a transwoman written by transwomen. As a transwoman, I feel invisible, except when someone, usually a religious someone, wants to terrorize and traumatize me. Then I want to run away and hide. But with the Wachowski's coming out and telling their story, I feel, well, visible—in a good way. Validated as someone who is real and someone who can be loved, just for who they are. They're telling the story of the future now."

"I'm sorry you've had to suffer so. And I'm sorry I didn't acknowledge the personal connection for you in the *Sense8* story."

"That's okay. I agree the story is about quantum physics and post-human spirituality—but in *Sense8* the audience must be able to conceive of quantum physics and post-human spirituality entangled within queer theory. And those watching must empathize with the pain and trauma."

"Tell me more."

"Have you seen Amrou Al-Kadhi on TEDx?"

I shook my head. "No."

"You should check them out. Amrou is British-Iraqi, Islamic, and queer. Amrou discovered that quantum theory provided a model and language for the beautiful contradiction of the multiplicity of their identity. They even found a path back into Islam through the Quran and Sufism. I love the last line of Amrou's presentation. 'Bask in who you are, for in multiplicity there is magic.' It's a beautiful story. It's my story. Stories like Amrou's and *Sense8* give me hope. But must hope always be preceded by terror and subsequent trauma? And why is the agent of trauma usually done in the name of God? Or is God the agent of trauma?"

IS GOD THE AGENT OF TRAUMA?

"Dear Eve, I rarely follow up a spiritual companioning conversation via email. Obviously, I'm making an exception. Admittedly, then, this email probably has more to do with me than with you. Most of my ideas about trauma are the result of doing research for my book about my sister, Dinah, who has Prader-Willi syndrome—particularly the trauma that encircled our mother, Dinah, and God. To rephrase a Jungian analyst I've been reading, the God-image is traumatic.[15] Such a statement gives some psychological weight to Walter Brueggemann's theological idiom, "We believe in an irascible God, found in illusive texts, that requires polyvalent interpretations." In quantum terms, we can experience the image of God simultaneously as both loving and traumatic. How so? I don't know, but just the thought of that idea itself traumatizes me. But at the same time the trauma energizes my soul with an odd cold anger that I have needed to dare go on the quest for the answer. Thanks for being brave and visible."

Saying that we want to understand God is the equivalent of saying we want to understand consciousness. We do want to have a better comprehension of both. Maybe if we understood one we could solve the riddle of the other. But neither appears possible—comprehension or solving the riddle. Maybe the historical search for God has been identical to the modern search for the meaning of consciousness—two pilgrimages, same path. Strangely, though, the underlying meaning of the desire to understand God may be "provoked" by the trauma of encountering either the presence of God or the absence of God.

Is it God who is at the root of trauma? Or is the causation of the trauma manifested from the images of God that we've been handed? Either the absent God who doesn't answer our prayers or the all-too-present God that seems to have wielded the sword of destruction. What we need or desire the most feels absent, causing deep psychic pain. The absence itself, therefore, can shift the blame, and the subsequent trauma is ascribed to the God that allowed—or caused—the tragedy. The experience of the trauma of the God-image can be the "event we can visibly point to." To cry out as the biblical poet, "My God, my God, why have you abandoned me?" and allow this tragedy to happen to me. The absence is real and the trauma feels circular, like a never-ending loop. Can the closed circle of chaos that caused the trauma be transmuted into a spiral? Can the event that creates the psychic chaos open a portal onto the labyrinth where we might go on a pilgrimage to search out meaning, purpose, even consciousness?

Please don't hear us wrong. We are not romanticizing trauma for the sake of saving God. Nor are we diminishing trauma's terrorizing affects. We are not offering any sanguine platitudes. We are, however, encouraging the work of granting trauma a seat in our circle by not denying its prevalence in the human condition. We do not need to seek out trauma—it finds us in almost every aspect of life in so many ways—emotionally, psychically, physically, spiritually. But when it does come can we dare seek out what Jeffrey Kripal terms "the gift of traumatic secret." What is the traumatic secret? We don't know. But we imagine it to be different for everyone. Both of us are still searching for the hidden pearl buried in the vast field of life. Maybe it's the pilgrimage of seeking the secret that's the secret? Dinah, the one who has suffered from much trauma, often tells us, "I not, not know." She is a wise elder and our spiritual companion. In the "not, not" our pilgrimage still continues.

WHAT'S NEXT, NEXT?

We spend a lot of time pondering the unknown, which leads us into considering what's possible, what is the potential yet to be revealed, what is the secret's gift. Particularly, what lies ahead in the treatment of people like Dinah, who have Prader-Willi syndrome. Our imagination confronts us with the potential that syndromes like PWS may not exist in some not-so-distant future. Is that the next? How would Dinah be different if she did not have PWS? Would she be posthuman? Or superhuman?

Should we imagine being spiritual companion to superhumans, the posthumans that replace sapiens? Aren't superhumans just comic book fantasy? Not according to Harari, and not considering the scientific possibilities that already exist. The potential for designer babies could eliminate all types of genetic birth issues, including Prader-Willi syndrome. Genetic manipulation could extend life by eradicating cancer, Alzheimer's, and a host of other diseases. But with such advances comes the perpetual monitoring of the algorithms of our everyday thought, action, and life. And who will make the decisions that will lead science in the development of superhumans? The economic drive of human desire? We've already started down that road and every day we hand over more and more private information that influences what we buy and how we live. And who will determine the ethical implications of such decisions. Harari in *Homo Deus* posits that with new science arises the potential for the emergence of new religions. Will these new religions worship the designers of superhumans, or the superhumans themselves, or the science that extends and sustains life itself long beyond our current expectations? And what ethics will arise from these new religions? And will spirituality be able to stand alongside or act as an alternative to whatever new religious dogmas might attempt to regulate our lives and choices as they do now? These are the questions that provoked the Young Contemplatives yearning for wise guides. We may not know the answers, or think we'll live long enough to be impacted by any of these potential realities. But one of us may be the spiritual companion of someone who will one day find themselves in the center of the labyrinth of a dilemma brought about by a future scientific discovery, or by the constrictions of some yet unthought of religion.

The notion of new religions and superhumans may be so far-fetched or so far in the future that we feel these ideas are not worth our time. But what about the times we live in? The world is in chaos, awash in crisis: we are forced to live with new viruses that go uncontained, an environmental crisis that will soon be out of reach of any attempt to correct it, global economic insecurity, the abounding threat of nuclear self-destruction, and the collapse of institutions that used to be our source of comfort. Has modernity come to an end? Is/was post-modernity a thing? Many younger philosophical minds have suggested that the idea of postmodernity has failed us: all critique and no hope. Some have posited the start of a new era they've designated Metamodernity. Religious historian Jason Josephson-Storm has boldly proposed a new era of Metamodernism, an interpretation of the modern and postmodern, which will be the salvation of academic humanities, religion, and art.[16] Spiritual writer Brendan Graham Dempsey coined the term Metamodern Spirituality and claimed that it is "designed to facilitate the collective artful co-creation of a religion that's not a religion."[17] Today's spiritual companion must be willing to transmute the essence of their spiritual being before they find themselves facing a pilgrimage path they are ill-equipped to travel. To put it another way, today's spiritual director/companion must evolve or become irrelevant.

CHAPTER TWO

PILGRIMAGE: A WAY OF LIFE

When we strive to become better than we are,
everything around us becomes better too.
—Paulo Coelho

N eil and Gil had walked for six days in Ireland. The first three days they journeyed the Wicklow Way from Dublin to Glendalough. Then, they turned west and walked along Saint Kevin's Way. It's a long and poorly marked trail from Glendalough to Kildare, the home of the patron saint of Ireland, Brigid. After being soaked through and through for almost one hundred miles, they decided it was time to take the train back to Dublin and spend a few days as proper tourists. Devitt's, a quaint pub with a rich history, was near their B&B. Under various names and owners, the pub had held the same location for over two hundred years. The dark mahogany, the historic pictures, the family vibe, and the good food drew the two in more than one night. The pub was the perfect place for them to reflect on their pilgrimage, journal, and muse about future adventures. One Friday evening, as the locals and the tourists began to pour in, singles, groups, and families with children filled every space to sit or stand. The table for four next to Neil and Gil was overcrowded with a dozen twenty-somethings.

"Cheers! Americans?" said the young Irishman sitting shoulder to shoulder with Gil.

"Cheers and yes, we're Americans," Gil answered over the band that was warming up for their first session of the evening.

"What do you make of your current president?"

"Not much."

Everyone at their table lifted their glasses. "Sláinte!"

"Sláinte!" Gil and Neil responded.

"Tourists?"

"Kinda. We just finished a six-day hike in the Wicklow Mountains."

"Ya' did, now. Raining a bit up there, you know."

"Indeed."

"Get wet?"

"Drowned, more like it."

"Sláinte, to the forthright Yanks. No offense meant."

"Sláinte. None taken."

"Couldn't help but notice you're writin' in your book. You mind me askin' what about?"

"No problem. I'm taking notes, ideas, for a future book."

"What would your book be about?"

"A woman priest."

The young Irish woman who had been listening in turned to her mates. "Have you ever heard of such a ting?"

Her friends laughed and another raised his glass. "To all the tings we can only hope would be true. And to Americans bold enough to imagine such impossibilities." They all stood and raised their glasses. And we stood with them, raising our glasses as well.

"To the tings we can only hope would be true," our new friend said. "Cheers!"

"Cheers!"

Two of the guys from the table went to the bar for more drinks. Another to the toilet. Gil noticed the two at the bar were standing behind an American tourist. He couldn't hear what the tourist said, but he saw that their two table mates were wagging their heads. Then he heard the man behind the bar say to the tourist. "I'll not serve you Hennessy with ice."

The tourist raised her voice. "I'm the customer and I want Hennessy on the rocks."

"This pub is 200 years old. And I've been tending bar here for twenty years and I'll not serve you Hennessy with ice."

The tourist stormed off to her table, where she engaged her companions in a hushed conversation. A man got up from her table and stood at the opposite end of the bar. He spoke to the bartender, who was heard to say to the man, "And I'll not serve you a perfect good Hennessy so that young woman can ruin it with ice."

Neil and Gil's new friends stood in unison and raised their glasses to the bartender. "Sláinte!" The bartender ignored them. And the tourist and her friends who wanted ice in their whiskey stormed out of Devitt's. The two young men returned from the bar. One placed a Jameson in front of Gil, neat of course, and a pint in front of his companion.

"Thank you, but that wasn't necessary," Gil said.

The young woman who had initiated the conversation raised her glass. "You're very welcome here—you and your brilliant ideas written in your book."

Don't make too much of the assignment of our ideas as brilliant—the Irish cast the word about as much as Americans do the word "literally." Though the Irish don't attach a literal meaning to the word brilliant. Metaphors abound to the Irish. Telling you an idea is brilliant is their polite way of saying, "thanks for the conversation." To which the typical response to the compliment is, "no boter." As in, it's never a bother to have a meaningful conversation while hill walking.

WRITING AS A SPIRITUAL PILGRIMAGE

Writing is a pilgrimage. Hard work intertwined with a fleeting satisfaction: researching a subject, writing drafts, revising the drafts, editing the drafts, submitting query letters, book proposals, dealing with rejection. Lots of rejection. And writing is a drug—every day, all day, blurred nights, haunted nightmares, disappointed visions. Writing is a psychic explosion—exhilaration, melancholy, heavenly highs and hellish lows—chaos on a page filled with scribbles, arrows, and lineouts. Writing is a spiritual experience—all of it, the ugly and the sublime, the simultaneous experience of all the opposites. Why write? We are compelled to write. We write to save our soul. Writing is a living force within that will not leave us alone until we vomit our ideas onto a piece of paper. We call that force of energy the Muse. But she's more often a daimon—she's part god, part lusty lover. But what does the Muse whisper in our ears? What does she inspire us to write? Our life. What else? But we cry in response, "It's so dangerous to write about our life: vulnerable, raw, transparent." Are we writing about our life or is our life writing us? How did we become spiritual but not religious? We walked with the souls of the disappointed, rejected, abused, weary, and the bored. We wandered and wondered with them. We wrote about them. And we realized we were writing about ourselves. We had become who we already were. It's a circle. No, it's a spiral. No, it's several spirals on multi-dimensional levels. No, it's four spheres as one life. Two lives, side by side, interconnected at some in-between vague spirit space—timelessness when it flows—paranormal. Pain when it doesn't hurt. Want to walk with us? Pick up your pack and join us. Fair warning. Walking works blisters on the imaginal. But it's brilliant and definitely no boter.

The spiritual companion is constantly reminding us that we must "do our work."

"What do you mean by 'work'? As in: to walk, build, write, create?"

"Yes, it could be one of those. Or all of those. Or none of those."

"What does "our" mean? Could it be my work? Your work? Our work together?"

"Yes, it could. Or not."

"And what is work? Fulfillment or drudgery? Avocation or vocation?"

"Yes, it could be. Or not."

"You're not very helpful."

My work is my work. Your work is your work. No matter how you might want to define your work, it is your work. If I were to suggest even one possibility of what your work might be, your mind will dissect that specific suggestion as if you are for or against, building lists of pluses and minuses, holy minded potential for hidden meaning, discernment of potentials, reasons to celebrate or rage against. Do your work? Pick up your pack. Strap it on tight. But not too tight. You have to breathe. Lean forward. In a balanced sort of way. You will be walking up hills and down into valleys. Start walking when you're ready. Make sure you are on your own path and not someone else's. Ancients may have walked this way before, but the "souls" of your feet are now adding the footprints of wisdom to the trail. You'll probably get lost at some point. Lost is good, because then you'll have to get un-lost. No need to panic. You are surrounded by water. Sit down for a bit. Reimagine where you are and where you want to be. And then begin again.

"We don't like where we're at and who we're expected to hang out with."

"Where is this place you're at?"

"My family's religion."

"And why don't you like being there?"

"Too traditional. No. Too conservative. No. Fundamentalist. No. Unwilling or unable to reimagine. Not relevant."

"Drill down. Be more specific."

"Too many cis, white, straight dudes that are way too old. Too patriarchal. Too hierarchical. Not congruent with my worldview, which is socially progressive, racially diverse, non-binary, spiritually open."

"Deeper."

"Soul-choking."

"Okay. So what are you going to do about it?"

"Walk away."

"What does that mean?"

"Just not 'there.' We don't know. We haven't heard ourselves on that yet."

"Hmm."

"We're writing about it. Then we'll know."

"Okay. Is that 'doing your work?' What you write about is what you are and what you're becoming. Or am I missing something?"

"Not polite to be a smart-ass."

Writers write for the sake of making their soul. Writers do not write for the sake of being published. Seeing your work in print is an extra unexpected benefit, but not a requirement. Writing is not about sharing your beliefs. Beliefs are opinions and everyone has them. Writing is about putting your experiences on paper. Some to be shared. Some to be burned.

The process of writing—whatever you're writing—is the writing of your personal narrative, your work. You might scribble your work in a secret journal. Maybe you'll draw it on a blank piece of paper. Possibly paint your story on a canvass. Chisel it in marble. Collage it in a notebook. Mold it in clay. Carve it in wood. Weave a rug. Knit a shawl. Twine a twin. Tattoo it on your skin. Take a hammer to a stone. Walk the Way.

All is art. Life is art. And every piece of art we create is part of the process of prying the hands of the choker away from our soul. A process of light and dark, filled with chaos and synchronicity.

PILGRIMAGE INTO THE DARK NIGHT

The paradox of chaos and synchronicity is the capacious cauldron that holds the mystery of spirituality. A mutual friend recommended our Wisdom's Way Interfaith School—a two-year program devoted to expanding our spiritual presence and practice—to Amanda. She reached out to us and we agreed to meet her at a local coffee shop. She showed up with her wife, who is a transwoman. Amanda is a leader in the Faery Tradition. She practices witchcraft. Amanda would fit the stereotypical depiction of a faery: small, very large eyes, infectious laugh, wispy presence, here, yet not. We instantly fell in love with her. She brought her Self to Wisdom School and magically created her place in the circle. Her ideas were whimsical and imaginative. Her emotions empathic. Her life on display. Somewhere along the way, she asked Gil to be her spiritual companion. Of course he would. Amanda is such a fascinating person, what a pleasure to listen and learn from her as a spiritual companion—mutuality, a give/give relationship.

"Gil. Did you ever work at Banner Thunderbird hospital?"

"I was a chaplain there for a while. Even after I left, I was in and out of Thunderbird all the time."

"Did you ever go to the psych ward?"

"At times I felt like I lived there. And I loved it—the people and the experience were real and raw. The unknown of it. The chaos of it. The paradoxical sublime beauty of it."

"I doubt you'll remember this...twelve years ago, we met there...in the ward...I had tried to commit suicide...failed... obviously...asked the nurse to see a priest...I was a recovering

Catholic overburdened with guilt. A few nights ago, I had a dream about being in the hospital, back then. I had taken a puzzle piece I found in the common area, believing it to be the missing puzzle-piece of my life. The man in the dream told me to go back and read my journal about that experience. Who wants to read about a time in their life when things were so bad that they would try to hurt themselves? I tried to ignore the dream, but it wouldn't let go of me. So, I dug out my journal. There, next to the puzzle piece I had taped into the journal, it said, "I met Father Gil tonight. He told me I was okay. That it was okay to be a witch. And the only hell I would go to would be the one I created here on earth. And that the only God I needed was in me, myself, the true me. But, he said, if I wanted to hurt myself, no one could stop me. But he would sit here with me as long as I wanted, because I was worth it. When I left the hospital, I got sober. I was initiated into Faery. I met our mutual friend. And he introduced me to you and Catherine. I wouldn't be here if you hadn't been there in that hospital twelve years ago. And now I'm being a companion for other people."

We wept.

PILGRIMAGE WITH THE MOTHER TREE

Life is a series of chaotic and synchronistic spirals, each experience ascending and descending the tree of our life. There's an ancient tree just off the Wicklow Way near the Knockree Hostel (about 16 miles south of Dublin). Estimates are the rowan tree is well over 400 years old. A few of her children grow nearby. This particular tree has grown over a rectangular stone that is six feet long, two feet wide and over three feet high, creating a large opening in the base of the tree. Over the centuries, the opening in the tree became a vortex, high enough that a six-foot-tall person can stand upon the stone and disappear into the energy of the tree. What has become known in our circle as the

Mother Tree, appears as a holy temple for the wandering pilgrims along the way and the stone is her ancient altar. We've made several pilgrimages to this tree. She often whispers mystical stories to us. She never disappoints as she brings marvels to those who walk with us—those who have ears to hear, those who wish they did, and the skeptic alike. The mythic story of the tree is not a metaphor, nor an allegory, it is the truth of our collective network of eternal existence—belief not required, only experience.

Another hour of walking south on the Wicklow Way, past the Mother Tree, is Crone's Forest. Here stand Sitka spruce and Douglas fir and lurch trees. The trees are comfortably separated by natural means. Yet, at the points where their roots are exposed, they reveal a communal network. Forests talk and the trees rely upon one another for needed minerals. Tendrils reach out through the Irish black loam, finger tips touch, passing sustenance one to another underneath the forest floor. Walk slowly, they ask. We have stories to tell you pilgrims. Bandits, revolutionaries, and lovers alike once hid under our canopy. Protected, one and all. Without discrimination—wished-for gods who truly love without condition. Now, we the trees, are reminding you that this is your story, your myth, your reality.

FROM ERIK TO ELYSSA

Who am I? Why am I here? Where am I going? Questions we often associate with the young. And much too often we think of the spiritual but not religious as being an "issue" related to being young. "Once they grow up," some are convinced, "they will return to the faith of their family." Polls are proving that such wishful thinking is simply wrong. There are many reasons for religious exodus, but one we hear over and over is that organized religion has lost touch with the twenty-first century. Why? Because "who am I, why am I here, and where am I going" are no longer questions with simple answers that are reliant upon the economies of family, culture, or religion. Answers that include the considerations of non-binary queerness, multiracial birth, multiethnic family, and religious pluralism have dismantled the "book of answers," leaving mostly blank pages of what has yet to be written. There is no undoing what the course of human evolution has long been working towards. What we now need, says religious historian Jeffrey Kripal, is "an entirely new language, an 'imaginaire,' a new way of seeing the history of religions that is neither bound to the symbolisms and theologies of religious past nor hypnotized by our present technologies and military violences."[1] The only ones who can write this new language, write the new book, are just now coming into their own, or are just now learning to walk, or are just now not yet born. Our role is not to teach them how to think, or how to write, or what to write. The role of the spiritual companion is to walk alongside them, and when they ask us a question about how to think, how to write, or what to write, we must ask them back, "how do you think you think, how do you write, what do you want to write?" If such notions trouble you, or make you feel uncomfortable, or make no sense to you, or you think such thinking is the root of all the world's current problems, consider this: 1) the past is over and you can't go back, and 2) at the current rate of our global self-destruction, the human race is rapidly heading for self-extinction. Given that, it's time for a new language and a new imaginaire, but we must start now.

Erik dropped by Saint Brigid's Community, a Thursday evening gathering for young adults. "A friend of mine said you'd listen to me without judgment," he told Gil.

"I'll take that as a compliment. I will do my best to listen without judgment and I will keep everything I hear in utmost confidentiality. Unless you intend to hurt yourself or someone else."

"That's fair. Only a few of my friends listen without judgment. But my family judges me. My church judges me. The world judges me."

When Erik showed up that Thursday night, he was in his mid-twenties, had just graduated from college, moved to Arizona, and had started his career as a high school teacher. Putting it mildly, Erik is a genius, brilliant in languages, and a wonderful writer. He's also an introvert and deals with depression. We spent hours talking about family, work, writing and politics. Erik had already begun his pilgrimage away from orthodox Christianity.

He grew up in a fundamentalist Christian home. Then attended a conservative Christian college that brought with it questions he could no longer keep to himself.

"I knew all along I was an outsider, that I didn't belong; you can't suppress that forever. I understand now that I'm hardly alone."

More than philosophical questions, Erik's journey was one that carried the heavy weight of sexual abuse and a church that denied the trauma and damage it caused to a young child at the hands of a trusted leader. Erik's is the story of too many children, young people, and adults who have been subjected to abuse by those who were supposed to protect and care for them in the name of God. And this crime became more heinous when it was covered up by the church. Instead, the church ignored, or worse yet, turned on the victims, making them feel as if they were the cause of the pain inflicted on them by others.

"Christianity lost me because it messed me up and then blamed me for its own shortcomings," Erik said.

At Saint Brigid's, Erik had found a community that accepted him. Then he met someone he imagined he could spend his life with. But tragically, she died unexpectedly. He never had a chance to say goodbye.

"I had been a successful young teacher with a promising career ahead of me. But when my soulmate and best friend died, my mental health tanked, and in time my job and professional reputation evaporated."

His world was cast into chaos. During that time, Catherine and Gil had decided to walk the Wicklow Way that summer. Several members of the Saint Brigid's Community asked if they could join us. Erik signed up. After the pilgrimage, Gil invited him to tell his story in *Wisdom Walking: Pilgrimage as a Way of Life.* In that book, Erik wrote honestly about his life, frustrations, and particularly his perspective of Jesus and Christianity.

> I have learned that my guide has not been the fake Jesus of the Christianity I used to follow, the one who swoops in and picks up his followers whenever the trail gets rough. If my guide is Christ, it's the one who works in inexplicable and frustrating ways. Who shows up in the form of people whom the world doesn't recognize as Christian. He is Christ who has trained us. Now we have to walk. I imagine that he derives far more satisfaction from sitting atop the cliff, watching his protégés pick their way across rocky trails without an ounce of help from him. He said we have to carry our own cross. I wouldn't have Him, or Her, any other way.

After walking the Wicklow Way, Erik returned to Arizona for a year and then left for China to teach English for three years. Long before going to China, Erik had begun questioning his sexual identity. While in China, he began to acknowledge that Erik was Elyssa.

Elyssa has been sharing her story with us. As a teenager, "I didn't have the vocabulary to express the idea of being transgender, but I knew deep down I was different. I have to remind myself constantly that the point of transitioning wasn't to be trans, it was to be a woman, and the point of living as a woman isn't just femininity for femininity's sake but rather to be in touch with my authentic sake."

Elyssa returned to the States. She writes, supports the marginalized, and continues to pursue her vocation. While she has left Christianity, her spirituality is thriving.

"After weaving in and out of Christianity in its various forms for most of my twenties, I am now confidently and comfortably spiritual but not religious."

But what does that mean for Elyssa? "The important point I can't emphasize enough is that my spiritual but not religious affiliation is not laziness, lack of commitment, or low standards: it's a very challenging commitment to pursue truth, goodness, beauty, and holiness without nearly as much guidance as is available to conventional believers."

This is the comment we hear over and over again. And that's why we continue to do our work as spiritual companions. Elyssa wrote:

I suspect many religious people who want to understand the SBNR demographic would like to understand how we got this way—but more than this I know for a fact that many traditional believers already have lots of assumptions about people like me that are largely untrue. The biggest of them: that we aren't religious anymore because we didn't have enough faith. Nope. It's because life forced us to choose between faith and belief, and we chose faith without belief instead of belief without faith. Faith is trust; belief is a cognitive statement. I do not believe in Christianity's God; I do not think that the statement "the universe is ruled by an omniscient and omnipotent trinitarian deity" is factually true. I do, however, trust in a loving Creator.

Elyssa does have an "active relationship with the divine" that she experiences through being a "spiritual eclectic." An evolving faith engaging a "plural number of deities from the Celtic, Norse, and Greek traditions," and among them "the Cosmic Christ." Elyssa, however, has not abandoned the stories she learned as a child. Instead, she's re-incorporated them into her daily life with new values:

> They are, if anything, more valuable to me today than they ever were in Sunday school. Belief and facts were never the point. My quest is motivated by ethics, not information. None of the knowledge I've accumulated over the years counts for anything if it doesn't change how I relate to people.

Pilgrimage is a way of life for all of us. And while Amanda, and Elyssa, and Catherine, and Gil, and others who have traveled with us, all have walked a different path. Our relationships are at the heart of every story. And when we listen to each other, walk with each other, cry with each other, we become fellow pilgrims.

AFTERGLOW OR HANGOVER

We've walked and experienced so many wonderful pilgrimages. And we've experienced a few terrifying moments on those journeys. Every pilgrimage feels like it was built upon the previous pilgrimage. In 2012, our first grandson was born in February, Gil's mother Loretta died in March, Catherine retired in June, and then we spent six weeks in Ireland. Gil's pilgrimage was his and Catherine's was hers. Yet, they were and are intertwined. Each of those experiences—birth, death, retirement, walking, driving—were pilgrimages. And each pilgrimage was built upon the prior experience.

Our first grandson's birth was Loretta's first great-grandchild, the only one she would ever hold. And Gil would baptize the baby only days following her funeral.

Catherine's retirement was a beautiful, emotion-washed experience. In Gil's opinion, she was the beloved. Employees, students, and colleagues alike poured out their love and appreciation for her long service to the school district where she served as its superintendent. And within a few weeks we were in Ireland.

Gil walked almost 400 miles taking five different trails across the island of forty shades of green. And Catherine made her own pilgrimage driving on the "opposite side" of the tiny and sometimes treacherous roads of Ireland in a small car she named "Cocoon." Each pilgrimage informed the next by adding a hidden weight to the backpack carried on the subsequent trail. And each and every pilgrimage ended in the odd paradoxical feeling of a simultaneous afterglow and hangover, but together they brewed the aroma of a divinely inspired melancholy. Maybe it feels impossible to imagine finding an afterglow while holding the hand of a dying loved one. But without the alchemical blending of the afterglow with the hangover brought on by grief, we might miss experiencing the salty tears of the divine dripping onto our face. We both became awash with the blending of emotions we experienced holding Loretta's hand as she died, as we did when our grandson was baptized, and when Catherine was being publicly adored, and finishing the final mile of a dream pilgrimage across Ireland. Different pilgrimages, yet each subsequent experience informed the next. As if the past and the future were brewed into the present.

Walking the spiritual pilgrimage with anyone, the religious and the not-religious alike, can conjure those same dizzying pilgrimage feelings of afterglow and hangover—the afterglow experience of sharing stories of growth and enlightenment; the hangover experience of suffering, trauma, and grief; the realization that somehow the afterglow cannot be experienced without the hangover. The question is, who will faithfully walk the pilgrimage with those who are on the path that rejects religion as any part of their life? And how will that person prepare to be their spiritual companion?

CHAPTER THREE

THE PILGRIMAGE OF BECOMING A SPIRITUAL COMPANION

ORDINATION NOT REQUIRED

Let the beauty of what you love be what you do.
—Rumi

The ancient tradition of spiritual direction is one of companionship—soul friends in an intimate conversation. Brigid of Kildare, patron saint of Ireland, who established the first monastery that included women and men, said that a "person without a soul friend (*anam cara*) is like a body without a head." The Celtic monk Pelagius (354-418), whose progressive views on freewill and universal salvation were at the root of his being declared a heretic, wrote in his letters, "Indeed we each need a special friend who may be called the friend of the soul, hiding nothing and revealing everything." Hildegard of Bingen (1098-1179), Teresa of Avila (1515-1582), and Julian of Norwich (1342-1416?) were all venerated mystics of wisdom and soul friends. And because of their vast spiritual knowledge, mystical experience, and prophetic approach, they were often considered out-of-bounds by the Catholic Church.

The history of spiritual companions is not limited to Christianity. The Sufi mystic Rumi (1207-1273) is one of the most often quoted poets regarding spiritual friendship. In Judaism, long before the rabbinic tradition, people would seek wise counsel from a spiritual friend. Those intimate relationships are found in the Biblical stories of David and Jonathan, Mordecai and Esther, Naomi and Ruth, and Elizabeth and Mary. And the long tradition of spiritual companionship is also a significant component in traditions other than the three Abrahamic faiths. Author and spiritual director John Mabry, in his book *Noticing the Divine*,[1] provides an excellent introduction into the vast number of traditions that regard spiritual companionship as vital for the evolution of their religious experience. While there are many similarities within the practice of spiritual companionship among all these traditions, the most common is that the spiritual director should be well trained—but not necessarily ordained. This is Catherine's story: exemplary preparation, ordination not required.

EARLY LESSONS IN BECOMING A SPIRITUAL COMPANION

For as long as I can remember, I've always wanted to be a teacher. This desire has been an unquenchable flame burning brightly within me. It is born out of my insatiable curiosity and hunger for learning. The joy of the "a-ha" moments and the creative power to figure something out which was difficult or confusing fueled this passion. The way I could get lost in a book and travel to another time and place or be someone else was a refuge when life was chaotic at home. Then there were the gifts of people interactions and relationships stirring the cauldron of transformation.

Somewhere around third or fourth grade I began "playing school." I was the teacher. Creating a school environment for my playmates became one of my favorite pastimes. The kitchen table and carefully placed chairs became their desks; handwritten worksheets copied from my own school experiences were their work. My lessons were a repetition of what I had experienced in my school room—adding or subtracting or maybe handwriting. My coloring books became "stay within the line" art lessons. Reading aloud to my class from some of my favorite books was accompanied by comprehension questions. The challenge was making sure everyone was listening. Lots of "sit down and be quiet" language was spoken. To be honest, there wasn't much tolerance if those playmates didn't go along with my plan.

As I graduated from college and moved into the world of teaching elementary school, I began to realize that my work was a lot more about listening than telling. Randy was one of my fourth-grade students who struggled with reading. He was a likeable, bright, and compliant student. His parents worried about his lack of interest in reading and what was beginning to be an inability to keep up with his peers. I knew a lot of reading techniques and strategies to get Randy on track but all of that only added to his frustration and lack of enthusiasm.

"Randy, let's stop for minute from you reading aloud."

"I know I'm just no good at reading."

"Well, you do know quite a bit about figuring out what the words are. Why do you think you are no good?"

"This book is for little kids and I'm not a little kid. My friends are reading a lot harder books than me."

"Okay, what kind of book do you want to read?"

"I want to learn more about football."

"Why do you want to know about football?"

Randy began a long energetic story about his Pop Warner football team. He was a wealth of information about plays, strategies, and his favorite football players. I saw an enthusiasm in him I had never seen before.

"Well, how about the next time we have library time, you check out a book you want to read about football? You get to choose."

"Really? Any book I want to read?"

"Yes."

This moment was when I quit "teaching" and started listening. It was a moment when Randy and I began to co-create for the benefit of his learning. I have to admit I was a bit worried when Randy chose a book much more difficult than I would have picked. Even his parents expressed their concerns that he wouldn't be able to read it and complete his book report on time. While I offered encouraging words of support for Randy, I had my doubts as well. Those doubts began to dissipate as I watched him eagerly engage in reading this challenging book. Every time there was a spare moment he had the book in his hands, diligently working to decode the words and understand what he was reading. When he finished his book report, it was a personal handoff to me, with a beaming smile. His confidence and new energy for reading only grew as the school year went on.

Here was an early lesson in companioning on my pilgrimage path. As my professional journey continued with more courses and training, that work provided more roadside markers. Studying motivation theory, seeking to connect to students' interests and background knowledge helped to open a new way of interacting with them. I learned how to pay attention to the feeling tone of the classroom, not just plow through the required curriculum and assignments. As I began to monitor what was happening beyond what I could see, I found creative ways to adjust and make the learning more engaging. I actively worked on the skill of asking open-ended questions to elicit student personal engagement and activate their problem-solving abilities. The dynamic interchange of listening to these responses often created learning I never anticipated. It was energetic and vibrant bringing new meaning to the work. At the time, I didn't realize how I was building a foundation for holding space for my companions to hear their wisdom and trust their intuition.

LISTENING WHILE WRITING DISSERTATION

My path to earn a doctorate took many twists and turns, uphill trudging and downward slides, stormy weather inside my head, and unexpected discoveries. It was a long slog to the finish, with many doubts that I would truly arrive at the destination. Little did I imagine that my choice of conducting a naturalistic inquiry would illuminate ways of listening thoughtfully without preconceived ideas. To be honest, the reason I chose this type of inquiry was because I had neither the desire nor the confidence to set up a quantitative statistical study. That approach felt cold and disconnected from any new understandings. I wanted real interactions with the participants of my research. I was examining how adults learn in the context of a college reading skills class. What strategies do adults use in learning? What kind of environment enhances adults' learning? What motivates adults to become involved in their learning? I collected the adults' reflections, conducted one-to-one interviews, gave reading skills and needs assessments, made observational notes, and reviewed classwork. I had boxes of raw data to sort through, examine, code, and reduce into data sets, looking for patterns. What was repetitive or unique or irrelevant? It was overwhelming so many times, like walking an unfamiliar maze, not knowing if I would ever be able to exit or if I would just keep bumping into dead ends.

Any pilgrimage requires us to keep moving, one step at a time and not always forward. As I kept sorting, organizing, pondering, and listening to the data, the road signs began to appear. A framework took shape creating a road map of adult learning. I discovered a framework that had categories of understanding oneself, interest in the learning, a structure to guide, the role of the teacher, and the feeling of success. This framework of strategies, environment, and motivation gave a full view of the adult learning territory.

As I look back at what the students shared with me in their journals and interviews, I see connections to being a spiritual companion. I hear their words speaking wisdom into my learning. I recognize understandings of how to be with others as they explore their ways of being and growth. Some of the students said:

- "A teacher's role is to be in the group as an equal."
- "Teachers need to gather more input from the class."
- "I learn through experience, using my way to do something, not just the teacher's way."
- "Even though I am an adult, I'm more apt to learn because I feel the teachers accept me."
- "Understanding self, what you are, what you need, gets a clear picture for learning."

All this work transformed not only my approach to teaching but how I engaged others in my daily walk. It was the work of listening with curiosity and seeking to understand others' perspectives, of gaining insights that helped me connect and be in compassionate relationships. Hearing both audibly and intuitively what was swirling through people's minds and hearts opened the door of deep understanding. I see how this path brought new vistas of spiritual companioning, which was becoming a way of life for me.

LEADERSHIP WORK SHAPING A COMPASSIONATE LISTENER

"I'm thinking seriously about retiring," I shared with my spiritual director.

"Interesting. Tell me more," Sr. Marion said.

"There are some practical considerations. One being that my superintendent contract is due for renewal and there are new laws that have been passed about how the Governing Board handles the new contract. I'm not interested in the public airing of negotiation. I've given so much over the last 35 years as an educator and any excitement for what lies ahead is just not there. Besides, I've always said I wanted to step off before everyone is complaining that I need to retire."

"Besides the practical, what else is stirring within you?"

"This particular job has been so consuming of my life and detrimental to my health at times. I want space to be, yet I want to take all that I've learned and experienced into a new chapter of my life. I just want to be a teacher again."

"So what do you imagine will be in this new chapter?"

"One urging I feel is maybe to become a spiritual director, but I'm not interested in ordination of any kind. I have no desire to be clergy."

Sr. Marion laughed, "Oh my dear Cathy, you already are a spiritual director and ordination is not ever necessary."

"What do you mean?"

"You've told me so many stories about listening to those who work with you. You've thoughtfully processed how to be present with others and how to compassionately guide them, or many times just to let them figure out what they needed to do with grace and patience."

"Well, I just thought that was part of being a good leader. If you don't listen and care about others, that always comes back to haunt you. More than one knot on my head learning that lesson."

What Sr. Marion said started me thinking about how my journey as an elementary public-school superintendent was being a spiritual director. Repeatedly I was told by those who worked with me, you are such a good listener.

- "I feel like you care what I think."
- "You let me figure out what I might do next."
- "Walking down the hallway to your office there is a tightening in my gut and a bit of fear that I'm in trouble. What will I say? How will you react? Can I be open and honest? Then as I leave your office, I get a feeling of a gentle touch on my cheek and at the same time, a big push from behind to be better."

The practice of seeking to understand before being understood was the foundation of listening. I learned how to ask open-ended questions rather than using directive questions as a manipulation to get what I wanted. I learned the discipline of holding silence to bring out the deeper insights. This leadership walk in my pilgrimage was rich in heart-wrenching and heart-warming experiences, repeatedly bringing me to live out spiritual companioning.

HIKING THE WICKLOW WAY: THE ONGOING WORK

For Gil's upcoming 60th birthday I asked him what he wanted. "I want to hike the Wicklow Way again. This time with our kids and their spouses if they want to come."

"That sounds like something absolutely perfect for you."

"Are you willing to be the support driver again?"

"Well, do you think I could hike it?"

I had no idea where those words came from. I wasn't the least bit athletic and certainly in no shape to take on a 100-mile hike through the mountains of County Wicklow. I knew the intense and grueling task it was for Gil when he hiked it on his pilgrimage walking across Ireland. As his support team of one, driving our rental car from the daily starting point to the evening destination, I saw what each day's hike took physically, mentally, and spiritually. How did I even think I could try? But there was something brewing deep in my soul calling me to take on the challenge.

"You can do anything you put your mind to. And the pilgrimage begins now."

I lost thirty pounds, exercised every day, and worked my way up to walking more than eight miles at a time. I was ready to go. Then a couple of obstacles arose. I had a painful bout of diverticulitis. As I regained my gut health and got clearance from my doctor, I was back on the walking regime until I ran my bare foot into the iron leg of the living room coffee table. Surely I just stubbed my toe? No such luck. It immediately began to swell and turned purple. We were six weeks from beginning the hike and I had a painful broken little toe. I had to wear a boot-cast to stabilize it and help the healing process. No walking exercise could happen. So now what? The blessing of physical therapy to build up my core and a stationary bike to keep the legs moving were lifesaving.

I remember the rush of excitement, gratitude, and anxiety as I stood in Dublin's Marlay Park, the beginning point of the Wicklow Way. I was ready to begin the eight day, 100-mile hike to Clonegal. Our daughter Alicia, our son-in-law Phil, and nine other friends gathered with Gil and me to begin this journey together. Gil was right that my pilgrimage began long before I stood there that day. It began with an urging towards accomplishing something I didn't think possible, continued with my dedication to become physically strong, and lasted through the painful diverticulitis flare-up and the ugly broken toe.

With only one more day until we reached Clonegal, we were hiking from Kyle's Farmhouse to Shillelagh. Mid-way through the fifteen miles, my right knee began screaming pain with every step I took. It was excruciating agony encircling my right knee joint as I placed my foot down. Each step caused me to catch my breath as the pain shot down my leg. An overwhelming fear welled up within me that my knee would buckle and I would fall. Even more frightening was the thought that we were a long way from our destination with few options to step off the trail and get help. My family rallied around me. Phil carried my backpack and Gil gave me his hiking stick. Someone walked beside me no matter how slow I was going, offering encouragement and distractions. There came this odd rhythm of walking with the pain for the next seven miles—left step no pain, right step agony, left step no pain, right step agony. I began to embrace the pain of the right step knowing my next step would be free from torment—right step eased by the left step—keep moving slow and steady.

That evening at our B&B, I was filled with anxiety, exhaustion, and despair. I broke down in grief-stricken tears. Tears filled with an abundance of raw emotions—real physical pain, grieving the possible loss of not completing the hike, disappointing my family, remorse, anger, feeling inadequate. How could this be? How did this happen?

Gil told me that crying wasn't going to help. "Nothing needs to be decided until morning. Breathe, calm down, and try to rest." During the night the waves of grief continued over me like a torrential Irish rain. I felt like I was ruining everyone's pilgrimage, especially my own. My heart ached to think I'd come so far and wouldn't make it to the end. My body had betrayed me once again. I was embarrassed and felt like a failure. Okay, this was not going to help. So I began telling myself to breathe, be still, let go and embrace the pain. Then a peace came as if the clouds dissipated and let the light in. It will be okay if I can't walk tomorrow. I will not ruin anyone else's pilgrimage. I don't want to be rescued along the way, creating drama and unwanted attention. I can get a cab and meet the others in Clonegal. I know how to navigate the roads of Ireland quite well. All will be well and all shall be well.

When I tried to get out of bed in the morning and take the first step, my knee hurt so bad that I screamed out. I naively thought my knee might heal overnight, maybe be a little sore but I'd be able to walk. Instead, it felt a hundred times worse. It felt like three strands of barbed wire were tightly wrapped around the inside of my knee—wire to bone piercing deeply with each step. Right then I made the decision not to walk further, bringing some ease to the pain.

That morning, Alicia and Phil came to my room to see how I was doing.

"I'm not going to walk the rest of the way. My knee is still screaming pain with each step. I don't want to ruin your pilgrimage or anyone else's. No drama on the trail."

Alicia said, "Mom, you have accomplished a great feat already. You don't need to walk the final fourteen miles to be successful."

"It's okay not to go. I totally understand," began Phil. "But if you want to, you can do this. It's just one more day. You know what the pain is like, so now you can adjust. Besides, when you finish, it will be a ticket you'll never have to punch again."

Gil pulled out the Wicklow Way trail map and the three of them began analyzing the route—the changes in elevation, the trail condition, where there might be points that a cab could be called to drive me the rest of the way if needed.

It was then something inside me warmed to the idea of finishing. I needed to embrace my feelings of not being a burden to others while accepting the love and encouragement of my family. They believed I could do it and gave me permission to stop walking. The toughest mountain to climb would be the first one on the trail. I had more than 30,000 steps ahead of me. The biggest challenge would be to take the first step. I wanted to punch that ticket. I wanted to finish what I started. Fourteen miles and seven hours later, I walked into Clonegal with all the others. Every single right step was a painful screaming to stop and every single left step pulled me forward to be able to "punch that ticket."

The words, "Do you think I could hike the Wicklow Way?" began an intense transformation of every part of my being. From an idea to a dream to the reality of preparation to disappointments and set-backs to doubts to exhilaration to exquisite soulful moments to exhaustion to agony to peace to completion of the journey—all of it becoming the swirling soup within my alchemical cauldron. All of it bursting open my heart and soul to rise up out of the cauldron into a transmutation of my very being. Like the phoenix, I begin again, more than before.

The work of being a spiritual companion involves an ongoing engagement of mindful presence to the ego while seeking the true Self. Thoughtful, intuitive listening to heart, mind, soul, and body is the work required to be a wisdom listener and spiritual presence for those who come seeking. Spending quality time reflecting on life's pilgrimage—past, present, and possibilities for the future—opens space for the Divine source to move and co-create spiritual transformations.

CRUISING WITH VOX PEREGRINI WICKLOW WAY PILGRIMS

"So, what do you do all day while we are hiking?" asked one of the Vox Peregrini singers.

The perfect judge in my head was taunting, "Nothing. At least nothing compared to the grueling, gorgeous hiking you have done. I just drove 20 minutes and hung out. Big whoopee!"

But I took a deep breath and said, "Oh, I made sure we were all checked out of the B&B. Then I had a lovely day of writing, reading, and enjoying the beautiful Irish countryside. Driving to this destination to be sure all is ready for your arrival."

"Thank you so much for all the arrangements. The accommodations are better than any of us could have imagined."

"No worries. So glad to do it."

A few days earlier, these thirteen professional singers from around the United States had traveled to Bunclody, County Wexford in Ireland, just a few miles from the southern start of the Wicklow Way. They were committed to walking the almost one hundred miles from Clonegal to Dublin over eight days, going the opposite direction Gil and I had walked two years before. The first evening they gathered at St. Mary's Catholic Church, which graciously granted space for Vox practice. They sat in a circle for their first vocal rehearsal together. Gil and I had the honor to join this choir circle as privileged listeners. Their director, Dr. John Wiles, tapped his tuning fork, hummed a note and waved his hand for them to begin. The voices joined each other in exquisite four-part harmony, transforming the space into an otherworldly experience. The stunningly melodious notes swirled around the room, dancing with each other, moving in and through our very souls, bringing tears to our eyes. They sang eleven songs for three hours with their director pointing out small nuances he wanted for subtle improvements.

Vox Peregrini is a pilgrimage choir of professionally trained singers. They were committed to transforming themselves through the exhilarating and exhausting experience of walking twelve to fifteen miles a day from village to village on ancient paths. All the while, they were rehearsing along the route in preparation for a concert at the end of the journey. (voxperegrini.com).

Gil was walking with these singer-hikers, and I was their support person in my little rental car. My pilgrimage had begun months before, planning and organizing all the arrangements needed by this group. Reserving nightly accommodations, evening meals, adjusting when the plan wasn't going to work out, sending accurate information to the singers about their daily financial obligations, and responding to any unique needs or concerns of the group.

I embraced my pilgrimage of doing. Truthfully, I got great satisfaction from helping others. The "thank you," and the "you're so wonderful," and "I can't imagine doing this without you," filled my heart with appreciation and love. And then there is that moment, when Gil and all of Vox Peregrini walk away and leave me alone. They'll be together all day in the glorious, wild beauty of Ireland, meeting the challenge of long days up and down the mountains, carrying their packs and burdens, facing their fears and personal struggles, and when it gets too tough, someone is there to walk alongside them. They will have no worries at the end of the day because I've traveled ahead in my little car and will have everything ready for them—a comfortable bed, a hot shower, and a good meal, even snacks for tomorrow's hike.

I'm alone all day, the drive to the next stop taking no longer than 25 minutes. All the major arrangements were made months ago in the quiet space of my home. The bulk of the support work has already been completed. Now, I am faced with just me. Lots of waiting, thinking, what-shall-I-do dilemmas with no one to talk to, which is excruciating for an extrovert and a think-aloud person. Who has my common experience, so I can create a bond with them? Who'll walk alongside of me when it gets too tough? Just me.

This is where my pilgrimage got real. I must face me. All of me. And listen to the fears I was trying to cover up and the feeling of loneliness I tried to ignore. I was working to make friends with the judge who lives in me, pointing out all my faults and mistakes. The replays of last evening's conversations where I babbled on about my day while all the others had so many more challenges and extraordinary experiences. As I leaned into this hard work of not being consumed by the critical voice in my head, I found those fears being eased—I could indeed be a very good companion to me. As Paulo Coelho has said, "Life is a long pilgrimage from fear to love."

As I embraced my pilgrimage of me, I began wondering how Vox Peregrini singers might sit in circle beyond rehearsing. A time to share their reflections about the day's experience. I posed my wondering to the director, John Wiles.

"John, would you be willing to let me invite the singers to sit in a conversation circle with me?"

"What do you mean?"

"I've had the opportunity to sit in circles with women, practicing the Circle Way. (More will be shared in Chapter 5.) I'd invite any of the singers who want to come after dinner or whenever the times seems right. No pressure to attend, definitely not a "have to," like rehearsals."

"Okay. But I'm wondering if anyone would have the energy for that after hiking all day."

"We would only meet for an hour or less. The practice is simple. What is said in circle, stays in circle. There is no fixing, saving, setting anyone straight or cross talk. We will use a talking piece so that only one person speaks at a time, and you can always pass if you don't want to speak. I'll be the host to begin the circle with a brief reading, then ask a check-in question. I'll ask one person to be the guardian to help us hold silence when it's needed by ringing a bell. Low key, open-ended questions, and we'll create brave safe space for anyone who comes."

"Okay, let's give it a try to see if anyone is interested."

An hour later, I offered the invitation at our dinner gathering. Everyone was invited to meet in the living room of our B&B, but without the expectation of attending. I arranged the seating in circle fashion and waited to see if anyone would show up. Slowly and quietly, seven singers made their way into the living room. There was a bit of apprehension and curiosity about what we would be doing. I explained the basics and got a volunteer to be the guardian. So it began. Holding brave safe space for those sitting in the circle. Offering time to be, time to reflect, time to listen to the Divine Source within and all around. The pilgrimage of one became the pilgrimage of community.

SPIRITUAL COMPANIONING AS A WAY OF LIFE:
COMPASSIONATE PRESENCE

This chapter's title indicates being a spiritual companion/director does not require ordination. While this is true, it does require engaging in a study program if your intention is to actively schedule appointments with those who are seeking a companion for their journey. Beginning in 2011, I attended a two-year program at the Tacheria Interfaith School of Spiritual Direction in Tucson, AZ. It was a time of intense spiritual growth, learning about many faith traditions, sacred practices, and experiencing the trusted companionship of others in the program. It was a time of engaging in (W)Holy listening, preparing to walk with others on their journey.

As I opened myself to the possibility of being a spiritual director/companion, I became an active member of Spiritual Directors International (SDI). This organization is a treasure trove of resources and support. "The Guidelines for Ethical Conduct" brochure provides important information for consideration in establishing a practice.

Spiritual direction is a ministry that helps people tell their sacred stories every day. To clarify the relationship between the spiritual director and seeker, SDI recommends the use of ethical guidelines and the use of an engagement agreement to clarify roles and responsibilities.[2]

We have used the SDI guidelines to create a covenant that we share with our spiritual companions. Our covenant makes it clear that we are committed to confidentiality, except for situations of abuse or self-harm that require reporting. We recognize that there may be times that the companion will share psychological and relational difficulties; however, we are not psychotherapists or counselors and do not provide those services. Having a therapist or counselor is advisable. We offer our assurance that we are faithful to our personal work toward soul transformation through routine spiritual practice and meeting with our spiritual guides. Our covenant is a visible commitment to our spiritual companioning as a way of life and as part of the pilgrimage path.

Across my life, I've been walking the daily steps on my pilgrimage. Drawing experiences, relationships, reflections, struggles, joys, paralyzing fear, questions, excruciating pain, and love into my cauldron. The heat of the fire, sometimes boiling and sometimes simmering the soup, transforming the very essence of my Self toward becoming deeply passionate about seeking Wisdom's way on my journey. I embrace being a pilgrim of compassionate presence as I open my heart and soul to the Divine Source within and all around me.

CHAPTER FOUR

LISTENING: (W)HOLY WISDOM

How many ways are there
to get saturated in another's mind?
—Maggie Nelson

"I have a therapist I've been seeing for over two years, and she has helped me a lot. But I feel the need for something deeper or... more or ... I'm not even sure what," said Joanne at our first meeting.

"What are you thinking the more might be?" asked Catherine.

"I'm beginning to see how I might live something different than what was instilled into me growing up. The doctrine of depravity preached at the church we attended continues to seep into my adult life."

"What would you want the different to be?"

After a long silence she said, "I recently read a phrase in a book that deeply touched my very core. It was as if the author wrote these words for me: 'I am beloved. I always have been and always will be. I come from love.' I want to learn how to live as the beloved."

So began the journey with Joanne as we engaged in a spiritual direction/companion relationship. She's in the second half of life and on a journey of self-discovery. By her own admission, she was operating out of great emotional pain. Holding safe space with no judgment offered Joanne time to explore those deep, dark corners of her life hidden from view. She wanted to see a new way forward. She longed for new insights that could bubble up from the deep well of wisdom within.

Kay Lindahl, author and founder of the Listening Center, offers a beautiful definition of what it means to listen at an empathic level. "Listening is an art, more than hearing words and more than an act. What do we mean by the word art? At-oneness. Those times when we are fully present with whatever we are doing are times of oneness...It's a shift from listening as an act, something we do, to an art, something that we "be."[1] When we listen with total attention focused on the person speaking, we can feel a sense of connection. As the spiritual companion, the listener, we are intentional about clearing our mind from distractions.

Like in meditation, our monkey mind might be swinging from tree to tree. Often our glorious problem-solving brain jumps around to try to plan ways to solve the problem or ask, "have you tried this, or thought about that"—always in their best interest, of course. When that happens, we remind ourselves, "Be here now." This gentle suggestion can return our intended focus back to the companion and their story. The listener's full presence is an offering, a gift of acceptance, appreciation, and compassionate curiosity. Our goal is to hold a space of loving energy where our companion can freely speak about their thoughts and feelings. As well as a space where they can be comfortable with not speaking. Silence can be a gift of healing—a shared oneness—creating a sense of something beyond our individual selves.

(W)Holy wisdom listening is an art of the integrated mind,

body, soul, and spirit. The beauty of being aware and intentional. As companions we listen wholly, incorporating our entire being while simultaneously inviting the Holy within our companion to be present. We create a (W)Holy space of closeness and connection between companions that is mutual. Both seeking insight for the journey, both creating a container of listening for wisdom from the other.

"I've been making mandalas. Would you like to see them?" Joanne asked.

"Sure."

"I was reading Kay Lindahl's book about listening. In the book there are these beautiful mandalas drawn by Amy Schanapper. The mandalas were so intricate and mesmerizing to me. Late one night when I couldn't sleep and all the struggles in my life seemed overwhelming, I thought I would try to make one. I took a piece of paper and drew a circle, put a dot in the center and began drawing. Lines and triangles and squares and more circles began forming around the center. Soon it seemed my pencil was moving on its own. I drew until it felt finished."

Joanne pulled out her first drawing, which was on a five-by-five piece of paper. As I gazed upon it, I found myself drawn into the mandala. I began to feel movement from the center of the art bursting outward, circles and lines and triangles swirling round and round with cones exploding. I felt an energy of expansion within me. After a few moments, I looked up at Joanne with genuine wonder. "Wow," was the only word I could offer.

"It's called 'Birth.'"

"Tell me more."

"Well, when I finished, it looked like birth canals to me. I felt like the mandala is a glimpse into my very soul. I didn't plan this. I just let my drawing flow. It feels like I'm seeing Spirit within me."

Over the course of the next five years, Joanne's mandalas

were her guides to becoming more of her authentic Self, of living beloved. The mandalas beckoned her to give "birth" as she listened deeply to Spirit within and all around her. The mandalas began as black and white drawings born out of pain and struggle. They called out names to Joanne, names like Fragmented, Standing, Pregnant, Awaken, Sad/Angry/Depressed. As she opened her imagination creating the mandalas, poetry began to appear as a partner with the art. After a year, colors appeared. Shades of blue and aqua, red and coral, green, gold, and black. Their names were Validation, Magnify, Fiery Depths of Love, and Mother God in all her glory.

As her companion, Catherine held safe space for Joanne to share, explore, and find the deep wisdom within. "To listen another's soul into a condition of disclosure and discovery may be almost the greatest service that any human being ever performs for another."[2] Catherine and Joanne entered into a connection that was something greater than themselves. That something greater is rooted in love and compassion. From this greater than connection, Catherine asked Joanne if she would create a mandala for our book. And once more a beautiful piece of spiritual art was birthed: "One Source>Diversity>Unity."

LISTENING TO GRIEF

"My father died before I could get to the hospital. I never got to tell him I loved him, one more time to say goodbye." Ruth's tears rolled down her cheeks.

Those words brought back the memory of Catherine losing her beloved mother-in-law in much the same way. Fresh pain and guilt that things could have been different flowed through me. I needed to feel this deep connection while maintaining composure for Ruth. The practice of quieting my mind, holding lightly my feelings and then leaning into the Divine Source to bring solace and space for Ruth's story. In the listening, I could offer an understanding without any words. My experience brought an insight into the pain of unexpressed grief and loss. I could hold Ruth's pain knowing that Divine Love would flow in and around us.

(W)Holy listening has brought all the dark places of our own journey into the light. Many times the companion's stories touch memories and places within us that may have been long forgotten or shoved away in denial. These feelings can catch us by surprise in the most unexpected ways. It is imperative in the work of spiritual companioning to have consistent ongoing times to meet with our own spiritual director/companion. A trusted place to process and sort what swirls within during our time listening to others. A place where wounds are gently viewed and brought into the light of healing. A place where shadows and blind spots are examined and brought into consciousness for transformation.

Catherine shared this story about a session with her spiritual companion, Sister Marion.

"I was sitting in a session with Ruth and I was hit so hard by grief when she began crying and telling me about losing her father. While she was telling her story, I was reliving the loss of my mother-in-law like it had just happened, and that was seven years ago." As I was telling Sister Marion my story, tears welled in her eyes and I couldn't continue.

Sister Marion said. "Let's sit in silence for a few moments and allow you to embrace those feelings."

It took a bit of time to regain my composure, but after a few minutes, I told her, "Thank you. I don't think I've given myself permission to acknowledge how much it still hurts. That helps. But my worry is—how do I not let those feelings overwhelm me when I need to be listening to someone else?"

"What have you done to process this grief that was helpful in the past?" Sister Marion asked.

"Writing down what happened and how I felt. Trying to be brutally honest about my guilt and shame for not telling her how I felt when she went into the hospital. Acting like everything was going to be fine. Putting on the happy face when I was anything but happy."

"What was the writing like for you?"

"Well, at first I stared at the blank page in my journal for a long time. I couldn't figure out how to start. There was so much swirling in me, so much confusion, just not knowing what to say. Finally, I just wrote, 'I'm so sorry.' The words began to flow then with tears streaming down my face. I wrote my regrets and my wishes that I had done things differently. As I poured my heart and soul out on the page, I began to feel the release of pain and grief. When I sat with my words and stilled my mind to imagine what my mother-in-law would say, I distinctly heard, 'You are a good girl.' Maybe it's time for another conversation with my mother-in-law."

Catherine told Sister Marion at a subsequent session, "What I have learned from our last session is that my soul work is intertwined with the soul work of my companions. The work is ongoing, sparked by the words we speak, the silence we hold, the experiences of each of us, the compassionate caring, and the seeking of Divine wisdom for our journeys. I learned that when I begin to feel overwhelmed by the listening, I can ask to sit in silence for a few moments and allow the quiet still voice within me to be heard and to heal me. I learned that I need to allow space to care for myself—to hold brave safe space for myself is the only way I'll ever be able to do so for someone else."

THE GIFT OF SILENCE

"How long can you hold silence?" Gil asked after I lamented my frustrations over a fellow administrator. I was the superintendent of a large K-8 public school district at the time.

"What? Hold silence? John doesn't know what to do so how will silence help him? He swirls in the 'not my fault, everybody is against me' world. Nothing is happening. Same problem, same results."

"How long can you hold silence?" was the response again.

"Silence to solve a problem? How would that work?"

"Try starting with 'help me understand.' Then hold silence beyond what feels comfortable for you."

At the next meeting with John, I opened the conversation with "help me understand" and then stopped talking. John, once again, offered lots of defensive, not my fault, nobody is helping me language. When he stopped talking, I held silence beyond comfortable. It was hard to do. I struggled not speaking but waiting for John to offer the first words.

"Well, I guess it sounds like I'm a little defensive." John said.

More silence.

"Yeah, well, I did try one of the ideas you suggested. It didn't seem to make a difference."

More silence.

"Maybe I didn't give it enough time. I guess I could try again."

"And how would you try again?" I asked.

This exchange was another insight in the learning to be a (W)Holy listener. I began to let go of fixing, saving, advising, or setting someone straight. I began to quit thinking of my response while the other person is talking. I began to let go of my curiosity to know whatever it is I felt I needed to know. I began to truly live into the question "help me understand." I began to honor silence as a gift for the quiet voice to be heard. I began to see beyond the obvious and cherish the space for more creativity. Marion Wright Edelman, founder of the Children's Defense Fund, said, "Learn to be quiet enough to hear the sound of the genuine within yourself so that you can hear it in others." In silence, I began to listen. And in listening, I began to honor and respect the other.

THE ART OF OPEN-ENDED QUESTIONS

We spend time practicing (W)Holy listening at our Wisdom School. Most of our students are spiritual seekers and not necessarily interested in becoming spiritual directors/companions. Almost all of them, though, express the desire to know themselves better, to have a deeper spiritual connection and find others who are willing to embrace the experience of diverse thoughts, feelings, and experiences without judgment. They seek to be a part of a community free of religious dogma, free from societal boundaries, where everyone can contribute, learn, and grow. There is a hunger for the freedom to be spiritually curious, to ask profound questions, and to be comfortable with being uncomfortable. Above all, they want to experience deep listening; they ache to be heard. But to be heard, one must learn to listen.

We begin practicing (W)Holy listening by learning the art of the open-ended question. And invariably our students tell us "that was way harder than I thought it would be." We think the reason asking open-ended questions is so difficult is that these types of questions can expose our hidden agendas. Questions like "I wonder if you ever thought of doing this…" reveal the agenda of directing our companion to find the "right answer." Of course, the worst question is no question, and we give in to telling our "dog story." Try this experiment: tell a friend a story about your beloved dog, or cat, or child, or grandchild and mark how many times the other person immediately follows with their story about their dog, cat, child, or grandchild. Practice this: the next time someone tells you such a story, keep yourself from telling your story. Instead, ask them an open-ended question and watch their reaction. It's important for us to notice when we choose to listen and when we choose not to listen. Pay attention when we start to interrupt someone and what happens when we don't. Asking, "Is there anything else?" Simply let go of our agenda and be a listening presence with the other.

The craft of asking open-ended questions is the work of being fully present to the person who is telling us their story by not rehearsing what we will say next. This type of presence is often new territory for us. The art of listening doesn't mean we have a blank mind, but simply a quiet mind deeply absorbing what the other is sharing. The dance of listening is to listen without leading. We rely on our own inner wisdom to bring forth the next question allowing our companion to hear from their own pool of wisdom.

To coax the deep wisdom from within the companion, open-ended questions invite them to discover their own answers buried within them. Parker Palmer, in his book, *A Hidden Wholeness: The Journey Toward An Undivided Life*, shares,

> What are the marks of an honest, open question? An honest question is one I can ask without possibly being able to say to myself, "I know the right answer to this question, and I sure hope you give it to me. ...A dishonest question insults your soul, partly because of my arrogance in assuming that I know what you need and partly because of my fraudulence in trying to disguise my counsel as a query. An open question is one that expands rather than restricts your arena of exploration, one that does not push or even nudge you toward a particular way of framing a situation.[3]

Beginning a session with "How are you?" which seems to be an open-ended question, many times gets the quick response of "Fine" or "Terrible." Now we are trapped in the one-word answer whirlpool. What if we begin with "How are you arriving today?" or "What's moving in your heart today?" or "How is your soul today?"

Simple open-ended requests like "tell me your story" or "tell me more," give an expansive opportunity for the companion to hear what is beyond the surface. Stretching the companion to delve beyond the literal with questions like, "What can you imagine as another ending to your story?" "Can you create an environment where you would feel safe?" "Pretend that you can do anything your heart desired. What would that be like?"

"I wonder" questions can offer the companion an opportunity to expand what they had first thought possible. Asking: I wonder if you carried through with your options, what might appear or disappear? I wonder what the best outcome might be for you. Or the worst outcome? Or something in-between the best and the worst?

The art of asking questions can protect us from getting ahead of the language the companion uses. By paying close attention to the words spoken, we can invite the other person to probe down into what they already know but haven't yet named. "What did you mean when you said…" is one way to help them discover other feelings or insights.

Asking, "Can you tell me more?" is an opportunity for the listener to explore their interior life. It's also an opportunity for both the listener and the storyteller to take more of their presence into the listening experience. It can help the companion to hear themselves tell the part of their own story they've never said out loud. The part they felt no one would ever listen to. Here the spiritual companion must draw upon a rarely used bandwidth to focus on what is not being said, to double down on their intuition to order to understand what the companion's words might not be saying. And this is when the companion's body language may be telling us more than what is being said.

At these moments of exploring the "more than what's being said," the practice of holding silence allows the companion to completely finish their thoughts. By holding silence when the other person has stopped talking, we offer them the opportunity to share something else, a thought that emerged in the safety of silence. And because we have focused on what the companion has been saying and not thinking about our next question, when we hold silence, the space and time allows the next question to arise within us. The practice of presence by holding silence builds our capacity for wisdom listening.

At the end of day, we have to be honest with ourselves as (W)Holy listeners—and admit that it's okay to be human. Sometimes our mind wanders. At those times, we need to lay aside our expectations of being the perfect listener, the wise sage who is the best spiritual companion. What we have found to be helpful in these circumstances is to think of listening as meditation—making ourselves aware of the distractions, acknowledge them, and then return to focus. Focused not on our breathing but on returning our attention fully to the companion's breathing. *New York Times* journalist Kate Murphy wrote,

> While being open and curious about someone else is a state of mind, the ability to acknowledge someone's point of view with a sensitive response that encourages trust and elaboration is a developed skill…it takes practice. It takes awareness, focus, and experience to unearth and understand what is really being communicated. Good listeners are not born that way, they become that way.[4]

Whether we're part of a two-year spiritual direction program or not, to engage in (W)Holy listening and to learn the art of asking open-ended questions take a tremendous amount of practice. Lindhal's Listening Center website offers suggestions for daily practices to learn the dance of listening. As David Augsberg says, "Being listened to is so close to being loved that most people cannot tell the difference."[5] Indeed, the ache to be heard lives within everyone.

WALKING EACH OTHER HOME

When we have brought all we have of ourselves into the listening experience we leave our companioning session exhausted. (W)Holy listening is the craftwork of the spiritual companion and it taxes every cell of our Mindbody.

Tom Blue Wolf, founder of Earthkeepers and Company, said, "We're all just walking each other home. We're all going somewhere but nobody knows where. It's kind of like dancing. You don't dance to arrive at a destination—you dance to enjoy every step of the way."[6] Learning the dance of (W)Holy listening may find us making some missteps and awkward movements. Yet, the dance of listening will bring brilliant moments of deep connection with our hearts and souls through experiencing the joy of being truly heard and being genuinely valued. We continue to study the ways of listening deeply. We practice daily. We learn to listen by listening. And we continue to dance the dance of listening to others and to ourselves.

CHAPTER FIVE

BUILDING COMMUNITY: THE CIRCLE WAY

Somewhere, there are people to whom we can speak with passion
without having the words catch in our throats.
Some place where we can be free.
—Starhawk

Catherine was on her way to the annual gathering of the Arizona Council of Grandmothers. This would be her first visit. It was the Council's twentieth anniversary.

Fifty miles south of Tucson, Arizona, I exited the Interstate at Tubac. Instead of going into the only sizable town before crossing the US/Mexico border at Nogales, I turned right onto a dusty road. It felt like I had traveled ten miles winding up and down through dry washes and small rises, but it was just a mile when I crossed a cattle guard into Kenyon Guest Ranch. I had an overwhelming sense that something magical was about to happen.

The Ranch sits in the high desert on a low-lying plateau surrounded by two rugged mountain ranges: Santa Rita Mountains to the east and Tumacacori Mountains to the west. The landscape is dotted with sagebrush, palo verde trees and scattered grasses with a few low-lying cacti mixed in. The high desert may be hot during the day, so shorts and sandals are welcomed. Then at night, the temperature plummets, so a warm jacket, long pants and shoes may be a necessity. As I got out of my car, I felt as if I had been transported back to the days of 1930 old west Arizona.

The adobe hacienda architecture of cabins and community lodge nestled around small courtyards added to the mystique of the upcoming gathering. There was a quickening in my heart and an excitement in my mind as I walked towards the dining hall to check in.

The Council calls themselves "The Grandmothers" but many are not biological grandmothers. They are, however, a collection of women who may not be old, but working on being an elder. My friends encouraged me to attend, telling of four days engaging in a powerful full moon ceremony, sitting in small circles holding safe space for stories to be shared, drumming circles, labyrinth walks, sweat lodge experiences, a Ceilidh celebration, luncheon honoring the elder women over 80, and a place to just be. Their invitation was irresistible. I knew I had to attend. I longed for more than a women's retreat—I longed for a deep connection with other women. I longed for a place to be me, or even to find me, beyond my roles, appearance, and expectations of others. I needed community.

I felt a stirring in my heart from the first moment of the opening ceremony. Thirty-five women sitting in a large circle. Our ancestors from the four directions were invited to be present. One by one, each woman was invited to walk around the table in the center of the circle. On the table were four candles and a bouquet of beautiful flowers. Each of us was asked to place on the table something that symbolized why we had come to the gathering. I felt a great anticipation for what would be shared.

When it was my turn, I circled the table speaking my name into the candle light. I laid down my Irish prayer rope with its green beads, brown Celtic cross, and tassel. It had traveled many miles with me, been dipped into holy Irish wells, Pacific Ocean waves, the lakes of Glendalough, and Mount Rainer's glacier streams. As I made my walk around the table, I felt the power of each woman holding compassionate space for me to speak freely. I felt the honoring of elders present and the ancient ones who had been called to join the circle. I felt the Spirit dancing in and through and around me. I felt the heart of the circle itself as a living being filled with our precious offerings. I felt my tears bubbling over. I felt like I belonged.

This was my first experience with women who engaged the principles, practices, and agreements of *The Circle Way: A Leader in Every Chair*[1] by Christina Baldwin and Ann Linnea. Their technique of sitting in circle captures a way for changing how we engage and learn. Christina and Ann tell us that when we sit in circle, we activate one of our most ancient social processes and archetypes, welcoming everyone to participate equally. Our modern, well entrenched norm is the triangle representing hierarchical power coming from the top to the bottom. The circle is a way to reestablish social partnerships and collaboration from all the participants, welcoming diversity and open-minded conversations leading us to the opportunity for growth and change. The principles of rotating leadership, sharing responsibility, and honoring the center of the circle are practiced in order to hold the energy of spirit, and connection, and magic.

The Council practices five keystones of The Circle Way, which are:

1. Personal stories and materials shared in the circle are confidential.

2. Attentive listening with compassion and curiosity, withholding judgment. No fixing, no saving, no advising, no setting each other straight.

3. Only one person at a time speaks with the intention to contribute what has relevance, heart, and meaning to the topic and situation of the moment. Ask for what you need and offer what you can give.

4. Using a talking piece, which is a small object passed from person to person as an invitation to share, at your own pace and without interruptions, or pass by giving the piece to the next person.

5. Everyone engages in conscious self-monitoring with the commitment of caring for the well-being of the circle.

One circle member volunteers to hold the role of the guardian, a person who safeguards the group energy and the keystone practices of the circle. If there is a need for a resting point or the circle becomes unfocused, the guardian rings a bell to create a pause where everyone stops to take a breath and rest in silence for a few moments. Then the bell is rung again to bring everyone back, with an explanation as to why the bell was rung. Anyone in the circle can ask for the bell.

After the opening ceremony of the Arizona Council of Grandmothers Gathering, I sat in the cozy living room space of a Kenyon Ranch cabin with five other women. We gathered in a small circle as another part of the Council retreat. The woman who was the host of the circle began with this check-in question: "What has been happening in your soul since the last time we gathered or in the last few months?" And the invitation to share began with the talking piece making its journey around the circle.

When it was my turn I said that my mother-in-law, Loretta, died six months ago. I wasn't able to be there and I felt so guilty.

I surprised myself as those words came out and tears began to flow. She was in the hospital receiving an experimental treatment for leukemia. The first couple of days had gone well. She was feeling very optimistic. She encouraged me to attend an upcoming education conference in California that weekend where I was to be a presenter. I was anxious about going, but she was very insistent. She told me how proud she was of me and really wanted me to show off as Dr. Stafford. Besides, she told me, my husband Gil and his dad Finis would be there with her. Later, I found out that she sent them home in the evening to take care of things. In the middle of the night she began to have severe breathing problems, a side effect of the treatment, which led to the ICU and a ventilator. She never had a chance to call Finis or Gil. In the early morning hours, the hospital telephoned Finis to come because she was unconscious and unresponsive. The ventilator was keeping her alive. Gil didn't get a call from his Dad until around noon. Driving back from California, I saw a voicemail on my phone when we stopped at a rest area. It was my son, Neil, asking me to call him. I barely choked out those last words.

The Guardian rang a bell and the other five women in our small circle held silent and compassionate space for me in my grief. I was handed a tissue with no words and allowed to cry and gather myself. The bell rang again accompanied by the words, "I rang the bell to offer comfort and love to you."

Holding the talking piece I was able to finish my story. I told them I felt so guilty that I had gone to the conference and wasn't there at the hospital. The family waited for me to get to the ICU before removing Loretta from the ventilator. So many what-ifs were still in my mind. With a deep breath I quietly said, "Thank you for listening," and passed the talking piece.

This community of spiritual but not religious women and their practice of The Circle Way gave me gracious space for healing—the healing of being able to hear what I was afraid to say anywhere else. The healing of being held without judgment. The healing of release with silent comfort. The healing of no platitudes…just compassionate presence.

These experiences gave birth for The Circle Way to become a part of my journey and work. I began wondering how I could create safe, brave space in my daily life. How could I create community not boxed in by an institution's rules or religion's dogma, or the academic structure of organized workshops where information is poured in with no heart? I had the tools; now I needed to trust the process.

After six years of attending Grandmother Circles in Tubac, I acted on my wondering. I invited eight friends who had attended the Arizona Council of Grandmothers Gathering to begin our own circle. We called ourselves the West Valley Grandmothers. We met for the first time in December 2018 on the rising of Grandmother Full Moon. Since then, each month we continue our circling. Every time we meet, it is an experience of vulnerability, compassion, sharing of leadership roles, deep wisdom learning, and belonging. We laugh, cry, hold silence for healing, express ourselves fully and honestly, and feel like we can be our true selves. The power of the circle has transformed our journeys and lives. Oh, there have been moments when we stumbled over the practices and apologized. Times where we felt unsure or fearful about what we wanted to share or felt inadequate to take on the role of host or guardian. We learned that there are no mistakes in circle, only opportunities to be ourselves, fully and honestly. The beauty about circle is in the compassion and acceptance that sits in the heart of the center; the energy of loving spirit within and all around, a place for the spiritual but not religious.

Every time I sit in a circle and honor the agreements with others gathered, I experience the spiritual but not religious. The language of spirituality becomes expansive and welcomes diverse experiences. For me, it becomes a space where I can open my heart and soul welcoming the wisdom of the Divine. It becomes an active way of integrating wisdom listening. It becomes the connection for unleashing the bonds of limitations and expectations. It becomes freedom to be.

From these experiences, circle has become a way of being in relationships with others who may not know The Circle Way. Sitting around the dinner table when our grown-up children visit includes lots of sharing of daily life and storytelling. As I listen, the urge to tell them what to do or not do is strong. Yet, I find myself practicing the deep listening of compassion and curiosity rather than giving "mom advice." There are times when I begin to offer a related experience from my past and a grandchild runs up demanding some attention, interrupting the storytelling. When returning to the adult conversation, the flow has gone in a different direction. My story has evaporated. My ego wants to say, "Wait a minute, let me finish my story." As I live the circle practice of speaking with intention for the well-being of the group, I wait to be asked to finish. When that doesn't happen, my ego feels the hurt of being forgotten or ignored. Yet, my ability to hold silence and recognize the flow of the conversation holds space for more opportunities for the wisdom of the moment to arise. As the Dalai Lama says, "When you talk, you are only repeating what you already know. But if you listen, you may learn something new."

Even when I am sitting in a one-to-one companion time, the circle practices of confidentiality, listening with compassionate attention, and tending to the well-being of the companion are evident. I consciously hold safe, brave space so the Divine wisdom within can be gently called out. While there is no bell or talking piece, honoring silence, and asking questions, rather than giving advice, are followed.

During one of these companion times, Rebecca sat on my sofa with tears welling up in her sapphire eyes. She has a quiet presence with a direct intense gaze. She folded her legs under herself and dabbed at her eyes with a tissue.

"I'm so miserable. My boss drives me crazy, expecting me to be something I'm not. I find myself arguing with my teenage children over the most mundane things. I don't know what to do. I keep playing a million scenarios over and over in my head."

Finding an open-ended question to help Rebecca explore what may be hiding in the shadows was the challenge. "I wonder if you could talk about what you think is being expected of you."

"What? Like in my job or as a mother or how to be good person?"

"Whichever…"

"Well, my boss has sent me to leadership workshops about building relationships and being the uber positive cheerleader. She wants me to be more enthusiastic and outgoing. That's just not me. And not what my job requires. I need to be thoughtful, analytical, and detail oriented. Our work requires precision and when one of my direct reports can't measure up, I tell them. I'm not rude, but direct, which is not accepted very well."

"How does that make you feel?"

"Feel? I don't know. I guess I don't feel, I think… and think… and think."

"A few minutes ago, you said you were miserable. Maybe explore that feeling?"

Silence. Holding compassionate silence gave space for Rebecca to begin finding the wisdom within herself. She was opening to a new way of listening, a way of trusting the wisdom of feeling rather than problem-solving.

"Well, like I said, I feel miserable… and sad…and burned-out… and depressed. Okay, there are feelings I'm not recognizing. But I'm stuck in a thinking loop getting nowhere. I've abandoned my spiritual practices. I can't sit still for meditation.

Journaling is a chore which I'm avoiding. I've even stopped walking the dog."

More silence and now the tears are flowing freely.

"I'm such a failure at feeling. I'm trapped in my head."

"Can you think of a time where being in your head felt good?"

As Rebecca told her story, she engaged in the process of self-reflection. Her life experiences could be examined to see what wisdom could be gleaned. She was moving from only thinking to the mindful integration of her feelings into her whole self, one story at a time.

Many times, the spiritual but not religious have few options for being a part of a community of seekers like themselves. In 2014, Gil and I sought the support of the Tacheria Interfaith Spirituality Center to begin such a community. And out of this nonprofit partnership, Wisdom's Way Interfaith School was born to create a circle of seekers.

The School is a two-year program meeting once a month from September to June. Our students are the spiritual but not religious looking to escape religious dogma. They're searching for ways to integrate a deeper sense of inclusive spirituality into their lives. Through guest speakers from a variety of traditions we are able to explore differing spiritual practices. Our practice of following The Circle Way creates an environment of safe brave space for everyone.

As each of our students wanders into the room where we meet, there is a vibe of joyful expectancy and longing for the expansive learning, as well as connection in this unique community of seekers. Gathering here are people from the early 30s to 70+, various sexual identities, and differing ethnic backgrounds. They come from a wide variety of professions: educators, office managers, program directors, business owners, software engineers, therapists, scientists, artists, and university professors. Their spiritual journeys have been diverse: fundamental and mainline denominations, nature-based spirituality, pagan explorations, and eastern religion experiences. They are the spiritual but not religious longing for a place to explore freely with acceptance.

We sit in a circle with a candle in the center. We settle with the sound of the bell, holding silence, and another ring to begin our time together. We breathe deep, releasing the tensions and cares we are carrying. We remind ourselves of our Circle agreements. With our bodies, presence, and imaginations, we create the rim of a cauldron, fire in the center. We open ourselves to the magic of circle and the flow of spirit within and all around us. We listen with our minds and hearts. We are invited to share our stories. We pass the talking piece to honor the speaker. We respect the call for pause with the bell. We embrace the possibilities of transformation.

We hear this over and over from the people who come to our Wisdom's Way Interfaith School. One student told us, "There is no place, no community, no friends or family in my life like this. I feel safe to be vulnerable, or silent, or an emotional wreck, or joyful, with no guilt. With no one trying to save me, offer advice, or setting me straight. I'm free to explore my deepest, darkest secrets and questions with no judgment." Their heartfelt storytelling and deep listening expand their spiritual experiences.

Our way of being together changed dramatically with the onset of the Covid pandemic. No longer were we able to meet in person. How would the practices and processes of the Circle work via a video conference platform?

Catherine began our first virtual session. "Imagine that we are sitting in a circle together. Imagine that we are the rim of a great cauldron where a fire is lit in the center. We welcome Spirit to move within and all around us, swirling compassionate connection. We will honor our agreements and hold brave safe space for all."

We held to the idea that there is a leader in every chair and this became the strength that held our virtual circle together. Each person took responsibility to create their own circle space along with their unique talking piece. They made sure to be in a physical space where they could honor confidentiality. And those who volunteered to be the Guardian, kept their bell or singing bowl ready.

When someone was ready to speak, they would unmute, hold their talking piece up to the camera and offer the words, "I pick up my talking piece." When they were finished, the words would be, "I'm placing my talking piece back in the center." Then they would mute themselves. The flow of storytelling and deep listening could be seen and felt. The power of circle held strong across the internet.

How did our participants feel about this new way of being together? Did the power of the circle in this virtual environment hold brave safe space for growing our spirituality? At the end of each session, we asked the question, "What one word would describe how you feel right now?" Calm, grateful, peaceful, expanded, loved, encouraged, connected. No matter whether we met in person or virtually in the midst of a pandemic, the words spoken were a mosaic of the power of circle. The words of comfort and connection.

NEW CIRCLES

Equipped with the knowledge and experience of The Circle Way, some of our students created their own circles. Their intent was to open new opportunities for the spiritual but not religious to find refuge and support. A place where they can nurture their heart, mind, and souls in a safe container for spiritual exploration and connection.

Danielle said, "My spiritual journey began in earnest about ten years ago. What I encountered as I sought a community was either the megachurches with their rock and roll bands—or as I refer to them, the drum kit churches—or the elderly crowd at the traditional, more ritualistic churches. Nothing clicked for me." She went on, "As I chatted with some of my peers, I found the same longing in them—they wanted a place to explore different spiritual practices that were more ancient, while being with trusted friends."

Danielle began a small group circle of women who came together once a month to find community for their spiritual journey in a safe space. They agreed to follow Parker Palmer's Circle of Trust Touchstones[2] as their guide and process.

These Touchstones defined their boundaries: Give and receive welcome. Be present as fully as possible. What is offered in the circle is by invitation, not demand. Speak your truth in ways that respect other people's truth, no fixing, saving, advising, or correcting. Learn to respond to others with honest, open questions.

Sally found herself in a traditional church setting that did not match her childhood experiences. From ages four to ten, her family lived in Muslim, Buddhist, and Hindu countries. Her experience as a young person instilled a profound sense of religious acceptance, tolerance, and curiosity in her. It wasn't about the religions, but a way of living. Later, as a new mother in the United States, she began attending a mainline church. She felt the need to be a part of a faith community that would support her young family. Over time she began to question: "Where is the spirituality of the community?" And disillusionment set in.

"I needed a connection to a community that was like-minded, but not necessarily similar in beliefs or philosophies. We just needed to be on a path searching for a deeper spirituality in our lives," Sally said. She created another small circle that began holding brave safe space where members could explore different spiritual practices. They developed meaningful connections bringing good feelings about humanity. As Sally says, "I needed more than just 'mascara friends.'"

The Circle Way has been a major contributor to our practice as spiritual companions. Catherine's drive down the dusty dirt road into Kenyon Ranch led to learning how to be in an accepting, life-giving community. The southern Arizona desert setting brought the stark realization of the desert within our own lives. We were thirsty for a good desert rain bringing the musky earthy smell of the creosote bushes to life as they soak up the moisture. Breathe deep into this reminder of spiritual refreshment for the journey. Hold close the memories of brave safe spaces of women who poured their love over thirsty souls.

The Grandmothers Gathering embodied The Circle Way. They offered a process and practice for building capacity to create communities that support the spiritual but not religious. From the Grandmothers, multiple new circles have formed. This has become a way of life and it ripples out into many lives. What if every conversation, every interaction, every human connection was steeped in curiosity and compassion without judgment? Now that's a world we want to live in.

CHAPTER SIX

MEDITATION, CONTEMPLATION & MINDFULNESS

INSPIRED IMAGINATION

We can live without religion and meditation,
but we cannot survive without human affection.
—Dalai Lama

Catherine and Gil live in the heart of the Southwestern desert. Thousands of people come to Arizona every winter to enjoy sunny holidays, golf, spring training baseball, hiking, and swimming in their heated backyard pool. Few of our winter visitors stick around for the long harsh summer. Penetrating heat, rising and falling thirty degrees in a few hours. One hundred and ten degrees is common. One hundred and twenty, becoming more so. Shade is a mirage. The birds gape their mouths, grounded by the oppressive sun. The only relief found in those brief moments is when the sun waits in anticipation, hiding below the morning's horizon. Birds sing only as the tiny colored lights emerge as shy fairies—lingering in the light of the not yet. An illusionary space that is not space, the moment of the *aurora consurgens*, the mystical dawn. Here, the hawks, the sparrows, the lizards, the snakes, the rabbits, and humans breathe a sigh in unison as a ritual of gratitude. A fleeting moment pregnant with magic that must not be wasted. For such a ritual to become a reality one must rise long before the sun. To survive the summer is the hoped-for outcome. Breathing is the only liturgy. To be consciously awake is the only requirement. To be daily present is the practice.

In the early of the morning, when it still feels like night, Gil woke from a dream but was still in the dream. Words and numbers were floating around him like mist. The symbols became a veiled sky of soft hues, hushed greys, and a spray of orange, and pale blue layered across a thin line of uncertain horizon. And as the dawn sprawled across the sky, the words and numbers began to form into patterns and fragments. He knew what he was seeing but couldn't make meaning of the vision. His body carried him out into the morning darkness. The warm hands of a still breeze embraced his face, and the first glimmer of the aurora kissed his lips. And he heard a tender voice whisper, "You are loved." And he saw the tarot's Chariot begin to move along the horizon.

Was this a ritual of meditation, contemplation, or mindfulness? Yes. And more. The more is the experience of inspired imagination, based upon what Carl Jung called Active Imagination. Inspired imagination is a space where the practices of meditation, contemplation, mindfulness can all find a seat in our circle of meaning-making. Each of these practices can, on their own, take us into an altered state of consciousness, but we've searched to find a bit more. We do believe there a distinct difference in the practices of meditation, contemplation, mindfulness, and inspired imagination. To begin, we will take a brief look at the first three of these ancient crafts of soul work. And then we will offer a quick overview of Jung's Active Imagination as background for what we call inspired imagination.

MEDITATION

The earliest recorded history of meditation came from India over 3,500 years ago. Whether or not this was the birthplace of mediation, the religious practice of sitting in silence spread from the East. *The Bhagavad Gita* was written between 400-100 BCE. This book of poetic sayings provides the reader with information about the philosophy of yoga, meditation, and the spiritual life. The author of these sacred teachings tells us that the goal of meditation is detachment from material possession, a filling of spiritual wisdom, self-realization, and being at one with the Reality of consciousness. In the following Hindu text, we find common goals that appear in most all other sacred teachings regarding meditation.

> Select a clean spot, neither too high nor too low, and seat yourself firmly on a cloth, a deerskin, and kusha grass. Then once seated, strive to still your thoughts. Make your mind one-pointed in meditation and your heart will be purified. Hold your body, head and neck firmly in a straight line, and keep your eyes from wandering. With all fears dissolved in the peace of the Self and all actions dedicated to Brahman, controlling the mind and fixing it on me, sit in meditation with me as your only goal. With senses and mind constantly controlled through meditation, united with the Self within, an aspirant attains nirvana, the state of abiding joy and peace in me.[1]

Today, meditation, for those with or without a religious intent, is the practice of resting the mind on "no-thing." The purpose of meditation is to release the mind from its daily activity, more commonly known as, "quieting the monkey mind." When we sit in meditation, a million thoughts can flood our mind. The idea of meditation is to acknowledge the thought, then dismiss it, so as to empty the mind. Most practitioners use a mantra, a word or a phrase, to assist them in releasing the distraction and return the mind to stillness, to focus on their breath, or on "no-thing." Some practitioners use the image of placing the thought in a boat and letting it float down a river. Meditation can be practiced daily from ten minutes to an hour, alone or in a group. And research has shown there are many benefits for the mind, body, soul, and spirit through practicing meditation on a regular basis.

Some of our best experiences with meditation have been in a group. Six or so of us met every Wednesday night. Our facilitator placed a candle in the middle of our circle and then began the session with three minutes of quiet music. We then had thirty minutes of silence, which she brought us out of with some more soft music. This was followed by a short reading (typically a poem). To close, she would invite anyone to share a few sentences about their experience.

These group "sits" were important to us at that time because we felt the collective was calming our body and quieting the mind. It was as if we could release our thoughts and feelings onto the wave of energy that our fellow practitioners were creating. Our thoughts joined theirs in a collective wave that would rise to the ceiling and then out into the world, floating away, replaced by a stillness of peace. That didn't happen every night, but when it did, we left our time together with a lightness we could rarely find elsewhere.

CONTEMPLATION

Contemplation is a practice shared by many spiritual traditions. While meditation is the focus on "no-thing," contemplation is the practice of focusing the mind on "one-thing." We described a form of contemplation in chapter one in Gil's conversation with Marcus about his experience with OHALAH. In Kabbalah, some practitioners contemplate by focusing their attention on one of the Divine Names.

In the art of contemplation the practitioner is encouraged to engage the six senses—sight, hearing, touch, smell, taste, and intuition—onto the examination of one-thing. The focus of our attention can be on an attribute (or Name) of the Divine, an image (an icon or a statue), a picture (a tarot card, or a picture of loved one), a story (a few lines of a poem or a paragraph from a novel), or a potential outcome from a decision we must make.

Whether we are focused on a name, an image, a picture, a story, or a decision, we can follow a three-step process, divided into sessions of equal length —five minutes, for example. (We are not suggesting in any way that this is the Kabbalah method of contemplation.) To begin the first session, ask yourself, "What am I seeing?" Following this first five-minute session, give yourself two minutes to write what you saw in your journal. Now in the second five minutes of contemplation, ask yourself "What am I hearing?" Again, in your journal, spend a few minutes in reflection. Finally, in the third session, ask yourself, "What am I feeling?" Allow yourself as much time as you need to reflect on the entire session.

Another unique way to practice this form of contemplation is using what is known as a "nested meditation." Psychologist Kevin Anderson developed this model.

> A way to move, in a few words, from surface observations or feelings into deeper layers of experience. These meditations are presented in a layered or "nested" format. They reveal themselves one line at a time, with each stanza containing the previous one, much like a set of Russian matryoshka doll.[2]

A nested meditation is brief written meditation that begins with a single phrase or sentence, then adds one line at a time.

As each line is added the meaning of the piece begins to shift. Here is how to create a nested meditation:

- Start with a pad of paper and a pen or pencil.
- Take a few deep slow breaths to calm your Mind/body.
- Observe what inner thoughts arise or what you perceived in the outer world. Feel the flow within and all around.
- Write one brief phrase or sentence. This phrase or sentence will be the first stanza of the meditation.
- Rewrite the first phrase and add one more phrase or sentence. This phrase does not need to connect logically to the one before or the one after. Trust the flow. These two phrases will be the second stanza.
- Rewrite the first two phrases and add one more phrase. These three phrases will be the third stanza.
- Rewrite the first three phrases and add one more phrase. These four phrases will become the final stanza.
- Remember to take your time, feel into the flow, and enjoy what shows up.

Here is an example of a nested meditation written by Catherine:

Moving within me

Moving within me
Holy, soulful stories

Moving within me
Holy, soulful stories
Connecting me with the eternal in others

Moving within me
Holy soulful stories
Connecting me with the eternal in others
Pouring light into my depths

Another method of contemplation is to "enter the story." This is a method similar to that practiced by the followers of Saint Ignatius of Loyola. Select a brief reading, no more than a few lines of poetry or prose. Follow the same three-step procedure described above. This time, however, read the poetry or prose before each session of silence. Then use these questions to allow yourself to enter the story: which character am I attracted to; how do I see myself as this character; what is this character trying to tell me?

This same method and set of questions can be used to contemplate a dream or a question or an issue that is troubling you. Let's take a common example—a relationship problem. First, write out the problem in your journal. In this type of meditation practice, this will only work if you write your problem so that you can read it aloud—simply remembering the act of writing and reading aloud will allow the problem to come alive and thereby create an energy all its own. After the first reading, ask yourself, "What word or phrase am I attracted to?" After the second reading, "What word or phrase is repelling me?" The third reading is followed by the question, "What are my senses revealing to me about this issue?" Then journal your reflection.

Using any of these four contemplative practices, the "reading" can be used on multiple days, especially in dealing with a dream, a question, or a problem. Several days in contemplation of the same dream, question, or issue, typically will bring some ideas, answers, or resolve. We frequently recommend this last practice of contemplation to folks when they are faced with a decision and are having trouble deciding what's best for them.

MINDFULNESS

Mindfulness is the practice of focusing on the now (speaking in the first person)—my body, my feelings, my thoughts, and my surroundings. I am aware of what I am experiencing right now in this very moment. I am not judging what I am experiencing. My response is to be gentle with myself, nourish myself. Mindfulness focuses our attention on where I am now, not the past, not the future. Mindfulness can bring us into alignment with our self, into a state of integration, away from fighting against my body, my thoughts, my feelings. I acknowledge what I'm experiencing and offer love to myself for who I am. Mindfulness can bring about positive results in reducing stress, lowering anxiety, as well as being extremely helpful in the process of healing the body. Medical research today suggests that we cannot fight our illness, because we would be fighting against our own body. The best way we can assist our physicians in healing our body is to engage in the mindfulness practice of acknowledging my aliment. Give it a name, invite my illness to speak to me, listen to what is troubling me, and ask it how I can assist in the healing process. By recognizing my disease, my pain, my fears—by addressing my disease with loving attention and by participating in my healing with loving kindness—I am in cooperation with my Mindbody, along with my physicians, and my higher being, to be about the process of healing the very essence of myself.

Some of our best mindfulness experiences have been while walking. We can ask ourselves, "What am I seeing?" A tree. Can I stop and admire the tree? Ask the tree what it has seen this day? What does the breeze against my skin feel like? How are my feet feeling walking along the surface? Do my feet feel different when I change surfaces? Mindfulness is the awareness of my Mindbody and my surroundings, and how they interact.

Which is the best of the three practices: meditation, contemplation, or mindfulness? There is an endless supply of magazines, books, and gurus that will tell us their method is the best, for all good reasons. We think you have to decide for yourself what is best for you. Your answer will take into consideration where you are in life, what's happening to you, and what you need. Can we practice all three at once? Or better, you might be asking yourself, "aren't these three practices simply a different take on the same thing?" In a sense, we guess they are. But when choosing which method is best for us, we ask ourselves which of these three practices we are attracted to at this moment in time. What best suits the situation I find myself in? We could ask ourselves the same question of physical exercise: "What's best for me at this time in my life?" Isn't exercise just exercise? It's all the same? I don't think so. When we were young, we kept fit using a different set of exercises than we do now as an older person. If we tried to do now what we did when we were twenty, well, that wouldn't end well. Running sprints is much different than running distance, which is much different than riding a bike, which is much different than walking. But aren't they all achieving the same result? When we were twenty, the expected results were much different than now, when we are over sixty-five, simply wanting to manage weight and staying fit enough to play with our grandsons.

As a spiritual companion, having experiences with all three forms can be helpful, especially when helping someone sort through all the options. Try one of the three practices (meditation, contemplation, mindfulness) for thirty minutes a day, or once a week. Then try the others. What differences did you experience between the various methods and techniques? How would you imagine using the three forms during certain situations in life?

Sometimes, though, we simply need to change things up and go deeper into our imagination, to connect with our Mindbody in yet another altered state of consciousness. Active Imagination, as taught by Carl Jung, is an opportunity for yet another meditative experience.

ACTIVE IMAGINATION

Active Imagination is a term that was coined by psychiatrist Carl Jung, describing the experience of his self-experimentation, of bringing the unconscious into consciousness. His experiences were moments of paranormal synchronicity, when the unexpected arrived unannounced with a specific symbolic message.

During a chaotic period in his late-thirties, Jung left his practice and teaching position at Burgholzli Mental Hospital. It was 1912 and his fragile relationship with the older Sigmund Freud had unraveled. Jung published *Symbols of Transformation* in which he asked the question, "What is my personal myth?" (In Chapter 13 we will discuss how to write your personal myth.)

In the midst of Europe's tumultuous time, Jung had three dreams that he considered to be premonitions of World War I. Jung's personal unconscious was being overrun by what he termed the collective unconscious, the realm of ancient archetypes. Jung journaled and spent time contemplating his dreams. During these experiences, the "spirit of the depths" spoke to him and the words were disturbing. Jung sought solace from his soul in *The Red Book*:

> And you, my soul...I found you where I least expected you. You climbed out of a dark shaft. You announced yourself to me in advance in dreams. They burned in my heart and drove me to all the boldest acts of daring and forced me to rise above myself. You let me see truths of which I had no previous inkling. You let me undertake journeys whose endless length would have scared me if the knowledge of them had not been secure in you.[3]

As Jung continued his dream work, figures began to appear

as visions in his waking world. Four characters became his companions, his allies: Elijah, Salome, the serpent, and Philemon. His interactions with these figures and others were the frightening "journeys [of] endless length." At times, his allies were consoling. On other occasions, they challenged him. And still other times, they were condemning. For two years, Jung recorded these conversations in personal journals. In 1921, the results of his self-experimentation were published in his foundational book *Psychological Types*, from which the *Myers-Briggs Type Indicator* was derived. It wasn't until 2008, fifty years after Jung died, that *The Red Book* was published. This unique volume included most of his handwritten journals (known as the *Black Books*), mandalas Jung painted, and interpretive text about his experience.

Active Imagination is not fantasy. Fantasy is what you create from your conscious mind. Active Imagination is what arises from your personal unconscious, and/or the collective unconscious, without a prompt. The experience is like a waking dream in which the personal unconscious is filled with the images and thoughts that have been suppressed or avoided—the images that have become shadows. The collective unconscious images are less personal, more universal archetype images.

Jung's self-experiment of active imagination was fueled by the images of Elijah, Salome, the serpent, and Philemon. Jung provided some clues as to how these images emerged from the unconscious into the light of consciousness. The unconscious, he tells us, surrounds us; we don't have to search for it, we only need to be open to its presence. For those who are more visual, he suggests entering into a hypnagogic trance, the space immediately before we drift into sleep. Today, experts in dream practice refer to this as liminal dream space. Within this space we may well see figures and they might speak to us. People who are more sensitive to audio-verbal responses may only hear the unconscious speaking to them. Those who are more kinesthetic may experience auto-writing.[4] This is how early twentieth-century abstract artist Hilma af Klint first received messages from the unconscious with instructions on how to paint "The Temple." Recently rediscovered, af Klint's art exposes the intersection of the paranormal and the imaginal, revealing a new potential of the scientific exploration of the psyche.

Jung referred to this illusive psychic space at the intersection of the conscious and the unconscious as the transcendent function. Jung suggested that our access to the transcendent function is manifest via our least preferred personality type. (More on personality typing in Chapter 7.) For example, Gil is an Introverted person whose interior functions are, first, Intuition, and second, Feeling (INF). His third preferred function would be Thinking. And his least preferred function is Sensing. This is based on the idea that Intuition is his dominant of the four interior functions (Intuition, Sensing, Thinking, Feeling). Therefore, while it is difficult to access the unconscious through the least preferred function, once he does, the experience can be very profound. That is why he has had some of his most exhilarating transcendent function experiences while on walking pilgrimages, where his Sensing Function was on overload. It was while he was walking across Ireland alone, fasting, exhausted, that his hearing, sight, smell, and touching senses were heightened. And here is where he saw visions and heard voices. Some of the visions and voices qualify as conscious experiences (ram, raven, standing stones, mother tree), while others fall into the unconscious realm of experience (voices in the mist and the trees and raven guides). The unconscious manifested in his conscious experience and became his integrated reality.

Jung also used Kundalini Yoga in his personal practice as a means of accessing the unconscious. As early as 1912, other analysts were already comparing Jung's psychological work to yoga, calling it the "new path."[5] We find contemporary examples of the use of yoga as a means of accessing the unconscious. In both, religious historian Jeffrey Kripal's *Secret Body* and Episcopal priest James Reho's *Tantric Jesus*,[6] each had physical paranormal experiences that included visions and voices. In each instance—Jung's, Kripal's, and Reho's, as well as Gil's—the images from the unconscious became life-altering experiences and the characters lifetime partners and allies. (We'll talk more about Ally work in Chapter 10.)

Jung's Active Imagination is the foundation for what Catherine and Gil are calling Inspired Imagination. This method draws not only on Jung, but also on meditation, contemplation, and mindfulness, in order to access our unconscious in processing the issues of daily life.

INSPIRED IMAGINATION

Not everyone may be aware of having had an experience of paranormal synchronicity— visible characters speaking to us with audible voices that appear without conjuring or provocation. Most of us, though, have probably had that unexplainable moment—a strange coincidence that defies our reasoning—a mystical experience. To acknowledge the experience without the need to reasonably find an explanation can open the door for experiencing Inspired Imagination.

Third century Neoplatonists initially used the phrase "Inspired Imagination" in reference to the spiritual practices they used in order to be in union with the Divine. Neoplatonist Iamblichus (240 – 325 CE) incorporated breathing techniques and extended prayer sessions to enhance his Inspired Imagination experience of being at one with God. As mentioned in the Introduction, the Celtic Bards used a trance practice known as *imbas forosna*. The ancient Celts considered this to be a clairvoyant gift of the poets. However, we met an Irish artist who considers the trance state a technique that can be taught and practiced.

The trance technique of Inspired Imagination is rather simple. All you need is an object to stare at and an open mind. Our experience has been that the best objects to use are either a small ceramic bowl, one that can be held in your hand and is preferably dark blue or black, or a lit candle, or a stone, again small enough that it can be held in the palm of your hand. If none of those are available, on a blank piece of paper, using a black marker, draw a six-inch circle and in its center a dime-sized dot. In a softly lit room, while sitting in a comfortable chair, hold your object in your hands, or in the case of the candle, place it on a table directly in front you. Using the meditation technique mentioned above, close your eyes and focus on "no-thing." After five minutes, slowly open your eyes to gaze upon your object. Direct your attention now to one thing: the bottom of the bowl, the flicker of the lit candle, the stone, the center of your circle. In your first attempt, keep your gaze on the object for five minutes. With practice, extend your gaze until you lose track of time, stepping into timelessness—the trance of Inspired Imagination. In the trance state, the imagination of the images, the senses, the words, become active agents of inspiration.

Jeffrey Kripal posits in his book, *Secret Body*, that "the deepest roots and reaches of the imagination are the roots and the reaches of consciousness itself."[7] We can use our imagination to explore the unconscious, process our dreams, and make meaning of the paranormal. Inspired Imagination provides a wholistic technique that includes a variety of methods that previously might be seen as stand-alone tools—personality type, dreams, movies, books, music, tarot, synchronistic events, and the paranormal—now working together in rhythmic fashion to narrate the story, or myth, of our life.

Let's say you're struggling to solve a problem at work. One night you have a dream that seems to offer a clue about your situation. The next evening you're watching a movie that appears to be totally unrelated to your job. Surprisingly, a most pleasant moment of insight shines a tiny bit of light on the clue your dream revealed. That night, before you go to sleep, you're finishing a novel you've been reading for a couple of weeks. Something in the story speaks to you, suggesting a piece of the puzzle you needed for your issue at work. You take all of these pieces into the trance of Inspired Imagination. We have found that entering the trance experience opens our consciousness to those deeper reaches of the imagination and brings us inspiration.

This little example can feel rather random. We can, however, go through a specific process to bring ourselves into these states of Inspired Imagination to assist us with life's questions. In this practice sample, we're going to incorporate a method borrowed from Karen Hering, author of *Writing to Wake the Soul*.[8] We've used Karen's method in several situations with very interesting results. This technique requires a half-sheet of paper, 5 ½ inches by 8 ½ inches, a second piece of paper 8 ½ by 11 inches, two colored pencils, and some scotch-tape. There are six steps to the process.

Let's say you're trying to decide whether to move to another city:

1. On the half-size piece of paper, write your options and all the pros and cons. To put them on paper helps release the mind from "keeping a running list." By doing so, we open some creative space for ourselves.
2. Take the piece of paper you just wrote on, and vertically, tear it in half. Holding the larger piece of paper (8 ½ by 11) horizontally, tape the two torn halves at the opposite ends, leaving space on the longer piece in between.
3. Using the colored pencils, on each half of the torn paper underline words or phrases that jump out at

you. You may not have noticed these words before, but now, separated, they may take on a different meaning.

4. Carry the paper project around with you for a week. Be aware of new possibilities and inspirations in unexpected places that might illuminate your decision: movies, books, dreams, off-hand conversations, something seen on a walk. We must be open to see without straining to see. In the inner open center section of the project paper, keep notes about what you "see" and where you see them. These moments are worth spending some serious time pondering possibilities—it gives you time to marinate.

5. Now enter the trance experience. Fully engage your imagination and rely on it to speak to you. Ask the characters in your dreams—or spirit guides, or angels, or some other allies who you feel are trying to help you manage the complexities of your life—questions about your options. Then wait to hear their input. Whatever you hear, make note of it in the center section of your paper.

6. Given the insights you have gathered, can you imagine making a commitment to one of your options and then live with that decision for a week through the act of contemplation. How are your senses responding to walking around in your new surroundings? Then give yourself time to contemplate another option. If you're not ready, not fully inspired and your choice has not been illuminated enough, try another option for a week. When you make your final decision, meditate on the "no-thing." Are you settled?

Using this technique, you can take as much time as you want, or as little as you have. You can take a month, or a day.

The idea is to slow your mind and allow your whole self to participate in the process of making critical decisions.

This practice and process has been very good for us personally and as spiritual companions. It has allowed us to incorporate several of our practices. Inspired Imagination can even be used while walking a labyrinth. The more we integrate the Mindbody, the better our life experience. The more we practice our practices, the further they will carry us into the imaginal realm, and the more inspired and illuminated life becomes. And because these techniques have been valuable for us, we have shared them at retreats, workshops, and in personal spiritual companionship.

Change is the one constant in our reality. The rapid pace of moving parts can be overwhelming. The burden of life can become too much. More than ever, we need spiritual practices that will allow us to calm our mind. Developing a regular practice that includes meditation, contemplation, mindfulness, Active Imagination, and Inspired Imagination can create the time and space we need to do more than survive. A daily or weekly practice can relieve stress while we're trying our best to live life well. And by calming ourselves, we can expand the capaciousness of our consciousness. We can breathe. We have more space to think. We can expand our capacity to handle the daily pressure of living life well. And we will have reliable tools that will assist us in discerning what's best for our lives. Breathe. Slow down. Reflect. Be good to yourself. All will be well.

CHAPTER SEVEN

PERSONALITY TYPING: DON'T PUT ME IN A BOX

The whole point is to live life and be—
to use all the colors in the crayon box.
—RuPaul

Our first student quit Wisdom's Way Interfaith School on the first day of our first class of our first year. The morning session was dedicated to becoming acquainted with the practices of The Circle Way. The second half of the morning and the afternoon we were reviewing our self-assessment of the *Myers-Briggs Type Indicator*.

At lunch, one of the students from that first class said emphatically, "Don't put me in a box."

"We're sorry you took the *MBTI* that way. As we said during our session, the functions of the *MBTI* are based completely on how you see yourself. These are your preferences. If you disagree with the assessment, please, let's talk about it. Do you mind sharing with us the function or functions you think the assessment missed about type?"

"I don't want to be put into any kind of box. If I knew we

were doing personality typing, I wouldn't have signed up for this program."

"We're not putting anyone in a box. The title of today's session is 'Our personality and our spirituality.' Our work is self-reflection, self-assessment, and self-actualization. The *MBTI* can simply be a good place to begin the exploration of our spirituality. Next year we'll look at the Enneagram as another way to examine our spirituality. The Enneagram uses a narrative model to help us determine our personality preferences, and like the *MBTI*, it can help us better understand the shadow sides of our personality and the complexity of our relationships. Hopefully, this self-awareness can help inform us about how to approach our spiritual practices."

"I don't care what kind of assessment or system you use. I don't want to be put into a personality typing box. I hope you'll be sensitive to my needs and refund my money."

We did refund the person's money. And in the afternoon session, we once again re-iterated that the *MBTI* personality types are based on the individual's preferences and that if they disagreed with the assessment, they were free to do so, without judgment of any kind. Whether we used the *MBTI* or the Enneagram, every year since that first year, someone has complained about using a personality typing assessment. Fortunately, no one else quit over that particular issue. Over the years of using both assessments our understanding of the values and pitfalls of these two tools has evolved. After all, they are just tools, simply a starting point to explore our spirituality. Our personal work with these two systems has helped us see where the two inform one another. At those intersections we have relied heavily on the shadow work presented by both the *Myers-Briggs* and the Enneagram. The next step we took in our focus moved us beyond personality typing as the central teaching of each tool. We began incorporating personality typing development and shadow work into the multileveled aspect of our daily spiritual practice. As we brought together the practices of meditation, contemplation, mindfulness and Active Imagination into Inspired Imagination, we also began to incorporate other tools into a wholistic spirituality experience, which makes room for the mystical and the paranormal. Our goal is to continue to build upon the convergent points of our practices and tools in order to bring about the union of our unconscious and conscious—the expansion of the Mindbody experience.

In this chapter, we will begin with a very brief introduction to the *Myers-Briggs Type Indicator* (MBTI) and the importance of what Carl Jung termed "the inferior function" and our subsequent work with the shadow side of our personality. The second half of the chapter will focus on the Enneagram in much the same way. The purpose of this chapter is to explore the relationship between those least preferred aspects of our personality and how we might expand the breadth of our spiritual practices.

James is brilliant. He has spent the first forty years of life preparing to become a surgeon. He told Gil that becoming and being a physician has been the driving force of his life—it is his purpose and his mission. Almost every decision in his life has been made in relationship to his life's work as a doctor.

"Thanks for telling me your story, James. Can you tell me why you wanted to see me?"

"In my life, decisions are made on the best information we have available to us. We work as a team, though admittedly, many times the immediacy and the emergency of the situation demands quick and precise action. To be exact, *my* quick and precise action. It's stressful. But I feed off the stress of problem-solving and saving people's lives."

"When you say you 'feed off the stress' what's that look like?"

"I'm not sure. I think that's why my partner suggested I visit you. What I do is move from patient to patient, so there's no time to process the experience. The only reflection is done in recording information about the patient, the diagnosis, and the treatment. Sometimes, though, it's very difficult when I have to tell the patient and their family that the outcomes weren't what we expected."

"How does that make you feel?"

"I try not to feel. Patients want my knowledge and expertise, not my feelings."

"Even though you try not to feel, when you do have feelings, how do you process them?"

"That's the problem. I don't know how to process my feelings."

"James, you know I'm not a therapist. Right?"

"I have a therapist. The reason I wanted to talk to you is that something outside the realm of the rational happened to me and I don't know what to make of it. I don't know how to make sense of what I do feel about the unexplainable."

"Something related to your work?"

"Everything in my life is related to work."

"Tell me about this unexplainable event."

"It was about two in the morning. I had just finished a long emergency surgery on a young patient. Lots of complications. Things weren't going as expected. But we kept working. Like we always do. Stay focused. Be calm. Think. Make good decisions. And we did. Our team is excellent—we saved this person's life. I was exhausted but on an adrenaline high. I got a cup of coffee and went outside to get some fresh air. I was sitting on the ground floor patio. Usually there's always someone out there, no matter what time of the day or night. But that morning, it was quiet. I was all alone. You know how those early summer nights are here in Arizona—still a hint of cool in the air. The tension in my shoulders released. I felt myself relaxing into the chair. I closed my eyes taking in the moment of a job well done. And then I heard some footsteps walking toward me and opened my eyes. As the person got near me, he smiled. He never stopped walking, but as he went past me he said, "Nice work tonight." And he walked on by me. I had no idea who he was. It couldn't have been more than fifteen seconds later when I turned around to ask him who he was, but he was gone. He had disappeared. Who was that guy? How did he know what I had done that night? Where did he come from? Where did he go? Was it my exhaustion? Had I fallen asleep and dreamt this? I don't know about weird stuff. But this felt, feels, weird to me. That's why I'm sitting here. I'm an atheist. But something happened. Because ever since that moment, I have felt that guy's presence. But that just can't be."

James and Gil spent several sessions together. James trying to make rational sense of his experience and Gil listening.

James said, "I know I'm in my head and the only way to make sense of this is to get out of my head and into my heart. I can't believe I said that, but I guess that's true? Let's say it is true. Just for the sake of argument. Then how do I get out of head, if just for a minute, to process my 'weird experience' in my heart?"

"James, how would describe your personality?"

We have learned that offering someone the opportunity to explore their personality, its shadows, and their spirituality, may not be the best way to begin a spiritual companioning relationship. Maybe if we had moved our exploration of the *MBTI* to later in our Wisdom School curriculum, our first student to leave the school wouldn't have. What we did change was to develop ways of using the *MBTI* to practice one's spirituality over the course of a lifetime, instead of exploring it in only one session. And that's the process that James was ready to engage in—the process of providing someone the tools to integrate the Mindbody: heart and head.

Before we start, here's our disclaimer. Personality testing is an assessment of someone's preferences, not a scientific evaluation of their personality. Personality preferences can be influenced by both nature and nurture. They can evolve over time. They can become more stable with maturity and can become rigid without a personal commitment to the process of development. Personality typing tools are not used to determine someone's mental health and should not be administered if that person is struggling with mental health issues. An evaluation of the personality can only be conducted by a licensed psychiatrist or psychologist. Their professional methods of evaluations are one part of a battery of assessments used to diagnose the patient's mental health. Catherine and Gil are not psychologists. We do not diagnose nor prescribe. We are spiritual companions who assist those we walk with in the process of self-discovery— their own preferred ways of living in the world as a spiritual being.

MYERS-BRIGGS TYPE INDICATOR

While the *Myers-Briggs Type Indicator* was originally based on the work of psychiatrist Carl Jung, he did not create the tool we use today, nor anything like it. American novelist Katherine Cook Briggs (1875 – 1968) began developing her perspective of personality typing while musing about the emotional growth of her young daughter Isabel Briggs Myers (1897 – 1980). After Isabel graduated from college and was married, the mother-daughter team began working on what would eventually become the *MBTI*. The first version of their evaluation appeared in 1943 but was not widely distributed until 1962. The expanded use of the *MBTI* began in the 1970s, and by the 2000s its popularity has grown to where more than two million people a year take the assessment.

The Briggs and Myers personality typing tool was based upon the work of Carl Jung and his book *Psychological Types*, which was originally published in 1921. Jung's book became the foundation for his development of analytical psychology and his theories about the personality typing of Extroversion, Introversion, Sensing, Intuition, Thinking, and Feeling. Each function has a pair, its opposite. While we use both of the pairs, we prefer one over the other. Extroversion paired with Introversion, Sensing with Intuition, and Thinking with Feeling.

Jung used the term "attitudes" for Extroversion and Introversion. These attitudes, or functions, are the external displays of our personality and the most easily recognizable.

He referred to Sensing, Intuition, Thinking, and Feeling as the interior functions. He paired Sensing and Intuition as the functions through which we receive information. He identified the functions of Thinking and Feeling as what we primarily rely upon to make decisions. Extroverts display their most preferred interior function to the external world, while Introverts internalize their most preferred function.

Sensations tell us that something exists. Thinking tells us what that something is. Feelings tell us whether that something is agreeable or not. And Intuition tells us where it came from and where it is going. Using the *MBTI* as a tool, we could provide James with a matrix for his work of making "sense of his weird experience." Only James could do his work of meaning-making in his life. As spiritual companions, all we could do was provide the resources.

Jung never developed an instrument such as the *MBTI* to make these determinations about one's personality. As an analyst, he relied upon therapeutic conversations and observations to assess a person's typology, which were on display in eight different types determined by the varying combination of Extroversion, Introversion, and the four interior types. But still, his evaluations were dependent upon the person's preferences; they were not a predictive assignment of the types.

The *Myers-Briggs Type Indicator* functions of Judging and Perceiving were not a part of Jung's lexicon in psychological typing. Myers and Briggs, however, believed Judging and

Perceiving were implied, though underdeveloped by Jung. "Specifically, they are built upon Jung's description of an *auxiliary function* that supported and complemented the dominant function in every type. The addition of the J-P [Judging-Perceiving] dichotomy in the *MBTI* instrument has been used to identify the dominant and auxiliary functions for each type." Simply put, the pair of Judging and Perceiving reveals how you deal with the outer world, either as an organized person (J) or a spontaneous person (P).[1] By adding the J-P functions as a pair, Jung's eight types were expanded to the *MBTI*'s sixteen types. The *MBTI* assessment has been updated over the years to better reflect the information gathered by the Myers-Briggs Company (who now owns the rights to the *Myers-Briggs Type Indicator*).

Critics of the *MBTI* abound and there's no reason to list all of the critiques here. However, the *MBTI*, in our opinion, should never be used to make decisions about employment nor determine one's mental health. Aside from the *MBTI*'s murky past associated with Katherine Briggs' novels and the shortfalls of the assessment itself, there can be value in working with personality preferences. Particularly, by understanding one's least preferred function, or what Jung referred to as "the inferior function." Here, according to Jung, is where we hide or repress unwanted thoughts and feelings that manifest into our "shadow."

Again, the interior functions are Sensing (S), Intuition (N), Thinking (T), and Feeling (F). Based on our responses to the questions on the assessment, one of these four types (functions) is dominant over the other three. The inferior function is the opposite of the dominant interior function.

Using the assessment and James' own analysis of the results, James determined that he is an INTP—someone who is Introvert, Intuitive, Thinking, Perceiving. In short, according to the *MBTI*, James is logical, analytical, ingenious, curious, independent, calm, insightful, and contemplative. He Introverts his

Thinking and Extroverts his Intuition. Sensing is his third function. And Feeling is his 'inferior function.' Simply put, James must explore his Feelings in order to make meaning from his weird experience. James, according to his own admission, "tries not to feel." He suppresses his feelings, making room for his shadow to form complexes around the multiple layers of his personality.

According to Jung, our best access to the unconscious is through the inferior function (James' Feeling) where we hide those things we don't want to deal with or aren't ready to confront. Our inferior function contains a vast storehouse of our shadows—in James, his feelings about his patients, his co-workers, and his partner. His feelings were his last resort for making sense of life. Only by accessing his feelings would he ever make meaning from those events that didn't make sense to him. What James came to discover is that when he slowed down to reflect upon his experience of that eventful day he could grant himself permission to tell himself, "nice work," and feel how good it felt. That revelation brought with it a tad bit of moisture to the eyes.

Both Jung and those who have created (and revised) the *MBTI* insist that the goal of understanding one's personality preferences is not to solidify one's personality type into perpetuity, but instead, to understand how to work with one's types and how to integrate all the functions into our best self. No matter our type, we each have all the functions within our personality.

Notice that Feelings do not appear as part of James's INTP personality type. What matters was the work James had to exert to access all his functions. While he was definitely a Thinker, he does have the Feeling function within him. But he had to learn how to access his Feelings when he needed them. But even with such work, Jung pointed out, whatever one's inferior function happens to be, it would most likely never be fully integrated into one's personality because of the endless complexity found in our shadows. In other words, James would have to spend some dedicated time in contemplation exploring how he felt about the events in his life in order to integrate his feelings into his everyday way of living.

The *MBTI* has been used by educational institutions, churches, employers, self-help programs, and spiritual directors. The temptation of personality typing is to label others and even ourselves as a particular type. While difficult to resist, we must not fall into the trap of assigning types to other people no matter how well we think we know them. James had to decide on his own that he was an INTP—his own particular and unique derivative of an INTP.

Accordingly, we should not use our type as a defense mechanism, or the means of explaining to others why we can or cannot behave in a certain way. Hence, there are good reasons for the resistance to being "typed" by some of our companions and Wisdom School students. This is one of the reasons we use more than one tool to explore personality preferences. Different tools can provide alternative means of seeing the essence of who we are. Not every tool can help us access every aspect of our spirituality. By using the MBTI *and* the Enneagram, we explore nuances and subtleties found in one tool and not the other.

THE CONTEMPORARY ENNEAGRAM

One of the maxims of The Circle Way is that there is a leader in every chair. To be a leader begins with knowing oneself. No one can lead others effectively without first understanding the deeper intricacies of one's own personality and how they function under stress.

Jessica is a university professor with an advanced degree in nursing. She had worked her way through the ranks toward tenure. While producing quality research, her goal as a tenured professor was to be able to focus on what she loved most—

teaching and her students. But sometimes achievements and expectations can collide, particularly if the goals of our employers don't match the desire of our heart.

"I've invested so much time and so many resources to get to this point in my career. But now that I have what I want the pressure just continues to intensify. I'm expected to deliver larger grants, which means more research and less time in the classroom. As the pressure mounts, I find myself being late for meetings, even missing meetings I had on my calendar. And then I overbook myself—volunteering for things I know I don't have time for, but I can't seem to say no. I feel like I'm losing it."

"What's that feel like? When you're losing it?"

"Like I'm not myself. Like I don't know who I am or why I'm doing all this."

"All what?"

"All my life, even under pressure, I was always reliable. I was where I was supposed to be, when I was supposed to be there, and doing what I was supposed to be doing. Now it feels like I don't know who this person is who is living in my skin."

"So, tell me more about the person who was living in your skin, when everything was as it was supposed to be."

"When I was a teenager, I would dream, daydream, about being a professor. My grandmother was a professor at a small college. We lived close by and sometimes she'd talk my mom into letting me spend the day with her at school. I always felt so special following my grandmother around while she taught classes and went to department meetings. The best days, though, were when she would let me help her with her research. They had an impressive library for a small college. It was so cool. Over time she introduced me to the librarians and their student assistants. My grandmother would give me a list of materials she needed. Most I could find on my own, but other times I'd have to ask one of the librarian assistants for help. And those college students would treat me like I was one of them and we would have some of the most amazing conversations."

"Was your grandmother also a nurse?"

"No. She was a sociologist. She came down with early dementia. And I sat by her side and watched her wither away. My mom was single and had to work long hours. I took a year off college to care for my grandmother. I was like her nurse. After she died and I went back to college I changed my major from sociology to nursing."

"How do you feel now about that switch in majors?"

That question began a series of conversations with Jessica unpacking her personality while building spiritual practices that would support her ever evolving understanding of herself. One important tool in her kit was the Enneagram.

The Enneagram

The Enneagram is a circle divided into nine parts and sometimes referred to a nine-pointed star. Its meaning and use have varied over at least the last 100 years, and its history has been as intriguing as its design. The disputed birth and development of the Enneagram has included stories about dervish Sufis, the "School of the Bees," the Metatron of the Kabbalah, shamans, gestalt theorists, and the intrigue of stolen secrets.[2]

While the contemporary personality typing model of the Enneagram is the concept most of us might be familiar with, the nine-pointed star has a rich history that is often passed over. While we don't have the space here to write a complete detailed comparative history of the three models of the Enneagram, we do think it's important to acknowledge that the Sufi Enneagram, Gurdjieff's Enneagram, and the contemporary personality typing Enneagram each have unique, yet entangled, purposes. To explore these nuances will allow us the opportunity to examine the Enneagram as more than a typing tool in Chapter 9. In this chapter, however, we will focus exclusively on the use of the contemporary Enneagram.

Today, the Enneagram has a broad popularity as a personality typing tool. It has a more recent origin than either the Sufi or Gurdjieff Enneagram but with an equally cloudy story. The birth of the Enneagram's popularity in the United States has an interesting connection to the Esalen Institute, located on the coast of Northern California. The Esalen Institute was founded in 1962 and has been credited with the development of the human potential movement. The Institute brought together world-class scientists and humanist scholars,[3] including the likes of businessman Steve Donovan (who helped found Starbucks), particle physicist Fritjof Capra (*The Tao of Physics*), quantum physicist Henry Stapp (part of the Bell's Theorem group), anthropologist Joseph Campbell, Beatle George Harrison, as well as leading psychologists, Olympians, astronauts, politicians, and religious leaders. The founders of Esalen committed themselves to "synthesizing the spiritual and the scientific, of wonder and reason." From their work emerged a type of "religion of no religion" and the acknowledgement of a mystical secularism.[4] The work of the Enneagram seemed to fit well with Esalen's purposes.

Chilean philosopher Oscar Ichazo (1931-2020) began teaching his form of the Enneagram as a personality typing model at Esalen in 1972. Ichazo had been introduced to Esalen by Chilean gestalt psychiatrist Claudio Naranjo (1932-2019). Titles of Ichazo's Esalen workshops include Arica Awareness Training and The Human Biocomputer (which may have included some instructions on the Enneagram).[5] Shortly after that introduction, Naranjo ended his time at Esalen and started the SAT Institute, "Seekers After Truth" (a term he borrowed from George Gurdjieff). At his Institute, Naranjo began teaching the Enneagram as a personality development tool that he had learned from Ichazo. But it would be Naranjo's students who would popularize the current contemporary personality tool we have today.

In 1984, the first book on the Enneagram as a personality typing tool was published. *The Enneagram: A Journey of Self Discovery* was written by Maria Beesing, Robert Nogosek, and Patrick O'Leary. In 1987, well-known Enneagram teacher Don Riso, who had learned about the Enneagram while attending a Jesuit seminary, published his first book, *Personality Types*. And in 1988, Helen Palmer, a student of Naranjo, published her first book, *The Enneagram*. All of these people had connections with Naranjo.

This early model of the Enneagram personality typing tool used the "narrative method" for determining one's Type, represented by numbers One through Nine. The method is still widely used today. This technique relies on paragraphs (narratives) that describe personality traits and preferences for the nine Types. The person taking the narrative assessment ranks the descriptive paragraphs in descending order, beginning with the paragraph that best describes the person's personality. The narrative method is a qualitative assessment, which for many, we've been told, feels "more spiritual" and less "academic."

Within the last ten years, however, a quantitative evaluation has emerged, similar to the *MBTI*. The test has 144 questions, the results of which rank the person's nine Types in descending order. It's not unusual for the person taking the test to have two or three different Types rank at or near the top. At this point, the person is given a narrative for ranking the top three chosen Types in order to select which best fits their personality. There has been an ongoing debate between those using the qualitative method and those ascribing to the quantitative method as to which assessment is the best for determining one's Enneagram Type.

After the third session with Jessica, she asked about the Enneagram.

"Maybe it would be easier if you started with what you know about the Enneagram."

"A close friend is like an expert in all things Enneagram. She invited me to an all-day workshop, so I went. It was cool. We used this small book, *The Essential Enneagram*, to determine our Type. I'm pretty sure I'm a Four with a Five wing. It all seemed pretty straight forward. But I'm sure there's more to it than that."

SOME BASICS OF THE CONTEMPORARY ENNEAGRAM PERSONALITY TYPING METHOD

The story of the Enneagram is complicated and its use as a personality typing method is no less complex. What follows is an extremely simplified explanation of the nine personality Types. For those of you who have done extensive work with the Enneagram, we do acknowledge the in-depth work required to understand all the nuances of this personality typing tool.

As a sophisticated tool, the contemporary personality typing model of the Enneagram can provide a starting point for exploring our spirituality and developing corresponding practices. Above, we mentioned the narrative method and the quantitative assessment as two techniques for determining one's preferred personality Type in accordance with the Enneagram. Regardless of the method, the outcomes should be the same. For simplicity's sake, the nine personality points of the Enneagram are typically referred to as:

1. Perfectionist or Reformer—those who focus on correcting error
2. Helper or Giver—focused on the priority of others needs
3. Performer or Achiever—focused on tasks and goals as a successful life
4. Romantic or Individualist—focused on what they feel is missing in their life
5. Investigator or Observer—focused on detachment and the intellect
6. Loyalist or Skeptic—focused on mitigating potential hazards
7. Enthusiast or Connoisseur—focused on life's positive options
8. Protector or Challenger—focused on who has the power and how to use it
9. Mediator or Peacemaker—focused on the external claims on life and finding harmony

In using either the narrative method or the quantitative assessment, the desired result is to determine our most preferred personality Type, the one we use in navigating through daily life. We all have at least a bit of each of the nine personality Types at our disposal. The purpose of the Enneagram is to help us determine those we use the most and to eventually learn how to access those we might rely on less.

"Jessica, why do you think you're a Four?"

"I still daydream a lot about what might be a better situation for me. I wonder what life would've been like if I'd stayed a sociology major. Or taken a job at a small university like the one where my grandmother taught. I'm always asking what if, or what's next."

The nine personality Types are found on the outside rim of the circle, representing the external manifestations of our personality—what other people might easily recognize about us. The two numbers immediately adjacent to our preferred Type are known as wings. At differing times in our life, we can consciously or unconsciously, slide into either of the wing Types. In certain situations, we might function out of one wing so much of the time that others will insist we are "that Type" as opposed to our preferred Type. This happens quite often at our job, especially when our work demands that we perform duties using skills related to one particular wing Type instead of our most preferred Type.

Like Jessica, maybe you're a nurse and you choose your field because you really want to help people. You took the Enneagram assessment, but unlike Jessica, it determined your preferred Type is Two. And you agreed that that fits with how you see yourself. You've been successful in your career and your supervisor asked you to make a presentation to other nurses in the hospital. Your workshop went extremely well and you were invited to repeat your presentation at another hospital. Following your presentation at the second hospital, several of the attendees invited you to lunch. The person sitting next to you, whom you've never met, strikes up a conversation about the Enneagram. They tell you they've just finished an Enneagram class and were very excited to discover that they were a Three on the Enneagram. They were very impressed by your speaking ability and wondered if you were a Three as well: a performer and achiever, focused on tasks and goals. You respond by saying, "That's just my wing shining through the workshop."

"Jessica, what led you to determine your wing to be a Five and not a Three?"

"Yeah, I know that was a tough call. Three is a performer and I love to teach. But I also love to spend my days in the library, like I did with my grandmother. I can lose myself for hours in the books. More than once the librarian has had to chase me out of the building so they could lock up."

While the outside ring of the Enneagram reveals our exterior personality, the interior lines (3-6-9 and 1-4-2-8-5-7-1) represent our psyche and where the complexes of our life (that others may know little or nothing about) are hiding out. These interior points equate to our *MBTI* inferior function. What Jung called complexes, or clusters, are the containers for the experiences we have repressed. More often than not, these events were traumatic in one form or another and because we don't want to remember or process them, we have suppressed them into the recesses of our mind, known as shadows. These shadows are typically found in our least preferred and lesser used personality Types. (There are several different theoretical schools regarding Enneagram personality typing and each school has their own take on how the interior numbers relate to our personality.)

"Jessica, what did it feel like when you were sitting with your grandmother while she was dying?"

"That was almost twenty years ago and I still don't think I can talk about it. Whenever it's the anniversary of her death or her birthday, I feel all melancholic. Sometimes I have to force myself out of bed—and some of those days I never make it out from under the covers."

"How's your mom these days?"

"She's in a memory care center."

By looking at the Enneagram shown above we can see that

the interior lines connecting the numbers associated with our most preferred Type are found in the triangles formed by either 3-6-9, or the triangles formed along the 1-4-2-8-5-7-1 line. For example, if your preferred Type is One, your interior numbers most accessed are Four and Seven (as seen in the lines 1-4 and 7-1). Typically, either the stress of failure or the stress of success will activate what we have repressed into the shadow(s). Continuing with our example of Type One, under stress, our shadows will arise from either Type Four or Seven. One is a perfectionist, but under the stress of failure, the One might daydream (type Four) of how to get out from under the stress. Or, under the stress of success, the One might move to Type Seven and become overly enthusiastic and positive about everything, even though normally as a perfectionist they would be conservative in their attitude toward the circumstances. Neither of these responses, daydreaming or being enthusiastic, is bad, but it is not the "daily" outward display for a Type One in a non-stressful situation. Extreme stress, however, can activate the shadows of our personality traits at the most awkward of times. The perfectionist who is daydreaming might let things slide. Their atypical lack of perfectionism might in turn create more stress. The usually punctual One might show up late for a meeting, or forget they even had a meeting. Or the perfectionist who is experiencing the pressure of success might begin to wonder if their success is fleeting, and their insecurities rise to the surface, they laugh at awkward times, then regret their behavior, and retreat into their Nine wing, and begin to mediate and micro-manage every situation from behind the scenes.

Long time Enneagram teacher and psychotherapist Jerome Wagner, in his book, *The Enneagram Spectrum of Personality Styles*,[6] provides a concise access to the shadows of each personality "Style," the word he uses instead of Type. Wagner assigns "Positive Core Value Tendencies" to each personality Style. Correspondingly, he lists the "Distorting Core Characteristics" of each Type. Our shadows, or blind spots, are found in the Distorting Core Characteristics. For example. Jessica lives predominately in the Four Style. She, like most Four Styles, is very individualistic and highly values originality, which is considered a Positive Core Value. The shadow in the Four Style is that she can overidentify with her romanticized self-image of feeling that she is special and unique. This distortion can be more than off-putting to others and it can bring her insecurity to the surface resulting in withdrawn and eccentric behavior (often displayed in her Five wing). In reviewing the Four Style, Wagner lists thirteen Positive Core Values and a corresponding Distorted Core Characteristic for each positive statement.

Working with each pair of Core statements will most likely prompt a denial somewhere along the line. One positive statement read, "You are sensitive toward the fragile feelings of hurt, pain, loss, and grief."

Jessica responded, "That's true. And that's why I feel I'm empathetic." The corresponding Distorted Core Characteristic statement read, "You are prone to melancholy. You believe your suffering makes you special." Jessica responded, "Yes to the first sentence and it took a long time for me to recognize that the second sentence is equally true. Only after working with the Enneagram did I come to realize that the continuing grief I have experienced since my grandmother's death did, in an odd way, make me feel 'special.' Deeply connected to her in a way I never was with my mother—but there was a disconnect between my grandmother and mother that I came to acknowledge was similar to that I had with my own mother."

When we're working with our shadows, other events and experiences we have repressed can begin to appear in the Types we haven't considered our preferred Style. Staying with the example of someone who has a Four Style where Type Two is their response under stress, Jessica may had taken Wagner's phrase, "What's the use? I'm beyond repair, so I'll help others."[7] And so, blind to this shadow, she decided to become a nurse.

She said, "The more I tried to hide my feelings, the more emotional I became. My therapist suggested I needed to heal myself before I could heal others. I told him I felt helpless to do so." The path of self-discovery, to the place of healing and wholeness, can be long, difficult, and sometimes uphill.

NINE TYPES DIVIDED BY THREE

Tri-Type, or center work, is one of the few vestiges of the Sufi and Gurdjieff models that have survived into today's nine-pointed star. In the contemporary Enneagram, Riso and Hudson divide the nine personality Types into three categories: The Instinctive Triad, 8-9-1; The Feeling Triad, 2-3-4; and The Thinking Triad, 5-6-7. A good question to ask is, "How does this part of my Tri-Type make decisions?"

- The Instinctive Triad—Types Eight, Nine, and One are concerned with maintaining resistance to reality. They tend to have problems with aggression and repression. Underneath their ego defenses they carry a great deal of rage. The Instinctive Triad has also been described as the Gut, or Body, Triad. This Triad often reacts to the world first with their gut reaction. They are relying on their Intuitions, whether good or bad, to guide them in making decisions.
- The Feeling Triad—Types Two, Three, and Four are concerned with self-image. The stories about themselves and their assumed qualities are their actual identity. Underneath their ego defenses they carry a great deal of shame. The Feeling Triad responds to the world with their emotions. And when they make decisions they are dependent upon how

they feel about a potential situation, as well as how it makes others around them feel. When they factor in their feelings and those who will be impacted by any decision, they feel they are ready to make the best decision possible for everyone involved.

- The Thinking Triad—Types Five, Six, and Seven are concerned with anxiety. They engage in behaviors that they believe will enhance their safety and security. Underneath their ego defenses these Types carry a great deal of fear. The Thinking Triad responds to the world based on what they consider to be rational ideas.

Again, if there is a "center point" in the contemporary Enneagram, it lies at the convergence of the work with the Tri-Types. The work of convergence, then, is to integrate each of the Tri-Types in the individual's decision-making process. Our Intuition, Feelings, and Thinking all have valuable voices to add in our discernment about what is best for us in any given situation. In other words, the Tri-Types keep us from being fixated on any one particular point of view. Such is the danger of the Enneagram personality typing tool.

Working with the Enneagram has much more to offer than simply dealing with our single Type or Style. The work includes the integration of our wings, stress points, our Tri-Types, as well as our shadows. The ultimate goal is to recognize that we each have all nine Styles within our Self. To integrate the nine Types, we must take the time to acquire the tools necessary to access the least developed Types of our personality. In working with these least formed Types we encounter the potential of integrating all nine Types into the center of our self. Indeed, the "center is everywhere and the circumference in nowhere."[8]

In Chapter 9 we will discuss the need for a more expanded way of working with the Enneagram and the *MBTI*, one in which we can access not only our conscious personality, but also our unconscious shadows, our dreams, and particularly the paranormal. The Enneagram (least preferred types) and the *MBTI* (inferior function) can be models for exploring telepathic communication with the living and the dead, as well as making sense of synchronistic events. We believe expanding the use of the Enneagram and *MBTI* to include the "extended functions of the psyche" can help us move beyond personality typing and more toward holistic soul-making.[9]

SOME PRACTICAL QUESTIONS FROM WISDOM SCHOOL STUDENTS

Admittedly, this has been a long and complicated chapter. You might be on information overload. And most likely you have more questions. We thought this might be a good place to include questions about the Enneagram that our Wisdom School students have asked. Hopefully, this will help a bit in your own work with personality development in this life and its extended existence.

1. I took the Quantitative Enneagram Assessment. Is the goal to have scores evenly distributed across all Types, or to work on recognizing pitfalls of the main Type/s and adjusting in a healthy way?

The later statement is the primary goal, or at least that's the way the contemporary Enneagram model is presented by its chief teachers and writers. (The books we've suggested present this model.) While the idea of having a personal balance across the nine Types might be considered as a goal, I doubt it's possible to achieve—or even desirable. Might be better to approach each Type by asking, "Where can I see myself in this Type?" The answer to this question will be especially helpful in discovering our shadows and blind spots, for they are most likely hiding in our least preferred Types. For there is our access to the unconscious and the mystical.

2. I am still unclear in regard to having a "tie" with say two or three Types at the top of the assessment. If I have three Types that are the same or close in number, do I use the Qualitative Assessment (paragraphs) to pick what I feel is the Type I most identify with?

This is a good question and often a point of confusion. In Enneagram theory, self-discovery is "the work." One way to discover your Type is, as you have suggested, to use the Qualitative Assessment. Another method of finding one's most preferred Type (in the case of same or very close scores on the Quantitative Assessment), is to look closely at the wings of each score. We may find some clues in helping us discover where we think/feel we best "land" on the circle. I think the most helpful process is to look at each of the Types where we have similar scores and start with the one we like the least. The Enneagram can/does reveal our shadows. Another technique is pick one Type and "wear it around" for a few weeks and see if it fits. Then try the other Type. You can always ask someone close to you. Finding one's Type is a process.

3. I scored highest on Type 9 (score 25). I scored second highest on Type 1 (22), and then Type 3 (20) and Type 6 (19). Are the stress/growth variations related to why I scored higher in Type 3 and Type 6?

In contemporary Enneagram theory, the simple answer is yes. In Gurdjieff's theory of the Enneagram, it's about energy generation. Each triangle of numbers (3-6-9 in your case) generates energy when dealing with issues/problems/new ideas. As a Nine Type issues/problems/ideas consciously are perceived at the 9 point. The Three Type presents a passive presence, typically in the unconscious (dreams, active imagination, daydreams). If the unconscious is ignored, it will try again, if we resist, the unconscious manifestation (archetype) will give up and become a shadow. If instead, we work with the unconscious, energy is then generated in the Six Type. There are other variants of this process.

4. If I am a Type 9, my wings would be Type 8 and Type 1. I am confused regarding what this means, especially after discussing the stress and growth variations.

One way of thinking about differentiating the wings and the stress and growth points is to see the wings as conscious awareness and stress/growth as more unconscious. In your reflection, you mentioned anger. Anger hangs out as both a positive and negative in Type 8. In your search for "my version of death metal karaoke," look in wing 8. Of course, preforming the karaoke would be enjoyed in Type 3. You also said, "I feel that mentally I can overcome just about anything." This reflects living in Type 1 as perfectionism; something others probably see in you as leader (always solving problems). Either the Type 8 or Type 1 wing will dominate over the other, but can change, intentionally, at different times in life. You might think of the wings as "my different personality types when I need them." Wings are exterior manifestations of our personality. Stress and Growth are the interior manifestations of our personality.

5. Why is 9 on the top?

Good question. Rarely does anyone ask. Gurdjieff used theosophical addition in creating his system. He combined the Law of Three, which he considered the "free trinity of the system," with the Law of Seven. Gurdjieff's octave (Law of Seven) was developed by creating seven equal parts (sevenths), as follows:

1/7—0.142857...
2/7—0.285714...
3/7—0.428571...
4/7—0.571428...
5/7—0.714285...
6/7—0.857142...
7/7—0.999999...

You will notice the similar pattern in the first six parts (1-4-2-8-5-7). You will also notice that by adding (1+4+2+8+5+7) the sum is 27. And by using theosophical addition (2+7) the sum is 9. The Law of Three (3-6-9 as the triangle) combined with the Law of Seven (1-4-2-8-5-7 the star). Nine steps lead to Ten, the circle is the sum of the whole and leads us to the next higher level, hence Nine is in the primary position of the circle as the top of the Tree. Just to complicate things a bit more, Gurdjieff also enveloped the Jewish mystical system of the Kabbalah into the Enneagram. The Kabbalah's Tree of Life has Ten Sephiroth, with Ten (Kether, the Crown) being at the top.

CHAPTER EIGHT

WALKING THE LABYRINTH: THE SERPENT'S PATH

Images burst forth: unwinding, uncoiling,
participating in the cosmic dance.
—Lauren Artress

G lendalough, Ireland is the home of Saint Kevin's monastery, which was founded in the sixth century. Every year, a million tourists walk the grounds and wander through the church ruins. Saint Kevin's Kitchen was built on the monastery grounds in the eleventh century and is still one of the only remaining structures in Ireland with its original stone roof. The building was a church and was never used as a kitchen. The name was dubbed so because the belfry tower looked more like a chimney. A few steps away from the Kitchen stands a stone watchtower, also built in the eleventh century. The tower is over one hundred feet tall. The cemetery is still in service and has held the remains of people for over 1500 years. The earliest headstones date to the tenth century. Glendalough is near the mid-point of the Wicklow Way and the perfect place for walking pilgrims to take a day off. It's also been the home of 2Wisdom's Way Sacred Cauldron weeklong retreats, where we spend time visiting the monastery, two other chapels near the grounds, and the village of Kildare, the home of Saint Brigid. Our retreat focuses on each person developing a personal ritual.

Just outside the entrance to the monastery grounds is the Glendalough Visitor Center. Nearby is a heart-shaped labyrinth, whose design mirrors some of the earliest known walking passages. Some historians have suggested that pilgrims used these labyrinths to pray while on their way to the monastery 1500 years ago. We have taken seven groups to Glendalough, and each time we walk the labyrinth next to the Visitor Center.

At one of our retreats, just after breakfast, our group of eight made its way to the labyrinth for a meditation walk. We chose that time because we would get our silent walking meditation in before the tourist buses began arriving. We gathered in silence at the entrance of this unique labyrinth. Catherine started the walk, and the others began to follow, waiting about twenty steps before entering the small path of six cycles.

Gil planned on being the last person to enter. David, who was on his second retreat with us, was standing serenely by the labyrinth entrance. David is a tall fit man in his early seventies. He always seems to have a gentle inviting smile on his face. As everyone else had already entered the walking path, he looked at Gil and smiled. Gil motioned for David to go ahead. But he returned the motion to Gil, who then entered the labyrinth. Just as David was about to start his walk, three boys, ages five to nine, lined up at the entrance behind him. The first one started about twenty steps behind David, then the second boy, then the third, all equal distance apart. They maintained their pace and walked in silence, following David as ducklings would their mother. As each person of our group finished their walk, they would stop at the entrance and bow, then move to the outer rim of the cosmic egg waiting for everyone to finish. David did the same.

As the boys exited, they bowed, and walked back to their parents who were standing under a large oak tree ten yards away. As our group broke silence and walked away from the labyrinth, the boy's mom ran over to David. With tears in her eyes she told him she couldn't believe her sons had walked with us in silence. Their family had never seen a labyrinth and were not religious. She was overwhelmed as her boys stood nearby, talking among themselves. David, being a very peaceful person, smiled and nodded. The woman told David he had a special presence, and he demurred. She thanked him. He thanked her. And the boys waved as their family walked toward the monastery grounds. We had walked this labyrinth dozens of times, but who could have known that on that day, our pilgrimage would be joined by three young pilgrims just beginning their journey?

IT'S A LABYRINTH, NOT A MAZE

A couple asked Gil if he knew of any really cool outdoor venues for their wedding. He suggested the labyrinth at Trinity Cathedral in downtown Phoenix, Arizona.

"Didn't Shakespeare use the labyrinth as a metaphor in *A Midsummer Night's Dream*? Why would we want to get married on a maze?"

"Why don't you go to the Cathedral and walk the labyrinth and then come back and we can talk about your experience?" Gil said.

"I don't get it," one of them said.

"You are correct about Shakespeare's use of the labyrinth as a metaphor. The word maze and labyrinth were used interchangeably throughout the Middle Ages and obviously into the Renaissance. Those two words, however, did have different meanings as long as 4,000 years ago. A maze has a series of twists and turns, dead ends and misleading paths. A labyrinth, however, has a singular path to the center which mirrors the path of an individual's life."

We've done a wide variety of rituals on a labyrinth, including weddings, baptisms, memorial services, and fire ceremonies. At one indoor labyrinth, our pilgrims walked the sacred circle barefoot. And before leaving the labyrinth, we washed their feet in honor of their spiritual journey.

Labyrinths have been around for centuries prior to the common era. Egypt is home to what could be the earliest labyrinth, built in the nineteenth century BCE. The Rocky Valley labyrinth in England was most likely constructed in sixth century BCE. Throughout Europe and Greece, coins and baskets have been uncovered with labyrinth designs from the fifth century BCE.

The Chartes Cathedral in France is the site of the most recognizable labyrinth. It was constructed in the early thirteenth century. The Chartes labyrinthine circle was built as an ancient pilgrim's path, a journey seeking the divine. The Chartes labyrinth is a sacred circle, home of the medieval alchemist's spiritual path. The circle is divided into quadrants, representing a mandala, the symbol of life's journey, as well as the four elements creating life, the four directions traveled in life across the four seasons of life.

The Chartes labyrinth is also a moon calendar, surrounded by 114 semi-circles. These 114 lunations are divided by the quadrants into the 28 moon cycles of a month. Three times around the circle represent a year's moon cycles. The exterior circle of the labyrinth became the moon calendar for calculating the day of Easter, which is the first Sunday after the first full moon following the Spring Equinox.

Traditionally, the Chartes labyrinth is known as an eleven-circuit path with a rosette center. The labyrinthine is a journey through the twists and turns of life that eventually leads the pilgrim into Rosicrucian's Rose, which represents the naval of God.[1]

These are the imaginative rituals of ancient peoples, the cycles reenacted of birth, life, death, and rebirth. The cyclical life stories bring the unconscious of the dreaming night into the light of the conscious daylight, holding the tension of the opposites for the realization of another dimension of experiencing reality—a layer of understanding found by taking a pilgrimage into the foggy shadows of our past, present, and future.

BUILD YOUR OWN LABYRINTH

Shelley wanted to gift her church a labyrinth. She didn't have a preconceived notion of what it would look like, or where it would be located, or even how much it would cost. What she knew was that when she walked a labyrinth, any labyrinth, every labyrinth, her body slowed down, her mind became quieter, and she could begin to imagine a future. Her beloved husband died from the results of Marfan syndrome. As the inherited disorder affected his connective tissue, his brilliant mind continued to shine its light and his heart never stopped radiating love. She felt his mind and heart continue to speak into her soul even after he died. As Shelley walked a labyrinth, its safe space created the quiet moments where she could hear Keith whispering a new future for her that wouldn't neglect the past.

Many who attended church with Shelley had never heard of a labyrinth. Some questioned whether it was really Christian; wondering if it was possibly something pagan or sinister. A few tried to persuade the leadership of the church to prevent the building of what they believed would "embarrass the church," cause members to leave, and prompt outsiders to mock "this thing," and by association, them personally.

But others asked questions. What is a labyrinth? What's it for?

Why would I want to walk around in a maze? Can I get lost in there? Is God okay with us walking this thing? How do you walk it? Is there a right way? A wrong way? Will God be there? Will God answer my questions? All good questions. Few have answers.

The approval of the proposed design and location of the labyrinth, as well as the church board's acceptance of Shelley's donation for the entire project, would take two years. But the questions never ceased. They never do because they never should. But do our questions evolve? Or are we still asking the same questions after millennia? The questions that keep changing not because we don't have answers, but because the old questions aren't relevant anymore? What are the evolved questions? Yuval Noah Harari dares to suggest in his best-selling book, *Sapiens*,[2] that "the real question facing us is not 'What do we want to become?' but 'What do we want to want?'" We might be brave enough to add to his question, "What do we want to want to ask?"

Are the saliant questions still about life and its meaning and purpose, vocation, mate, children, death, and the afterlife? For those of us who have asked these questions of priests, pastors, and shamans, we've heard the spectrum of answers, from the expected, to the kind but not helpful, to the suspicious.

LIFE'S LABYRINTH

Taylor leaned forward in the chair. "Do you think God has a plan for your life?"

"Why do you ask?"

"Last week, I went to church with my brother. It was his birthday and he asked me to go with him. I really didn't want to but I love my brother so I figured, how bad could it be? It's a non-denom church, kinda conservative. The music's good. Anyway, the pastor preached about following God's will in your life. It sounded okay, you know. At first it was, live a good life, do what's right, stuff we all should do, Christian or otherwise. Then he started saying that we need to listen to God's specific plan for our life. He said that if we asked God to give us his map for our life, he would. I wasn't buying the God, 'he' thing. But I don't know what to do with the God 'who has one and only one plan for our life', thing. What'd you think about that?"

"It's more important what you think."

"Well, I guess it would be interesting to know what God thinks? About me, I mean. Does God really care about what kind of job I have or who I live with or don't?"

"What if God told you to change jobs? Would you?"

"I love my work. Why would God tell me to do something different?"

"If you follow the idea that God has a very detailed plan for your life, then you have to accept the possibility that you made the wrong choice, even though it's something you really love."

"My brother buys into that theory. He was trying to make this really important decision but he wouldn't tell me what it was. But he did tell me that he knew, deep down in his soul, that God has a plan for his life. And if God would just tell him what it was, he would do whatever God told him to do. But then my brother said, kinda under his breath, "Why won't God tell me what it is?"

"Why do you think God won't answer his question?"

"Has God ever directly answered any of your questions?"

"Not really."

"Alright. Have you ever asked God a direct question?"

"I asked God why my sister was born with Prader-Willi syndrome."

"Did God answer your question?"

"No."

"Did you get mad at God?"

"I was already really pissed-off at God before I asked the question. Soon after my sister was born some Christian told our mom that if she would pray more and fast more often Dinah would be healed. But what really got me angry was when a supposed Christian told us that my sister was possessed."

"How long you been carrying that around?"

"More years than you've been alive."

"So...what do you do? About God not answering your question."

"I walk."

"Walk?"

"The labyrinth."

The labyrinth is a container for questions that have no answers. The more difficult part is being willing to accept that our questions have no answers. And then, on top of that, we discover that we still must be willing to carry the question around because it is so significant for our very existence. If Gil lets go of the question, then he feels like he's dismissing the pain and suffering of his parents, Dinah, and everyone else who has ever experienced the maddening frustration of the unanswerable question, "WHY!" Sometimes letting go is the wrong thing to do. And truthfully, it feels so impossible to do. Sometimes we need to carry it because we want to, we need to, or have no choice to. But many times we need to set it down for a while; somewhere that is safe. Somewhere we know the question will be there when we come back for it. But maybe, just maybe, can we hope that the weight of our unanswerable question will be at least one ounce lighter because it has rested in the center of the labyrinth's magic? While it may feel like we're walking alone, we never are. Many have walked before us and many will follow. And the wisdom of their questions will swirl with the wisdom of our questions—and from the wisdom generated by the questions themselves will arise a waft of fresh mountain air, a lightening of the load.

We have found that the labyrinth is a safe place to wrestle with God about our most painful, unjust, and frustrating questions. Fortunately we have been very privileged to be friends with author, clinical psychologist, and "Veriditas-Certified Advanced Labyrinth Facilitator" Robin Dilley. She is the creator of labyrinth workshops, "Discover Your Inner Wizard" and "Rediscover the Compassionate Mother Within." And she has taught us the 4Rs of labyrinth work. Catherine adapted Dr. Dilley's work for use at a quiet day for those being ordained into the Episcopal Church in the Diocese of Arizona.

Remember as you stand at the opening to the labyrinth:

What has led you to this point?

What has been the easiest?

What has brought you the most joy?

What has been the most difficult and what did you learn?

What transitions are you facing now?

Release your fears and anxiety about what has led you to this point as you walk toward the center of the labyrinth. You may want to carry a stone or some other symbol of what has brought you to the labyrinth.

Receive what you need when you arrive in the center. Everyone has a different faith perspective so let the center be for you what it needs to be. For example, the center might be God's womb, or the naval of God. The center might be a garden where you can pick what you need to nourish yourself in your current situation. It can be whatever you need it to be. The center is a gift that contains mysteries, so take from it what you need. Leave what you have brought with you in the center of the labyrinth.

Return on the walk out, retracing the same path that took you to the center. Return with what you need to make the changes in your life. Allow yourself to reflect for a few minutes about what this experience was like for you. Perhaps it seemed meaningless or perhaps it was filled with mystery. There is no right or wrong experience. Just let it be.

The labyrinth can be a friend, a confident, a spirit guide, the spirit, or a representative of the Divine. The value of the labyrinth is that it brings together our whole self into the spiritual experience of processing some of the most difficult questions and concerns of our life. Whether we're walking, crawling, rolling, limping, breathing, praying, singing, crying, wailing, questioning, doubting, denying, disbelieving, loving, hating—the labyrinth can absorb whatever we bring into it. And we can feel a bit better for being heard.

LABYRINTH: A SAFE SPACE FOR BRAVE CONVERSATIONS

Shelley's vision of a labyrinth for her church intersected with her walking a pilgrimage on Ireland's Wicklow Way—a path that takes pilgrims through ancient forests and offers the opportunity to embrace standing stones, while the soul is nourished and softened by a gentle mist and leaf-covered paths. The spirit of the fog seems to descend from above, while the ancient materials of limestone and quartz rise from below. The safe and brave space where the spiritual and the material are held together in creative tension—not to become one, but to acknowledge that they are within the One, which allows them to cocreate as one. The entanglement of everything became interwoven into the story of Shelley and Keith. Life and death for them took on another narrative of the before, the now, and the beyond, a yet to be imagined future—a timelessness.

Here's a mind experiment. Without thinking in images of the afterlife, but instead the experience of life/death as a state of timelessness, let's ask ourselves these questions. As Keith was experiencing life/death was he walking toward the center of his labyrinth? Or was the end of his walking the labyrinth of his life on earth followed by a transition onto a labyrinth in another dimension? Is it possible for us to imagine that Keith might discover that the labyrinth is not a one-dimensional, flat path, but instead a multi-dimensional, spherical continuation of multiple pilgrimages? Could the essence of our life on earth be more than the expression of a single life, a longer life, an endless consciousness? Was Keith the only one walking this labyrinth? Could Keith have been walking on the cosmic labyrinth—the labyrinth of all consciousness as One Cosmic Consciousness? Are we all walking on the same labyrinth with all that was, is, and will ever be? Are we all a part of the whole, like cells in a body—the body of a Living Labyrinth?

Shelley's labyrinth was built on the church courtyard with a standing stone at its center. The rustic red and white brick floor of the labyrinth is surrounded by three granite stones and two benches—connecting the church to the community's open space: a park and a pond. The labyrinth's location appears to belong to no one and at the same time to everyone. Few people know Shelley and Keith's story, but everyone who walks the labyrinth is invited to bring their own story onto the path, to slow down, become quieter, and sort out life, to imagine a hopeful future, and to ponder their secrets. While we may walk the labyrinth alone, we are traveling in the footsteps of hundreds of pilgrims, both past and future.

How can a one-dimensional path that goes nowhere be anything other than a waste of space, time, and resources? We won't try to convince you otherwise. We're better at telling stories and asking questions. Is there a place in your life where you are free to slow down, become quieter, sort out life, imagine a hopeful future, and ponder your secrets? A place where you can integrate the movements of your body with the wondering of your mind? What are the questions you are afraid to ask? What are your secret questions? Your "WHY!" questions? And what if your secret questions and your why questions are the same—those secret questions you believe you can never ask anyone, not even God? But what if those secret questions are the key to your past, present, future? Your timeless Now.

Once the ground was prepared for Shelley's labyrinth, the workmen dug a four-foot-deep, four-by-four square hole in the center of what was to become a labyrinth. A two-ton, ten-foot-tall standing stone would be set in the hole. Shelley arrived at the same time as did the truck hauling the stone from a local quarry. As the workers held steady the "mother stone," now resting on the ground at the bottom of the hole, Shelley slipped down and stood at the base of the monolith. At the foot of the stone, Shelley laid a sealed bag that contained the wedding ring Keith had given her and the dress she wore on that most special day. She rested her forehead against the stone, face-to-face. The stone reached out to her. Shelley stretched out her arms reaching halfway round, embracing the stone, imagining Keith on the other side, completing their circle within a circle. Her tears dripped onto the stone. In a moment of new energy, she leaned back, stepped away from the giant granite, gathered herself, and climbed out of the hole. We saw more than one worker brush a sleeve across their eyes before the concrete began pouring in. A ritual of endings and a ritual of beginnings: some known, some unknown. Her ritual did not have words, or music, and only the workers and a few friends attended. Her ritual arose from a place of experience and new-found wisdom. The ritual appeared as if from the time before time existed; before everything had begun; a ritual before rituals that was in itself a ritual. When Wisdom Sophia drew a circle on the face of the Cosmos—and in the now—Shelley imagined what was and what might be.

This is not a beginning nor an ending. Shelley's work, Keith's work, our work, is built on the work of many others, those with imaginations and wild thoughts, those who dream, and those who have had visions, artists, scientists, writers, musicians, those who doodle, and those who have no words, and those who have yet to discover the gifts they have brought into the cosmos. Some known, some unknown. The influence of each flow through our mind, body, soul, spirit. They form a cloud of witnesses standing around us while we live, move, and have our being in this world, doing this work of crafting rituals to be enacted on sacred ground in spaces like labyrinths. This chapter, however, is not an ending—our intentions are that others will take up at least one idea offered here and make it their own ritual for the future.

CHAPTER NINE

REIMAGINING PERSONALITY TYPING

SURVIVAL OF THE MINDBODY

The dead do manifest themselves occasionally
in parapsychological events...
—Maria-Louise von Franz

Hugh O'Doherty, of Harvard Kennedy School, has spent a lifetime working for peace and reconciliation in troubled areas, particularly his home country of Northern Ireland. Hugh is slight built man of average height. He has snow white hair that accentuates his warm smile. His soft Irish brogue is near hypnotic. And his presence is as soothing as a cup of tea on a cool misty fall afternoon. Hugh was a facilitator and mentor for a four-week workshop Gil attended at a retreat center in rural Connecticut. He goes on to tell this story.

The group gathered each morning in a room large enough for thirty people to sit in a circle and enjoy friendly conversations. And after two weeks, our group had been meeting long enough to have gotten well acquainted. This particular morning, Hugh stood at a break between two tables, quietly waiting for the group to naturally come to rest. Within a few minutes he had the group's attention. Everyone was quiet and Hugh held silence. He began to look around the room, silently, intentionally, looking each person in the eye. He gazed into the eyes of each person for a good fifteen seconds before turning to the next person. Everyone sat in silence for ten minutes.

When Hugh had gone around the room, he said softly, "We're going to play a game. There are twenty-six of us here. The game is simple, we're going to count to twenty-six. But to do so, we have to close our eyes, and then without going around the circle, we have to count to twenty-six. If at any time, two people speak at the same time, then we have to begin again. We'll keep going until we have successfully counted to twenty-six without interrupting one another. Any questions before we begin? None? Okay, everyone close your eyes. And when someone feels like it, say One. And then someone else, Two, and we'll see how far we get."

Between each of the six failed attempts, there were awkward chuckles, sighs of discomfort, and attempts to resettle in stiff chairs. On the seventh round, the group made it to twenty-six, without interruptions. But what was Hugh's point?

He said that this was the first time he had tried the game. He asked the group what they thought they might have learned from the experiment. One person said they experienced listening with their whole being. Another said they focused on listening for an opening that felt safe for them to speak their voice. The person sitting next to Gil said they thought people were establishing their personal number and once they had done so, they kept that number on each round. And eventually, Gil's table mate said, "We found our way to twenty-six when everyone had found their number." A few people quickly said they had used a different number each time we counted. Someone suggested the exercise was easier for Introverts than

Extroverts. Gil wondered to himself how that might equally apply to Ones and Fives on the Enneagram.

Catherine and Gil have tried this experiment with several retreat groups. The smaller the group, the fewer rounds of counting it takes for them to be successful. Only one group we've worked with successfully counted to the finish without interruption on the first attempt. That group had forty-one people, the most of any group with which we've tried this experiment. They were a young adult group that had been meeting weekly for a few years. And over time, they had established some tight bonds.

We think the point of this experiment is dependent upon whatever each person takes away from it. But we also think this little game provides evidence of telepathy among the people sitting in a circle. How long can we hold silence? Can we hold silence long enough to hear the other person thinking that they're going to speak the next number?

If we see everyone sitting in the circle as separate distinct individuals, hearing what the other person is thinking might seem impossible or ridiculous. Imagining forty-one people sitting in a circle and counting without interruption also seems highly improbable or possibly absurd. But what if we're not isolated human beings, sitting in hard backed chairs, separated by tables, and impenetrable space? What if, instead, we are networked into a cosmic consciousness like the circle, triangles, and lines of the Enneagram. Instead of attempting to transmit messages brain to brain across occluded space, we are, what psychical researcher and contributor to *Beyond Physicality*, Eleanor Sidgwick suggests, "partially united at some deep level, thinking and feeling together behind the scenes."[1] Psychologist William James (1842 – 1910) said that while it may appear we are singular trees in the forest, we comingle our "roots in the darkness of the underground." There is, James goes on, "a continuum of cosmic consciousness."[2] Silence is no longer something to be avoided but something that expands our ability to communicate within the forest of trees and the continuum of cosmic consciousness. This is the language of the wisdom listening and George Gurdjieff believed the Enneagram provided the space for such an imaginative experience of the Mindbody.

The language of wisdom listening, like the Enneagram, is a map for the process of integrating the Mind and the Body, which are no more separable than the trees in the forest. The conscious integration of the Mindbody is the realization of what already is, as well as that which affords the ongoing evolution of our unique transcendent personhood. Our Mindbody, our personhood, as suggested by the researchers of *Beyond Physicality*, can transcend bodily death into the realm of the "living dead." We're not talking about the dualistic separation of the Mind, or soul, from the body at death. What we're suggesting is a cellular integration of the body's dying process into the energy of the psyche. As our body dies, the essence of our Mindbody energy spirals us toward the expansion of our own consciousness into the multiple altered states of consciousness of cosmic consciousness.[3] What we're suggesting is that the image of the Enneagram as a multi-dimensional spiral enmeshed into a labyrinth can provide us with an artistic depiction of the movement and communication between the living and the living dead.

The Enneagram as presented on a piece of paper is a one-dimensional image. George Gurdjieff envisioned the Enneagram as a hologram of three worlds. The first is the material world we live in. The second world is of the spirit, that which we do not see, the dimension of angels and the dead. The third world is filled with the potential for our transformation. Gurdjieff's goal was for us to be in a continual state of spiraling upward through the processes of the three worlds. Whirling dance movements were a vital component of his teaching and group practice, which were inspired by the Sufi dervish. He believed the Enneagram must be felt in the body. He would draw the Enneagram on the floor and have his students dance through the interior lines. He manifested this work in his ballet, the "Struggle of the Magicians."[4]

Catherine and Gil are proposing that we extend Gurdjieff's imagination of the nine-pointed star that exists in three separate dimensions, into a multi-spiraled figure existing within a singular, yet infinite, cosmic consciousness. Each individual being one spiral, within an endless number of spirals, the forest, that constitute the One Spiral, cosmic consciousness. We borrowed this image from Romantic poet W.B. Yeats and his book, *A Vision*.[5] In our model, our individual Enneagram is a spiral. Our Enneagram spiral exists within an infinitesimal number of Enneagram spirals—a multidimensional manifestation of a unified reality (the forest). And our forest of connected Enneagrams is one with all other forests of Enneagrams, the total of which we call Cosmic Consciousness. We want to envision walking (or dancing) our Enneagram/labyrinth as a model for communicating with the collective unconscious, spirit guides, and the living dead. Said in another way, we want to explore a new imaginaire for personality development, one that survives death.

WHEN THE ENNEAGRAM MEETS THE LABYRINTH ON THE OTHER SIDE

In the previous chapter we told the story of Shelley and Keith, walking the labyrinth of life and death and onto the next unseen labyrinth. Walking the pilgrimage of the labyrinth is not a race. And neither is it a marathon. Dancing the Enneagram/labyrinth is an infinite way of being without end. Every holy pilgrimage on the Enneagram/labyrinth is walked in a spiritual desert. Never in the heat of the day but always in the darkness of night. A dark night of the New Moon inhabited by dragons. To enter the Enneagram/labyrinth we must pass through a narrow gate that requires the key of Wisdom. This is a pilgrimage of soul-making.

Soul-making is the lifetime process of integrating the Mind-body. Our work incorporates our spiritual practices but it also includes our physical work. We walk, hike, and do yoga as well as pay close attention to what and how we eat. Every act of living and dying can be considered a spiritual practice and should be treated as equally important in the process of evolving into integrated beings.

In 1968, the controversial Episcopal Bishop James Pike (1913-1969), a regular at California's Esalen Institute from its earliest days, wrote what would be both a prophetic and yet still unrealized statement about the need to create a new practice and a new personality tool to accompany that spiritual practice.

> Perhaps what is really needed is a new way of looking at the human personality—a way which we can at one and the same time take account of both the highly individuated, decision-making, conscious personal focus and the more diffuse but person-connected constellation of fluid factors from the individual's unconscious mind and from the collective unconscious.[6]

Pike clearly understood an extraordinarily unique tool would be needed for an age that would accommodate the conscious and unconscious aspects of the personality. He also suggested in his book, *The Other Side,* that personality development extended into the afterlife.[7] Pike's ideas were based on his personal experiences with psychic contact, through mediums during seances, with his only child Jim, who, two years prior, had taken his own life.

As spiritual companions, we're not suggesting that anyone need participate in a séance. Nor are we going to provide you with concrete evidence proving our ideas about personality development that survives death. All we're asking is for you to participate in our experiment with the imagination for the sake of those who may come knocking at your door with experiences of the unexplainable.

"My cousin died a month ago. We were very close," my companion said.

"I'm sorry. How are you feeling?"

"I'm sad. She died too soon. She was forty-three. We're practically the same age."

"What else are you feeling?"

"Grief. Anger. Loneliness. She lived far away. We couldn't get together that often. I mean we talked on the phone, Facetime, you know. But it's just not the same."

"How have you been processing the grief? The anger? The loneliness?"

"I haven't had time."

"What's preventing you from taking the time to process?"

"Well...in a bizarre way...this is hard to say...she's still here and she wants my attention. She doesn't know what happened to her and she's not ready...to die...she never believed in God and definitely not in the afterlife. But now she's experiencing... something else...and she's afraid."

"Have you had a conversation with her?"

"Well. It's taken me awhile to get over the...shock...no... the...the weirdness...that's it, I guess...the weirdness of the whole thing. No one who has died has ever talked to me. You told me you've talked to dead. What do you say to them?"

"Hmm. They talk to me. I only answer questions. So, it depends on what they want? Sounds to me like your cousin has told you pretty clearly what she wants."

"Tell her not to be afraid? How can I tell her that? I have no idea what she's experiencing."

"When does your cousin talk to you?"

"At work. Well, not exactly at work. Every day, at noon, I go to a park across the street from our office. There's a lovely old tree. I do a little meditation. Eat my lunch. Journal a bit. That's when I hear her voice. During meditation. I stopped meditating. Then I heard her while I journaled. So, I stopped journaling. Then I heard her while I ate. I've been thinking about giving up lunch."

"Your cousin's pretty persistent. How's that make you feel?"

"That's so her. I guess when your dea...I mean...on the Other Side...you're pretty much the same? Honestly, now it's become kind of annoying. I really used to look forward to my lunch time. Especially the meditation. I've got a stressful job and the time alone, outside, under the tree, has helped me keep my sanity. Now maybe I need to change my routine."

"Did you ask her why she always show's up at your lunch time?"

"Yep, I did. And she said I seemed too busy at any other time to listen to her."

"And?"

"Well, yeah, that's probably true. I try not to think about her being gone. But now I want her to leave me alone. Well...not totally. But not every day...at lunch. I don't know. I don't want her to be afraid. I want her to feel...safe...I guess that's it... safe...loved...loved. That's it, safe and loved."

"Can you tell her that you love her?"

"I have."

"And that she's safe?"

"I haven't told her that. But how do I get her to stop consuming my lunch...hour that is."

"You walk the labyrinth pretty regularly, don't you?"

"Yeah."

"Maybe the next time your cousin shows up at lunch you can ask her if she'll meet you at the labyrinth and there you will talk to her about where she's at and about her fear. How's does that sound?"

"Fine. But what do I tell her?"

"I think you can reassure her that her work is not finished. That she's still able to grow and learn. But she needs to figure out for herself what that means. If she does show up in the labyrinth, pay attention to what location she appears. Do you know what her Enneagram type is?"

"Definitely a One."

"Okay. So when you enter the labyrinth, consider the top of the Enneagram as the Nine point. And the One will be to your left as you walk in. Before you start in, orientate yourself as if you're walking the Enneagram. See where your cousin encounters you and ask her why she picked that point to talk to you. Just listen. Reassure her she's safe in the labyrinth and that you'll be back to walk with her again, in the same place. Then call me and we'll talk about your experience."

"Will it work?"

"It has for others."

This kind of conversation did not take place within the restrictions or preconceived dogmas of any religious belief about the afterlife. Embracing the reality that we are living a polyvalent life of transcendent personhood does not require belief or hope. These ideas and subsequent practices are based on more than a hundred years of research.

In William James', *The Varieties of the Religious Experience,* he has provided the groundwork for many of today's philosophers, psychologists, and scientists who study the inter-related areas of the paranormal, panpsychism, panentheism, Process theory, dream work, quantum theory and spirituality, and consciousness.[8] Each of these topics are being actively researched and have their own contemporary specialists housed at major universities like Duke, Rice, and the University of Virginia. The more recent materials can be found in resources like *Beyond Physicalism: Toward Reconciliation of Science and Spiritualism* and *Irreducible Mind: Toward a Psychology for the 21st Century* as well as from the Parapsychological Association website. Our point here is to suggest that there is room for serious conversation about the transcendental personhood, the potential extension of the essence of human personality beyond death, near-death-experience (NDE), out-of-body-experience, (OBE) the paranormal, and synchronistic events without the necessity of any religious reference.

Historian and philosopher Jeffrey Kripal has told the story of his own paranormal encounter as well as that of multiple scientist and rationalists who have had their perspectives "flipped" regarding the validity of encounters with the weird. In his book, The Flip, he challenges us, and scientists, to consider a "new worldview, a new real" that will lead us closer to understanding the mind and consciousness as more than a brain within a body.[9] He offers us five answers that moves us beyond the dualism of the material (brain in a body) and the spiritual (it's a miracle). The two that are most applicable in our discussion are "dual-aspect monism" and "quantum mind."

For most religions and particularly the modern person the world is divided into the material world and the spiritual world, and never the two shall meet. Dual-aspect monism, however, is an alternative to the dualistic way a viewing life. Simply put, proponents of dual-aspect monism state that while it might appear reality is dualistic—it is, instead, united into one.

Ultimately there is no inside or outside, no subject or object. Ultimately, there is no stream of time and no structured space. There is only a fundamental oneness that is neither mental nor material.[10]

Kripal builds upon the work of some of the leading quantum theorists to explain dual-aspect monism with quantum mind theory.

Mind is an expression of the quantum wave function. Matter is an expression of its collapse and observable measurement as a particle. Mind and matter are thus the "same thing" expressed and known by us in two very different ways—that is, within two different types of physics and mathematics.[11]

Let's try and put the concept of dual-aspect monism into Gurdjieff's model of the Enneagram. Two of the major axioms of Gurdjieff's teaching about the Enneagram are: The Law of Three (Law of Creation) and the Law of Seven (Law of Manifestation). Gurdjieff has intertwined the two laws in order to create a wholistic process.

In Gurdjieff's Enneagram, every number is connected to a geometrical figure. For Gurdjieff, the symbol of the circle represents the unified universe, cosmic consciousness: "the unity of everything, unity in diversity."[12] The symbol of the triangle within the circle represents the diversity within the unity. The triangle generates the psychic energy force needed for every action within the unifying circle of the Enneagram.

While the circle of the Enneagram is obvious, the triangles are a bit more subtle. There are multiple triangles within the Enneagram. The easiest to recognize is the (3-6-9) connection. But the star (1-4-2-8-5-7-1) is also a constellation of triangles, for example (1-4-2) and (8-5-7). Each triangle is capable of generating its own psychic energy.

The stages of the Law of Three that create energy are: the energy force of chaos, the matter force of synchronicity, and the information force of synergy. Each triad creates energy used to lift us through Gurdjieff's three worlds.

For example, a problem arises in your life (this world), entering the system at point Three. (The numbers of Gurdjieff's model have nothing to do with the personality typing of the contemporary Enneagram.) The problem creates active chaos in the system. The shock of the chaos induces energy. This energy flows to point Six where it is confronted by its passive opposite. The tension between the chaos and its passive opposite generate synchronistic events that demand meaning-making. The thirst for a synthesis (meaning-making) begins to develop as the

WALKING WITH THE SPIRITUAL BUT NOT RELIGIOUS   157

energy moves toward point Nine (synthesis). The potential for transformational energy available at Point Nine, creates yet another triad of energy. Without the synergistic energy at point Nine, creation of any new energy is impossible. The energy at point Nine was not the creation of point Three and Six, but the result of the collective of the energies at all three points. The energy manifested by each triangle, in turn, contributes to the force needed for the seven stages of the interior process. The goal for the Law of Three and the Law of Seven is for us to manifest the energy (physical and psychic) needed to rise into the spiral of the next dimension (world), into a higher state of consciousness. The combination of the process of the Law of Three and Law of Seven equals Ten, the number of completion as well as the number of beginning (Ten is $[1+0=1]$). Gurdjieff relied heavily upon "theosophical addition," the sum of any number with two of more digits, in his interpretation of the Enneagram.

Using Gurdjieff's Law of Three, we could say then that the "mind-matter problem" is the point of chaos where the energy of force is generated. That energy moves towards the passive resistance, which is Newtonian classical physics. When the problem and a rationale response merge, a matter force of synchronicity combine. The two create an environment where centuries of research can evolve and the information force emerges as a synergistic force. Quantum theory is continually unfolding as a reality (synergistic force) that reveals the oneness of a universal consciousness.

> Who of us can imagine a deep sociology in which there are and are not true individuals, where everyone is a material body and brain but also a nonmaterial wave function that can be "every-one" and "everywhere" at the same time?"[13]

Indeed, who of us can imagine being everyone and everywhere at the same time—but some of us, like Kripal, have had these kinds of experiences. And this idea is in sync with the mystical axiom: "the center is everywhere and the circumference is nowhere." The multiplicity of personal Enneagrams that we are proposing provides an image for this imaginaire of walking the infinite pilgrimage of the Enneagram/labyrinth.

Some of you reading this book have had experiences with the living dead, like the conversation above or as written about in James Pike's *The Other Side*. Others have had a paranormal encounter—you know it happened but maybe you're afraid to talk about it for fear of what others might say. A few may have experienced a near-death or out-of-body experience. (Often times they're experienced simultaneously.) There are many of you who have known the dizzying after-effects of a weird synchronistic event. Unfortunately, contemporary religion typically has had two responses to these events: either 1) you need to see a psychiatrist, or 2) you're possessed by a demon. What we're saying here is that these events are happening daily to countless number of people who are neither mentally ill nor possessed by evil. Some of us consider these happenings to be spiritual experiences and we want to be taken seriously. Instead of being looked at suspiciously, we want someone to listen to our story and help us sort out our experience without judgement.

We are walking a living labyrinth with nine paths. Within the spherical Enneagram are multiple spherical labyrinthine Enneagrams, which is a glimpse of the reality of a panentheistic cosmos. Every Type (number) of the Enneagram has its own nine-pointed star, an Enneagram within an Enneagram. All lines of 1-4-2-8-5-7-1 and 3-6-9 intersect and all are in relationship with one another, as well as with all other Enneagrams of the individual and the collective, (the animate, inanimate, as well as the conscious and the unconscious in connection at all times). Picture your body as the collective of each and every cell within the body. Each cell is a living Enneagram within itself, within the larger organ it inhabits, which is also an Enneagram. The model of the Enneagram is a portrait of panentheism, a picture of the spirituality of everything within the reality of cosmic consciousness. Everything is connected to everything else through the synchronicity of the center of the Enneagram, "unity in everything, unity in diversity." As we do the work of integration (recognizing the unity in ourselves), we bring our shadows of darkness into the light, integrating our Mindbody. We move closer to the center from where we can enter into a state of integrated consciousness, the space where we can spiral to the next level of consciousness.

"Sorry to call so late."

"Ah, yeah. What time is it?"

"I apologize, but I had to call. I just talked to my cousin. We were in the labyrinth. You know the weirdest part of all this?"

"Ah. I'm afraid to ask, but more afraid not to."

"My cousin was, I thought, a One of the Enneagram. But she was the oldest child with three siblings, the last one being an after-thought, who my cousin raised almost as her own. My cousin believed she had to be perfect. Large and in charge. But really, she was, is, a Two. She wants me to help her. Better yet, she wants me to know that I'm right...well about the afterlife thing. And she wants to talk to her baby sister. She wants to help her sister through life...like she was when she was living... but more helpful, loving. Get this...she wants her sister to know that she is loved. I can't believe this...this whole thing is too much...no, not too much...because it's not over with yet...I guess it never will be."

We live, move, and have our being in a cosmic soup that flows with the living and the living dead. We're living in the spiral of the Enneagram/labyrinth. Admittedly, not everyone may have an encounter with a pesky loved one who shows up at lunch time, nor want one. The idea of the survival of death isn't something we necessarily need to believe it—according to Kripal it requires an experience to be flipped. Maybe you'll never have that flipping experience. But if you do, therapy or exorcism might not be the best options. What we are definitely suggesting in this book is that by combining tools like the Enneagram and the labyrinth our personality development will evolve into another state of consciousness, thereby creating space for potentially unexplainable events to have a seat in our circle. And that the tools we're using in this book can also accommodate the space for our exploration of the multiverse within which we are negotiating our lives in context with our unexplainable events. All of this may sound more than a bit weird. But Carl Jung wrote in *The Red Book*, "As day requires night and night requires day, so meaning requires absurdity and absurdity requires meaning...meaning is a moment and transition from absurdity to absurdity, and absurdity only a moment and transition from meaning to meaning."[14] We'll take that leap even further in the next chapter when we add dreaming into the mix of the weirdness of meaning-making and absurdity.

A PRACTICAL QUESTIONS FROM A WISDOM SCHOOL STUDENT

A student wrote, "One of my classmates and I spoke at the same time during the number game. And then we came up with the same reflection work at the end of our class. She had asked if there was a tie-in with the Enneagram. Was our speaking at the same time in the number game, synchronistic expression of what would then later be manifest in our similar reflection work?"

As I said in class, I first learned about the number game from a mentor, Hugh O'Doherty. We had twenty-six people in our class. He asked us to close our eyes. Then he explained that our task was to count to twenty-six, one-by-one, without speaking at the same time. The first time we got to six before two people called out the number at the same time. We tried two more times, and in each attempt got a bit further. On the seventh try, we made it to twenty-six, without stumbling over each other. I've used the number game with several groups and only one group counted through the process on the first attempt. Some never made it and simply gave up.

The number game has several possible implications. Using it in conjunction with the Enneagram and its reliance on number symbolism is a good group experiment. My use of it in connection with the Enneagram is to ask the question, "Are our Minds connected to one another?" The Sufi's suggest that each Enneagram number has its own Enneagram, which is then connected to other Enneagrams, which I interpret as Mind-to-Mind connection. Potentially a descriptor for telepathy. Gurdjieff saw the Enneagram as holographic, multi-dimensional. WB Yeats in *Visions* interpreted our connectivity as Cones (spirals) evolving out of each other—our connections to one another, Mind to Mind, the living to the dead. The same metaphysics exist in the Kabbalah, Hermeticism, theosophical philosophy, and panentheism. The number exercise can be a conscious means of manifesting our personal unconscious connection to the collective unconscious—in other words, an outward manifestation of the reality that we all a part of the Cosmic Consciousness. The simple answer to your question is, Yes, you and your classmate are connected and your work with the counting game and the Enneagram are expressions of that reality.

CHAPTER TEN

DREAM WORK: FRENCH-KISSING YOUR DEMON

*The subject of the dream is not the dreamer
but the dream itself.*
—Stephania Pandolfo

Years ago, Gil began having a recurring dream. In the dream, he was following a person shrouded in a black hooded robe. The person was carrying a lantern down a long dark hallway. He could see they were headed toward a faint light. Upon reaching the light, the hooded person led Gil into a dimly lit ancient library with bookcases stacked from floor to ceiling. He followed whoever was leading him to a bookcase that contained a single red-leather book. When they reached the bookcase, the hooded person handed him the book, but he couldn't make out the title. He had this dream four times. Each time, he processed the dream in his journal. Without any success, he tried to make meaning out of the dream, always finding himself feeling empty and frustrated.

Finally, he shared the dream with his spiritual companion. He had been trained in dream work and was an excellent analyst. Gil trusted his insight about dreams.

"How delicious," he said. "'Every dream is a riddle'.[1] I think Jung said that or maybe Edinger. No matter. You know how I love reoccurring dreams; the magical cosmic soup of synchronicity and the unconscious are in relentless pursuit of your consciousness. Before we get started, though, I'm curious if you've started working on your third book?"

"No. I've been pretty busy finishing the final edits on *Wisdom Walking*. I mean I've given some passing thoughts about what might be next, but I don't know. I could easily write a sequel to the book on pilgrimage. I've got a lot of new material."

"Maybe the dream and the unconscious have something to say about that? I know I'm repeating myself, but the unconscious knows more than the conscious. Okay, so let's break down the dream. What do you think the long hallway means?"

"I've been working with the idea that it represents the long process I've gone through each time I've written a book."

"What's that process feel like?

"Painful. It always starts with thousands of words being deleted. I'm the poster child for Annie Lamott's 'shitty first draft,' except I write three shitty first drafts. The first book I wrote, my editor sent back my third chapter with the comment, 'the best thing I can tell you is to delete these 25,000 words and start over.'"

"Hmm, that's rough."

"Yeah, but she was right. Kind of seems to be the process I have to go through. My second book wasn't any easier. I must have deleted 50,000 words before I even got through the first draft. My son told me I shouldn't write books about alchemy if I didn't want to go through the fire of the alchemical process."

"Your son is pretty insightful. Do you think alchemy has anything to do with this dream?"

"Well, I've been thinking the hooded one might be the Hermit in the tarot deck."

"Let's dig a bit deeper. Who could the Hermit be?"

"You mean like somebody I know?"

"Maybe. Or maybe archetypal?"

"You mean, like you?"

"That's funny," Gil's therapist said. "And I doubt it. Do you think that the recurring dream you had last summer has some connection to this dream?"

"The dream I had while walking across Ireland?"

"Yes. There is a connection. Both dreams relate to walking."

"You mean my dream about Saint Brigid's daughter?"

"She's your Ally, right? Your advocate and connection to the divine and the unconscious."

"Yeah. She is my spirit guide. But it's a mutual thing, you know. I can't help but feel like at times she's getting something out of this."

"According to Jeffrey Raff and those who work with the Allies, she probably does. Do you think she could be the hooded person leading you down the dark hallway?

"Okay, maybe. I'll go with that."

"Where's she leading you?"

"Into a library."

"Have you been in that library before?

"I hadn't made the connection before, but it could be the library at Trinity College in Dublin."

"And where she's leading you?"

"To a bookcase."

"To do what?"

"Okay, I get it. Brigid is leading me into the process of writing another book. But how does that connect to my original dream about Brigid's daughter?"

"If I remember correctly, didn't she have a baby in that dream?"

"Yes, she did. Is the baby the book?"

"Could be? Play with idea a bit more."

"The symbol of the baby has always eluded me. But if the

baby is the book, I'm still not sure what the book would be about. I can't read the title. And I definitely haven't a clue as to what the writing process would look like if Brigid's daughter is going to be my writing guide. Is she the muse?"

"What's the cover of the book look like in your dream?"

"Red leather."

"*The Red Book*? Your Red Book."

"Jung's *Red Book*?[2] Because you think I'm going mad? Or because writing my own Red Book would drive me insane?"

"Okay, we'll back away from that idea for a moment. You mentioned you were thinking maybe the next book would be about pilgrimage. Any other topics cross your mind?"

"I've always considered writing my memoir—*Coach, President, Priest, Alchemist*. But I don't think I'm ready for that yet."

"Are there other people you might write about? Family members maybe?"

"My mom would probably be at the top of the list. She lived a life of courage. And I've toyed with the idea of writing a novelized version of my great-grandfather's life. He was an interesting character, bootlegger, always on the run from the law. That would be fun."

"What about your sister?"

"My mom wrote that book. I don't want to go there."

"Could yours be the *Red Book* version?" he asked.

My therapist reached for his copy of *The Red Book* sitting next to his coffee cup. He flipped easily through the heavily marked and annotated copy. Within a moment he found the page he was looking for. "We also live in our dreams; we do not only live by day. Sometimes we accomplish our greatest deeds in dreams."[3]

Every dream is a riddle. The key to the riddle is found while living in the dream, walking toward the center of the dark labyrinthine path of the soul-making. Once at the zero point of our psyche's sphere we will discover the secret ingredients needed to brew the alchemist's concoction of Dream Magic. The path to the illusive center is arduous and the work to decipher the secret symbols is complex. The most important symbols are the keys that will unlock the doors that separate a conscious understanding of the dream from the mystical unconscious.

The goal of our work with the dream is to distill a delicious liqueur from its contents. To successfully achieve our goal, we need the book of recipes, a cauldron to cook the brew, and a partner. The dreamer's work is dangerous: the wrong contents, too much heat, an ill-prepared companion—a myriad of things could cause the contents to explode in the alchemist's face.

What we also must consider is the weird notion that our dreams are a vital component to the narrative of our life. Our dreams are not isolated one-offs. Our dreams might feel like singular stories but instead they are the blended memoir of the narrative non-fiction of our life. Our dreams are mini-narratives woven into an ultra-long queer docudrama. Carl Jung considered the "long dream series" to be the process of psychic development that he attributed to individuation.[4] We must work with our dreams, not in isolation, but see them as intertwined with one another; one dream cannot be understood without the others. I'll admit, this kind of work can be frustrating at best and mind-numbing at worst. But the payoff for all the intense focus is mind-expanding. This is dream magic. A hallucinogenic experience, sans the drugs.

DREAM MAGIC

A companion and Gil were talking over FaceTime. This person asked Gil a mildly intimidating question.

"Gil, do you tell your spiritual companion about every dream you have had, especially the dreams about sex?"

Gil looked away as if he were pondering an answer. Under his breath, he sighed. He needed time to decide how much to tell. Turning back to his companion he said, "I don't share every dream I have with my spiritual companion. I mean, processing daily dreams can be like sorting through the mail. Some of it feels like mundane junk that I can throw in the trash, while other pieces appear exciting or dreaded. But when my therapist explained to me that my dreams are a perpetual stream from the unconscious, well, that changed everything. Every dream has meaning. Every dream is a significant part of a million-piece puzzle. Nothing can be discarded."

"That sounds crazy," Gil's companion said.

"It is crazy, kind of. And that's why I don't tell him everything. No one has time to listen to all of my dreams. But I tell him about the big dreams, the epic ones."

"Like?"

"Well, when I met with my spiritual companion last week, I told him about a dream I had that was so appalling, I had struggled about how to write about it. But I summoned up the courage and let it all out in my journal. And then I read it to him."

"Well, do you mind telling me what the dream was about?"

"Why?" I asked.

"Just curious. Was it about sex?"

"What's your thing about sex dreams?"

Gil's companion said, "I journal most of my dreams, but some of them I just can't bring myself to put on paper, like you said. And especially my dreams about sex and death."

"Are you dreaming about dying when you're having sex? Or sex after death?" Gil mused.

"Ah, I've never had one of those? Have you?"

"Well, kind of," Gil said.

"Okay, you're creeping me out. I knew you were weird."

Gil said, "Alright, I guess I kind of have to tell it to you now. It does fit in the sex-death category. Juicy enough for you?" The companion nodded. "Okay, here goes—I was eating a dead person's ashes out of a carton with a spoon."

"That's sick," the companion said. "And what does that dream have to do with sex?"

"It's obvious. Think about it."

The Director of the UC Berkeley Medical Anthropology Program, Stephania Pandolfo, wrote in *The Knot of the Soul* that our "dreams and delusions are poems of existence."[5] She's suggesting that we can consider our sleeping dreams and the waking fragments of psychic brokenness as a container for the language of our life. The images in the dreams are mystical poetry. Pandolfo explains that dreams are a knot of the past twisted into our imagination of the future. I might ask of myself, "Whose ashes am I eating in the dream?" I don't know. I haven't eaten anyone's ashes in my waking life. Is the dream a foretelling of the future? Or more likely asking me to go deeper into the symbolic passage of the unconscious.

Pandolfo would most likely ask me not whose ashes I ate, but "What do the ashes represent?" My therapist would be asking me, "What's the buried stuff that I need to process?"

A process that mirrors eating my way through the four paths of alchemy:

- chaos: appalling dream revealing an unconscious shadow,
- experiencing a glimmer of light: talking to my spiritual companion,
- recognizing the strangeness of a situation: realizing this is a death-sex dream with deeper implications, and
- embracing the new normal: imagining how the reorientation of my thinking process will benefit my life in the now.

And how do I process such a dream? Carl Jung suggested that every character in the dream can be an aspect of our psyche:

- the anima: the soul,
- the shadow: what was or is avoided or denied,
- the ego: our primary driving force,
- the persona: our masks,
- and the archetypes: universal images, like a parent, child, teacher, house, forest.

The characters in the dream can appear as people we know, or strangers. They can also emerge as symbols (trees, stones, weapons, planets), animals (including amphibians and reptiles), and mythical figures (gods, goddesses, dragons). Each of the characters that appear in a dream most likely represent an aspect of our psyche. Everyone in the dream is the person dreaming the dream. The "friend or stranger" who appears in the dream is not a person in my waking life. (There are exceptions to this which we will discuss below.) The image of the person in my dream is what my psyche is projecting of my shadow onto the person in my dream. Pandolfo writes that "the subject of the dream is not the dreamer but the dream itself." I am not dreaming the dream; the dream is dreaming me. But I am processing what the dream, the unconscious, is trying to help me become aware of, to become conscious of. How do I sort out these messages that appear in my dreams? Jung called this process dream amplification.

First, as soon as we wake up from a dream, before we get out of bed, recount the dream so that we won't forget it before we can take it to our journal. We've learned this the hard way because we've forgotten dreams from the bed to the journal, even with it sitting on the desk in the next room.

Second, meditate on the dream. Walk your way through what you can remember. Often pieces we didn't remember appears in the meditation. The unconscious is always eager to fill in the blanks.

Third, in our journal, identify who the characters in the

dream represent. Either highlight or underline names, key words, or phrases. As we continue to process the dream, we have found that who we initially thought the characters represented can change. When Gil first wrote the dream about the ashes in his journal, he thought the ashes represented his shadow, then after working with the dream he imagined the ashes were his soul, now he thinks they are both—the opposites of soul and shadow consumed in the alchemical fire to become one.

Fourth, we return to the dream time and time again, even as we have other dreams. We've both kept journals most of our lives. That's a lot of dreams. Gil has gone back through his journals, creating a life arc of dreams—processing them as the narrative of his psychic life.

Fifth, we talk to our spiritual companions regularly about our dreams. W.B. Yeats wrote that "our responsibilities begin with dreams." He was writing a poem, and it's hard to know what Yeats meant by that line, but I imagine if we keep ruminating on it, our dreams will dream it and help us sort it out, usually while talking about our dreams with our spiritual companion.

NIGHTMARES

Nightmares speak volumes if we have the courage to confront the shadow of our personal unconscious—like French-kissing our demons. Gil shares this experience.

> I had a nightmare dream in 2005. It was so disturbing I tore it out of my journal, stuffed it in a coffee can, and buried it in the backyard. We sold the house and moved. The dream reappeared in 2016. I lied to myself about what it might have to tell me. At all costs, I avoided telling my spiritual companion. I got a secure safe, dug a deeper hole, and buried the dream in the park

behind our house. We haven't moved yet. But I finally did process the dream with my spiritual companion.

Jesus said that if we sweep the one demon who lives in our house out into the street (or try to bury the demon dream in a coffee can in the backyard), seven more demons will appear. A strange saying indeed, but perhaps the thought experiment suggests we might be better off dealing with our personal identifiable demons and nightmares rather than ignoring them. Who knows what might show up next?

The COVID pandemic experience might qualify as a nightmare. And from some of the articles we've read, there are a lot of you out there who are having dreams about the pandemic.

Gil had one dream he easily categorized as a COVID dream, and on deeper analysis probably several others. This one dream wasn't the recurring nightmare dream he mentioned above, but it did have something to say.

> I was living in a church but was preparing to move out. I saw a priest who was vested and then went into the sanctuary to say Mass. Later, the priest came out of the sanctuary. I put out my hand to shake the priest's hand. Stopping, the priest looked at me in disbelief and slapped away my hand. I immediately started looking for a sink to wash my hands and could never find one. I woke up and had this compulsion to wash my hands.

Obviously, the message to wash my hands has been seared into my (and everyone else's) unconscious. We've washed our hands and used hand sanitizer so much our hands are raw and chapped. Maybe the PSAs on TV could start saying, "Social distance, wear a mask, wash your hands, and carry hand lotion with you at all times. You'll need it."

An underlying message from the dream could possibly be that I have some hidden anxiety about going back to church.

Maybe the priest will slap away my hands if I extend them to receive the Eucharist. How does that relate to washing my hands? Maybe the church has washed its hands of me? Or me of them having moved out of their house? Hmm. More work to do with this dream. COVID dreams are most likely to reveal the need for systemic and foundational change in our lives.

ACTIVE IMAGINATION

Active Imagination in dream interpretation is a precursor to lucid dreaming (which will be discussed below) and Ally conversation (which we'll discuss in the following chapter). As we covered in Chapter 6, Active Imagination is a term used by Carl Jung to describe his personal experiment with the unconscious. His work with Active Imagination consisted of his experiences and conversations with visionary characters, forming the basis of *The Red Book*.

Here's an example from Gil about how Active Imagination works. I had a dream about a nun who was floating above me. First, I relax into a meditative state for five minutes. Next, for five minutes I contemplate the image of the nun floating in front of me. Then, I ask the nun a question. I wait for her answer. And then I continue the conversation.

"What's your name?"

"Esther."

"Why are you in my dream?"

"From your days as president at Canyon, you considered yourself an Esther figure."

"I've tried to forget about that whole experience."

"I'm here to make sure you don't."

"Why? Those days are long gone."

"The calling is still the same."

"I'm retired. I'm not a leader."

"In case you forgot, Mordecai said to Esther, 'You were called for such a time as this.'"

"How could I forget?"

"You don't have to be a leader for a calling of the times to still be necessary."

"What do you mean?"

"You're writing this book. You are called for such a time as this. It's pretty simple."

"I hadn't thought of writing in those kinds of terms."

"I know, that's why I'm in your dream. I am here to remind you."

"Thank you. I think?"

I have had so many conversations with dream figures that I trust they will respond to me when I ask a question. I don't expect or demand an answer. I simply ask the question and wait patiently. Sometimes, I don't get a response. In those circumstances, I move on to another character and come back later to the one who didn't answer. On occasions, I never get an answer. Whether the dream image answers me or not, I always thank them. Who knows, they might show up in a subsequent dream, maybe years later. The one thing I never do is to question whether the experience is real. When I've had those doubts in the past, the images disappear and are usually replaced in my dreams with some horrible nightmarish ghoul. Or worse, the dreamworld goes silent. It's then that I feel alone and disconnected from my soul. For the dream characters are each a facet of the many faces of my soul. Even the shadow characters.

SHADOW INTEGRATION IN DREAM WORK

Our shadows are those memories we have suppressed into our unconscious. Most of the memories we bury carry some level of trauma with them. Because dealing with trauma is painful and requires work, we often hide it as deep as we can within our interior self. We suppress those memories for so long that the memories feel ignored. The memory becomes suppressed, ignored, and avoided for such a long period of time that the memory becomes a shadow. Instead of disappearing, the shadow haunts our dreams. The shadow grows larger and darker than the original memory. The shadowed memory begins to take over our psychic space by feeding off of our fears associated with the complex of emotions generated by our unprocessed experiences. The refusal to deal with the trauma of the original memory creates its own trauma. And the shadow becomes the nightmare that stalks us in our waking hours.

Our shadows will never disappear because they are not our enemies. Our shadows are as much a part of us as our lungs. While it may be our good feelings that we cherish, it is our shadows that strengthen our soul if we have the courage to integrate those events we've suppressed into our conscious being. To bring our memories and traumas out of the shadows requires a therapist and the support of a skilled spiritual companion—professionals that can listen deeply without judgment. They ask appropriate open-ended questions and offer carefully chosen words of gentle wisdom that are the keys to unlocking the riddles of our dreams.

LUCID DREAMING

Lucid dreaming is both a learned technique and an acquired art. The techniques are not complicated, but the art requires practice. Simply put, lucid dreaming is becoming aware of being in a dream while you are dreaming. The art of this awareness provides an in-depth participation in the dream that takes us beyond the typical experience of feeling that we are at the whim of the dream.

There are two techniques most often practiced by lucid dreamers. In the first method, immediately upon waking from the dream, while still in a near-sleep state, the dreamer reenters the dream, while not returning to sleep. Once in the dream, we can be more aware of what we see and feel while in the dream. We can take notice of more details regarding the images and experiences of the dream. We can open a door, or walk down a hallway, or read the title of book, possibly taking a truncated conversation further.

The second lucid dream technique can be practiced sometime after we've had the dream and worked with it in our journal. The best time to use this method is around your favorite nap time and place you enjoy the most. When you're relaxed, but before you go to sleep, recall your dream. Then allow yourself to drift into the space just before you go to sleep. At this point reenter the dream and become an active agent as mentioned above.

The idea in lucid dreaming is not to change the dream, but instead, to learn more about the dream experience and who and what is in the dream. If your participation in the dream, however, alters the dream, then you've engaged in Active Imagination. Both lucid dreaming and Active Imagination are forms of contemplation as discussed in Chapter 6.

DREAMING DREAMS OF THE LIVING AND THE DEAD

Gil's mother had a brother who was nearly ten years younger than she was. He had served in the Army and did a tour of duty in Vietnam. Gil was a freshman in high school when his uncle was in Vietnam. Gil tells this story about his uncle.

My uncle and mother exchanged letters while he was in Vietnam. She wrote more than he did—but she always wrote more letters than anyone that corresponded with her. During the nearly eighteen months he was in the war zone, we were all worried and my mother was extremely anxious during that time. But my uncle returned home safely and all returned to normal, all was well. Four years later my uncle was still in the Army, a Captain and a helicopter pilot.

One night, my mom woke up in a fright. In her dream, she had seen her brother standing at the foot of her bed. He told her he loved her and then disappeared. My mother had a tough time going back to sleep, tossing and turning the remainder of the night. At daybreak, my mom's sister called to tell her their brother had been killed in a freak helicopter crash during the night. He had died about the time he appeared in my mom's dream.

Swiss Jungian psychologist Marie-Louise von Franz (1915-1998) writes in her book, *On Dreams and Death*, that the dead can appear in dreams and other parapsychological events as themselves, with messages for the living.[6] Von Franz cites several situations that are similar to my mother's dream. But she also discusses other dreams that are not as dramatic, but equally profound. Von Franz and Jung use these dreams in the consideration that we do survive death as the living dead.

There are times when our living relatives and friends have important messages they deliver to us through our dreams. My sister Dinah has Prader-Willi syndrome and I'm her legal guardian. She appears in my dreams every once in a while. Sometimes she shows up with one or both of my parents. On rare occasions my sister appears in my dream without the effects of Prader-Willi. Those are always interesting dreams that require a lot of amplification.

In one dream she didn't physically appear in the dream. Instead, there were four small boxes about the size of a Rubik's Cube in the dream. Each box represented one of the bills that needed to be paid each month for my sister's care. I was in quite a panic because I wasn't sure if all the bills had been paid. What might happen if something went unpaid? Would her electricity be turned off? When I thought I was awake, I was still worried. I had to wake myself fully to realize that no, all the bills I'm responsible for had been paid. When I got out of bed that morning, I was still worried about my sister. So I called her house and asked the caregiver how Dinah was doing. She told me it was interesting that I called because the previous night Dinah had a rough time. She had a new caregiver on the night shift and Dinah was afraid the new person wouldn't know how to keep my sister from falling.

Dreams between siblings are not uncommon. Particularly, this can happen when the sibling's parents have died. And it's not unheard of for people who have lived and slept together for a long period of time to share dreams. The rarest of shared dreams is for two people who are very close to dream the same dream on the same night. Sharing another person's dream can be considered part of the realm of paranormal experiences, similar to telepathy.

DREAMING AS AN ACTIVE AGENT IN YOUR WAKING WORLD

Our dream life and our everyday waking world are not separate experiences. Our dreams, while not always easy to connect with our waking world, can inform and enrich how we live, move, and have our being as an integrated human. We work with our dreams so that they can be incorporated into our lives as interpretative agents. While our dreams rarely forecast our future, they can inform and interpret what is happening in our interior life, which in turns assists how we function in our exterior world. In a manner of speaking, our dreams can give us clues on how to live our lives. Spending time to record, review, and work with our dreams can be one of the most valuable spiritual experiences we can add to our daily practice. Coupling dream work with Active Imagination and contemplation can enhance our mindfulness and expand our consciousness. And working with a spiritual companion can be of great benefit to us. Spiritual companions with adequate training and experience sometimes aren't easy to find. We want to support our colleagues in gaining the knowledge needed to be insightful in dream work as well as asking helpful open-ended questions so that the companion can unpack the meaning of their own dreams. Dream interpretation is best done by the dreamer.

CHAPTER ELEVEN

ALLY WORK: THE SOULMATE YOU CAN'T SEE

Autonomous imagination is alam al-mithal,
the intermediate world of images,
where divine presence manifests itself in concrete form.
—Stephania Pandolfo

D o you feel alone on your spiritual journey? Or do you feel like you have an angel or spirit guide traveling with you? And if so, are you afraid to tell anybody for fear of how they might respond? Who are your allies in this troubling world? Are they spirit animals? Angels? Ancient guides? Dead relatives? Who walks with you and who can be your Ally in the unseen world? Ally work is an ancient practice that can be incorporated into our everyday modern lives. With the posthumous publication of Carl Jung's *The Red Book*, we've been afforded a model of how to converse with our spirit Ally. Post-Jungian analyst and author Jeffrey Raff brought this spiritual practice into the contemporary world through his four books. In this chapter we'll take a brief look at both Jung and Raff while sharing our personal stories of working with the Ally.

DINAH'S ALLY

At 67, Dinah Stafford is the oldest known living person with Prader-Willi syndrome. She's Gil's younger sister and only sibling. Dinah is neurodivergent not only due to PWS, but also as a result of a 108-degree temperature at nine months of age. She also has difficulty speaking. Because of her verbal challenges, she has often been frustrated in communicating with others. Carrying on a conversation with Dinah requires the listener to be patient, imaginative, and to hold silence. A few of Dinah's words are distinguishable by the untrained ear, but most require an experienced translator. A long sentence would be three words, which is often the combination of a word fragment, a sound, a hand motion, and a facial expression as subtle as a raised eyebrow. Her family has learned to share what new 'words' they've uncovered in Dinah's lexicon. Dinah's mom, Loretta, had been her ally, advocate, confidant, and interpreter. The two would often sit at the kitchen table, enjoying their morning coffee, looking out the window at the park behind the house, and having a chat. And then, when Dinah was 57, her mother died and those conversations came to an end.

Two years after Loretta died, my wife and I moved into the family home and Dinah would stay with us for holidays and vacations. On the morning we celebrated her sixty-fifth birthday, we were sitting at the kitchen table. Breakfast was over and we were sipping another cup of coffee while starring out at the park. After a few minutes of silence, Dinah started talking. Not to us. But to someone who seemed to be sitting across from Dinah. Someone who we could not see. There was a significant pause between each of Dinah's sentences, as if the unseen person was responding.

Mor momma.
I like my caca (coffee).

Oh boy.

I li dat.

Neat.

Tank U.

Cool.

Wow. Dat petty park.

My big day.

Dat puppy no hear me.

No fall down.

No way.

Goo day today.

Ham a eggs.

Weird dog.

Dog beg. No beg, my ham.

No bad

Dat no work.

I ear U.

Oh my.

See kids, my kids, aunie.

No min.

Sorry momma.

Sorry momma.

Sorry momma.

Paree, mine.

Wow, I appy.

See my daddy, cool.

I reaee.

Yeah momma.

Bye momma.

Sorry momma.

Dat goo momma.

Oh momma

We big paree momma.

Mo momma see dat.

Sorry momma.

Sorry momma.

Home, home, home.

Not, not, know me.

Kids no see me, night clothes.

I ear hone.

Apparently, Dinah was speaking to her mother, who had always been her ally, advocate, confidant, and interpreter. Her mother was evidently still her ally, advocate, confidant, and interpreter—but now from the world of the unseen, the realm of the living dead. The mother-daughter relationship had evolved beyond the seen world.

Does everyone have an Ally in the unseen world? We don't know. Do you have an Ally who walks among the living dead? Only you can answer that question. The psychological concept of Ally work is derived from Carl Jung and *The Red Book*. Jung's colleague, Maria-Louise von Franz, amplified Jung's ideas, and her student, Jeffrey Raff, carried the work further. Raff's four books are some the best and most accessible resources available on Ally work. Jung, von Franz, and Raff have provided the historical background, the psychological application, and the methods for having a relationship with one's Ally. Our role is to open ourselves to the Active Imagination within and to begin the conversation.

In the previous chapter, we practiced dream work. There we entered into the liminal space in order to reenter a dream and begin asking questions of the characters in our dream experience. The hard part, most likely, was trying to get past that repetitive nagging question, "Is this real or am I making this up?" That question is normal. The only way to mitigate the doubt, move beyond it, is to lean into the experiences of the mystical and the paranormal. Ally work includes acknowledging the paranormal as an ingredient of the conscious experience.

Jung, von Franz, and Raff never suggested that having an Ally was a paranormal experience. We, however, think mystical experiences seem to fit in the category of the paranormal. Philosopher Jeffrey Kripal and psychologist Edward Kelly both make the case for broadening the umbrella of the paranormal as the means of moving beyond a materialism that excludes the spiritual. Kripal's *The Flip* and Kelly's *Beyond Physicalism* offer a research-based approach that includes quantum theory, near-death experiences, out-of-body experiences, telepathy, communication with the dead, and unidentified aerial phenomena within the mystical realm. Kripal, Kelly, and their colleagues are positing the means of moving beyond the question, "Is this real?" Now we can ask: How can I expand my capacity for conscious experience, which encompasses the mystical as the paranormal and the paranormal as the mystical?

WHO IS AN ALLY?

Allies live, move, and have their being in the milieu of the cosmic soup we live in. As in Dinah's experience, Allies are advocates, confidants, and interpreters. They are the intimate friends who listen deeply and offer sage advice. They're also the friend that's not afraid to point out our blind spots. Our Ally will help us in our process of soul-making. And like a friend, the relationship is mutual. What we say and do will have an impact on our Ally. Our spiritual companions of the mystical realm, however, will not solve our problems, fix our troubles, or alter the forces of nature.

An Ally might be a dead loved one, like Dinah's mom. An Ally could be a spirit animal, an angel, a figure from the past. An Ally could be a tree or a standing stone. Allies seek us out. We do not choose them. It would be much easier if we could decide who our Ally will be and then we could put whatever words into their mouths we want to. But an Ally is not a genie in a bottle.

They will not show up at our beck and call nor acquiesce to our every whim. They are our Ally, they have our back, but they'll also tell us the truth we may not want to hear. Our relationship and experiences with our Ally will be as complicated as with any other intimate friend that we can both love and hate at the same time.

Allies make themselves known to us in our conscious world in all sorts of ways. We might not recognize them at first or realize that they are our Ally. The Ally may appear in a dream. They could arrive in an altered state of consciousness brought on by meditation, yoga, fasting, extreme exercise, a vision, or the use of a hallucinogenic. Allies might appear in a séance, as they did with abstract artist Hilma af Klint. (We will visit with her later in this chapter.) Allies show up when and how they so choose. Our task is threefold: 1) to ask the Ally to appear, 2) to be consciously aware of their potential to be present, and 3) to be patient.

HOW DO I KNOW THIS IS MY ALLY?

"I just got back from my annual visit to my mother's. I almost called you while I was there. My relationship with my mother, from my perspective, is strained at the best. I'm fifty-five for God's sake and she still treats me like she did when I was fifteen! I went to a college that was a thousand miles away and then when I graduated I took a job 2,000 miles away. And every time I visit my mom I'm reminded why I've never regretted living on the other side of the country. But this time something happened that was so weird I almost called you while I was at her house."

"What happened?"

"She was on one of her typical critiques of my sister's life, everything she's ever done wrong and how it has wounded my mother's heart. Her monologue is so predictable. When she says 'wounded my heart' she always reaches for a tissue to dab at her eyes. And then she says, without fail, 'your sister is exactly like my sister was."

"What do you think your mother meant by that?"

"Oh, I don't have to think about what she meant by that, she told me exactly what she meant. But this time I was so exhausted by her diatribe, I cut her off by asking a question."

"What'd you ask her?"

"I asked her about her relationship with her mom."

"And?"

"She got up and walked out of the room."

"What was her relationship with her mom?"

"I don't know. She's never told me. In all fairness, her mother died when she was twelve. Her dad went absent and her aunt stepped in to raise her. But then her aunt died when my mom was sixteen."

"What was your mom and your aunt's relationship like?"

"The only thing my mom has ever said about her aunt is that she was 'off her rocker.'"

"Any idea what she meant by that?"

"Well. I had never asked before. But here's where the weird thing happened. About half an hour after my mom had left the room, she came back carrying a tray with some tea for us. After we'd had a sip or two of tea, I got really bold and asked my mom what her aunt was like. I was hoping she wouldn't storm out of the room again. But without saying anything, she got up and left the room. Surprisingly, though, in about five minutes, she came back carrying a book. She handed me the book and told me her aunt had written it, and if I wanted to know why my aunt was 'off her rocker' then I should read the book. And then she left. The tattered black cover was held together by a frayed ribbon; though it had originally been red, now it was transparent from age. It took me a bit to undo the knot. I had to be careful when I opened the book because the pages could have easily fallen out. Every page was written on, front and back. My great aunt used a fountain pen, so on some of the pages the ink had bled through. By the entry dates, the journal covered the twelve years from when she was twenty-four to when she died. I sat there for the next three hours reading the strangest story I've ever read."

"What do you mean by strange?"

"She had an invisible friend. Like a child would."

"Did her friend have a name?"

"Jesse."

"Man or a woman?"

"I can't tell."

"Can me tell something about what you read?"

"The book was a stream of dialogues. My great aunt had pretty frequent conversations with her imaginary friend. The conversations were about important stuff. Like when my grand-mother died and my mom came to live with my aunt. There wasn't any of the usual journal stuff like the weather. There's was nothing mundane in any of the entries."

"How did it make you feel when you read it?"

"Creepy. Why would a woman that age have an imaginary friend? Was she that lonely? Her family was religious. I mean if she would have been talking to God, I could understand. But who the hell was Jesse?"

"Who do you think Jesse was?"

"I told you. Her imaginary friend. My mom is right. My great aunt was off her rocker."

"What if Jesse was your great aunt's Ally? Someone she could relate to. Maybe even see?"

"Okay. Right. I know you're into the weird-o-sphere, but you can't be serious."

If nothing else, Allies are persistent. A month later at our next appointment, more of the story emerged, with a twist.

"I hate to tell you this because I can only imagine where

you're going to go with it, but I had a dream. And Jesse spoke to me."

"Tell me more."

"Don't grin at me."

"Sorry."

"I couldn't see Jesse clearly. But I knew it was the person in my great aunt's journal. All they said was, 'hello.' That was it."

"Did you ask Jesse anything?"

"No."

"Are you willing to try an experiment?"

"Depends."

"Tonight. Before you go to bed, open your journal. Visualize Jesse from your dream. Write what you see. Then write in your journal, 'Jesse, are you my Ally?' And wait for an answer. You might "hear" the answer immediately. Or later in another dream. When you do hear the answer, write about what you've heard. If the answer is, 'Yes, I want to be your Ally.' Then ask, 'What do you want me to know?' And wait for an answer. At this point, you have begun to write the ongoing dialogue between you and your Ally, if Jesse is your Ally. What do you think? Willing to play along?

"No. That creeps me out. I don't want an imaginary friend."

"I can loan you a book about Allies. The concept is based on Jung's *Red Book*. It's simple and straightforward."

"I'm not interested."

"Okay. I won't mention it again. I promise."

And I never saw this person again. Of course I'm curious about what happened to them. But we have a rule—the companion is in charge. The only time we follow up is if someone is going into the hospital, or they've lost a loved one— more pastoral care than companioning. I do still hope this person will reach out again. But I have to be patient and trust our covenant that the companion is always in charge of the rela- tionship.

Following Carl Jung's lead, the journey into the unconscious is an experiment. His *Red Book* is the collection of three years of journaled dialogue between him and several Allies, as well as contrarian figures who appeared in his nighttime visions. His journals included drawings of his Allies as well as abstract soul mandalas. And what followed his experiment would be thirty years of research and depth psychology that would fill volumes and shape the practice of psychology.

If we are willing, our journal can be the cauldron for a liberated expression of our soul-making experience. In our own Red Book we can include the fullness of our experience; there's no need to limit our imagination. In Catherine and Gil's personal Red Books they've included not only drawings and diagrams but also pictures and articles copied or cut out of books and magazines. Their journals have become the home for their relationship with the Allies.

The sublimity of the Ally relationship is in its uncertainty. As the companion is in charge of our relationship with them, so too is the Ally in control of our fragile experiment. These relationships can last for long periods of time, like the companion's great aunt and her Ally, Jesse. But sometimes our Ally exists in the world we see and live in every day. For over twenty years, the Raven has been Gil's spirit guide in the world of the seen. Here's his story.

I've written about my relationship with ravens in other places, but what has stood out in every story is that the spirit of the Raven has been present at the most unexpected of times. While I've long been fascinated with these beautiful, mystical, and funny birds, I never thought they were "my spirit guides." Then one day, that all changed. This story appeared in *Wisdom Walking*, but every good story is worth repeating.

In 2012, when I was preparing for my walk across Ireland, I spent a lot of time at our family cabin hiking through the familiar Bradshaw Mountains. The terrain, the elevation climbs and descents, and the altitude made this the perfect place to train for my pilgrimage.

One morning just before sunrise, I stepped out the front door of our cabin and was surprised to be greeted by four large ravens. They were foraging the ground for breakfast. When they saw me, the four birds flew about twenty yards beyond the house, where they landed on the ground and continued their search for insects. I eased towards them and was amazed that I got within ten feet of the birds. I imagined they were allowing me into their circle. For five minutes, they kept an eye on me while they picked the ground for bugs. Finally, the largest bird let out a very loud "Prawck" that startled me. My sudden movement caused the ravens to fly up into a nearby tree. I stood still. They watched me for a bit and then flew off.

The experience was exhilarating. I had so many questions swirling in my head. I wondered why they would let me get so close. Were they trying to tell me something? I had hoped they would show up the next day, but they didn't.

A few months later, however, I was at the cabin again. I started my hike just before dawn. I was headed down the hill towards one of my favorite walks. About a mile away from the cabin I saw what I was fairly sure were the same four ravens searching the ground for something to eat. I wandered in their direction. As I got close, they "prawcked" at me, almost like they were laughing. I got within thirty feet before they flew off, low to the ground, through the trees. I passed them again a few hundred yards down the road. By then they were resting in the trees. I stopped and stood under the tree where the largest raven was sitting. Kind of in jest, I told the bird that in all the years I had walked through the area they had never left me a feather. The raven prawcked. Who was I to ask for such a thing?

I kept going down the mountain road for another three miles, when one of the ravens flew just ahead of me and then crossed my path. The bird landed in a tree just off the road.

When I got to where it was perched, to my pleasant surprise, I found a large black feather on the ground. To say the least, I was amazed and humbled. I bowed to the raven and thanked the bird for the gift. I walked another few dozen steps, admiring the feather. The raven swooped in front of me again and landed in a tree on the other side of the road. The bird was squawking what seemed to be a warning alarm. I felt like I was being called to the raven's side of the road. For some reason, though, I didn't heed my intuition and started to walk away. The raven changed its tone to what sounded like someone screaming. The piercing sound rattled me enough that I walked across the road toward the raven. By then the large black bird had moved to the backside of the tree away from the road. I walked around to the raven's side of the tree and stood there, staring up at the bird who was looking down at me.

Suddenly, I heard a truck barreling down the road. I turned in time to see a small pickup truck clip the rocks on the blind, narrow side of the road—exactly where I would have been standing. The driver would have never seen me in time to swerve away.

My heart dropped. My stomach rose. My soul smelt eternity. I leaned against the tree. I thought I was going to pass out. I knew I was going to throw up. What had happened? Could that raven have knowingly saved my life? Maybe it was synchronicity? Possibly my intuition had been working in my best interest. I know someone reading this is saying, "God saved you." Could be. I don't know. Raven, synchronicity, intuition, the Divine— I'm glad someone or all of them stepped in and I'm glad to be alive.

Carl Jung wrote in *Man and His Symbols* that intuition is an irrational involuntary event, a hunch.[1] Then he offered a clear and concise explanation of the four interior functions: "Sensation tells you that something exists; Thinking tells you what it is; Feeling tells you whether it is agreeable or not; and Intuition tells you whence it comes and where it is going."[2] My senses had been in tune with the raven. I was seeing and hearing him/her while I was touching the feather. Who asks a bird for a feather? That was a random event, I guess. Maybe not? I had thought about walking past the bird while it was squawking at me. Do birds give warnings to humans about impending traffic accidents? I don't know. But fortunately I was curious; my thinking was drawing me across the road toward the bird. My feelings were also involved. I was grateful for the feather and I was feeling affectionate about this particular bird. Honestly, though, I don't remember having any inclination, or intuition, that a truck was coming down that road. I guess I could have heard it, but I was focused on the bird, and besides, the raven was yelling so loudly, screaming even, that I couldn't hear anything else. My experience that day seems to defy rational thought. But at that moment, I believe the wisdom of nature was flowing into my Mindbody.

I've always enjoyed being out of doors, in nature. I have admired wild birds, their beauty, and flight patterns. But I never imagined I would have had such an encounter with four wild ravens. After my experience that day on the mountain road, I've spent a lot of time researching and studying ravens, watching them, listening to them, wondering about them. That momentous day in my life brought about a revelation—an epiphany—that comes from the ancients' wisdom. I have become convinced from my experience that all of creation, trees, stones, animals, birds, every blade of grass, everything has a soul, and we are all connected. I am also quite certain that some of those souls, ravens in particular, communicate with my soul. Soul to soul—the raven is my guide, an Ally. The raven is not my god. But we, meaning humans, animals, birds, stones and trees, are all a part of creation and we are all connected and we can all communicate with one another. This revelation is not new. It's not something I discovered. The native Yavapai and Apache peoples hold these beliefs. Pre-Christian Celtic people understood their connection to the world in this way. Christians like Pelagius (354 – 420 CE) wrote about the intertwined relationship of all God's creations. "There is no creature on earth (or plant) in whom God is absent."[3] Therefore, if the Creator is present in all of creation, then humans can be at one with all of creation. And the ravens can be my guide any time they want to, visible or otherwise.

HILMA AF KLINT: THE ALLY EXPERIENCE

Hilma af Klint[4] (1862 – 1944) was born in Sweden. She was a slight woman, barely five feet tall, with clear blue eyes. When Hilma was just turning eighteen, her ten-year-old sister, Hermina, died in a "terrible incident." Hilma said nothing else about her sister's death in the extensive journals she kept. In her paintings, however, the letters "bw" represented the "difficulties at the beginning of the earthly work, (that) could be called grief."[5] It may have been the loss of her sister that prompted Hilma to begin attending seances, which eventually led to the discovery of her gift of mediumship—the gift of communicating with the dead.[6] Her grief might have also triggered the onset of synesthesia, a neurological phenomenon in which the stimulation of one sensory pathway leads to the automatic involuntary experience in another, a blending of the senses. A sensation that the af Klint family believes Hilma knew well. A sensation that could have contributed to her genius vision of art. Grief is a disability and it may also accompany a benefit. One such "benefit" may be that the artistic creative processes of the unconscious psyche are often synchronistic flashes of inspiration arising autonomously from beyond the control of the artist, providing an extended period of an altered state of consciousness.[7]

The voices that inspired af Klint are universal images of existence within the collective unconscious, voices that have spoken and continue to speak to the artist who has an open mind, body, soul, and spirit. The relationship with the unseen Ally, or spirit guide, is limitless and unrestrained by time and space. The experience of being in communication with the spirits and archetypal images who reside within the collective unconscious carries with it not only the weight of personal interior transmutation, but also the desire and urgings to create outward symbolic expressions of this relationship—art in all its forms.

When Hilma af Klint's sibling died, the grieving sister dressed in the customary black dress. Hilma was so moved that she never wore another color the remainder of her life. She also marked her grief by becoming a vegetarian. At age twenty, Hilma was a member of the first generation of women to attend Sweden's Royal Academy of Fine Art. There she studied the Romantic technique of painting. She graduated after four years and received a prestigious scholarship, which afforded her a prominent studio in downtown Stockholm. For the next few years, she would enjoy a fair degree of success exhibiting and selling her landscape painting, botanical art, veterinary diagrams, color illustrations, and portraits. But for af Klint, there were two distinct periods in her art career. The first being her mainstream Romantic art, painted from 1887 to 1906. Then, in 1902, she began the second phase of her career, abstract art, which was inspired by her spiritual experiences and her love of natural science.

While she was still in the first phase of her career, at the age of twenty-four, during a séance she encountered a guardian spirit who identified itself as Lorenz. Three years later, she founded a weekly séance group, *De Fem*, the "Five Women," who were also students of the Royal Art Academy. These women were devotees of esoteric Christianity and technicians of the unknown. They spoke to the dead,[8] channeled higher forces, and received messages in the form of automatic writings and drawings.[9] For ten years, they met every Friday.[10] At these meetings, they wore long robes, sat around a homemade altar adorned with candles, a white-rose cross, and a statue. (From available pictures, the statue appears to be either Jesus or Mary.) In later years, the altar would feature four large pieces of Hilma's art, created specifically under the direction of one of their spirits. *The Five* began each session with prayer and meditation. They would read a Christian sermon and study the New Testament. Af Klint was very explicit about her views of the authors of the four Christian Gospels. She wrote in her journal on May 22, 1920:

> John, more than all the others, possessed belief in his ability to receive awareness. Mark tried to show that earthly bliss can be won only through distribution of the power of one's own being. Matthew [showed a] grateful reception of enlightenment. Luke tried to show that dullness can be overcome through a desire for the elevation of the life of feelings.[11]

Following their Bible study, they would conduct a séance. The women took turns being the medium, until 1902, when Hilma became the sole conduit of spiritual messages. *The Five* shared responsibility of taking notes, which included copying messages from the spirits as well as keeping copies of the women's automatic drawings. Their spirit guides were named Georg, Gregor, Amaliel, Ester, Theohatius, and Anana, the last being the name of Buddha's favorite pupil.[12]

In the twenty-first century we can expect varied reactions to af Klint's art and a wide range of responses to her means of inspiration. But we must keep in mind that both art and mediumship in the nineteenth century were ways to empower women.[13] Both created the possibility for women to gather in exclusively feminine spiritual gatherings where they could develop their own rites and rituals. Here women could set themselves apart from oppressive patriarchal religious systems. Absent male suppression, they could express themselves freely in speech, actions, writing, and painting. And for some women, mediumship was their only means of financial support.

When Hilma was forty-four, the spirit Amaliel commissioned her to create the *Paintings for the Temple*. Hilma wrote that Amaliel spoke to her the following words in a séance. "You will commence a task that will bring great blessings on coming generations...You were brought here to do this."[14] What followed was a series of 193 paintings. The collection was finished in 1915 and would serve as the spiritual foundation for af Klint's vision of the future. [15] The experience of receiving the messages and then painting the visions expanded her spiritual cosmos to include higher beings, vibrations, waves, auras, chakras, elemental spirits, nature spirits, guardian spirits, angels, and gnomes.[16] In 1908, af Klint's explained that "the pictures were painted directly through me, without any preliminary drawings, and with great force. I had no idea what the paintings were supposed to depict. Nevertheless, I worked swiftly and surely, without changing a single brush stroke." However, she went on to clarify that "it was not the case that I was to blindly obey the High Lords of the Mysteries but that I was to imagine that they were standing by my side."[17] Hearing voices from other dimensions can take many forms: audible, inner dialogue, urgings, intuitions. But regardless of the delivery, it always comes with an undeniable sense of being inside the flow of spiritual energy. It is an energy which is both empowering and draining—in many cases (as with af Klint) the energy manifests itself through cycles of manic energy that are countered by depressive moods.

Within the 193 *Paintings for the Temple*, there is a miniseries of twenty-one paintings. The title of this subset is *The Seven-Pointed Star*. For af Klint, any singular concept would require a series of images, a narrative, exploring the complexity of a multi-dimensional evolution—thus, the sets and subsets. To paint in such a manner gave evidence of Hilma's ability to "see" the holographic fourth dimension. She "willingly listen[ed] to the super-physical powers that she [wrote] directly onto the painting."[18] The Seven-Pointed Star is a commentary on the complete set of Paintings for the Temple. Hilma's Seven-Pointed Star is an archetypal image, depicting a circle in the fourth spiritual dimension. The circle is revolving continuously within the dimensional spheres of the union of the opposites.[19] Af Klint was able to conceive of and illustrate this multidimensional world using diagrammatic forms as geometric states of consciousness.[20] Circles as spirals, like the Nautilus, reveal the integration of polarities that give rise to another state of consciousness.[21]

Her Seven-Pointed Star series evolved into her painting the archetypal fourth dimension of a crucified androgynous Christ.[22] Here, we see the quaternity of a cubed cross. Hanging between each section is an x-ray of an androgynous figure. These x-ray figures symbolize the multidimensional union of the seen and the unseen. To the right of the four-dimensional cross is a one-dimensional x-ray figure who is yellow, representing the male. And to the left is a blue figure, representing the female. These two figures manifest the alchemical work of the union of opposites which is necessary in order to evolve into the fourth dimension—the Center, the space where everything is set against the paradox of absolute emptiness, the archetype of the androgynous Christ.

Af Klint's connection to the transpersonal space of the fourth dimension enhanced her varying states of consciousness, the spaces of the in-between, spaces where she experienced non-duality. These altered states of awareness were made possible when her conscious Self was brought into a direct, unfiltered relationship with the dynamic unconscious.[23] Through mediumship and meditation she was able to enter a lucid psychospiritual consciousness.[24] She could experience an altered state of consciousness while being fully alert. She had brought the conscious (the seen) into an interface with the collective unconscious (the unseen). In her journal she wrote, "The will power of feeling. The will power of thought."[25] This is a personal testament to the psychic energy needed to engage in the process of integrating the mind, body, soul, and spirit, the union of the conscious and the unconscious.

In the final painting of the *Seven-Pointed Star* series (described above), we can visually experience the integration of the feminine and masculine in perfect union via the sacrifice of the dualistic construct, which is represented by the figures at the side of the central image. From this multi-dimensional union, the feminine androgynous aesthetic emerges, breaking free of the dominant masculine androgynous model.

According to Jadranka Ryle, a scholar of nineteenth-century art history, "af Klint's feminine androgynous hybrid of myth, spirituality, and science led to her creation of an innovative abstract aesthetics."[26] Her art blurred the boundaries between science (material) and the abstract (spirit).[27] Her abstract art evolved as the opposites of nature unified with the spirals of the spirits, which continued to progress higher. She imagined the spiral with no beginning and no ending—art that only exists in the eternal Now. Hilma believed her art would inspire and enlighten, "proliferat[ing] like a [new] language," developing the center space of the spirit between the two circles. "Every atom has its own midpoint, but each midpoint is directly connected to the midpoint of the universe."[28] The center is everywhere. We each have our own center, but our center is connected to everyone's center. *The Seven-Pointed Star* is a circle of souls evolving into Oneness.

Af Klint's art has only recently been rediscovered, creating such a stir as to fill some scholars with the urgency to rewrite art history.[29] Her originality, scope, and depth of form has demanded a reconsideration of art's canon. Abstract art was once a field dominated by men like Wassily Kandinsky, who had been considered its founder. Evidence now points to af Klint as being the pioneer of abstract art. Like most everything else in modernity, art has been negatively influenced by the dogmatic insistence on the perspective of dualism. This overreach of the human ego, primarily masculine, is emblematic of the repression from which af Klint fought to liberate herself. She wrote, "Freedom comes only to those who have fought to reach it."[30] Af Klint was a woman of force, imagination, keen focus, and boundless energy. She was a most unique human being who was on pilgrimage to find the outside boundaries of consciousness by peering through the veil of the unconscious.

The long arc of her work included ideas from Christianity, Buddhism, Judaism, Rosicrucianism, the Hermetic philosophies, and Theosophical writings. Her art and life culminated in a new spirituality, one which expanded her consciousness and mapped a new imagination. Her mystical experiences also charted a path for the liberation from patriarchal domination and religion's inherent racism. Her new world, her new aesthetic, birthed this new spirituality complete with its own art and language. Af Klint imagined a new abstraction, one that would open a possibility for change and subversive thought. In this new world there would be a break from racism, misogyny, patriarchal religion, nationalism, and a world where dualism would be overcome. This new world would offer a feminine alternative to patriarchal domination. Her authentic imaginaire would embrace the reality of a polymorphous androgyne, a world that is gender ambivalent, an openly queer world.[31]

Ryle argues that af Klint released a revelation of thought and imagination that re-envisioned the future. First, af Klint developed a hybrid aesthetics of the feminine androgyne. In doing so, she eliminated gender bias from her art and her perspective of life. She replaced the masculine notion of androgyne—where the primordial male remains dominate in the androgynous form—

and replaced it with diagrammatic symbolism, thereby expanding the consciousness of a gender fluid Reality.[32] In other words, her art reflects the queerness of the union of the material and the spiritual. Second, in her life, her philosophy, and her art, she made a break from the inherent racism that exists in mainstream and esoteric Christianity. This break may have been more symbolic than actual given the absence of diversity in Sweden at that time; still, she recognized the dangers of any form of oppression and elitism by making a subversive statement of art against injustice. And third, her dramatic shifts in thought, life, and art opened the awareness of unexplored dimensions where her subversive political aesthetic could manifest.[33] She truly did the work of embracing many archetypal opposites.

She confronted a male-dominated world. She stood against a racist culture. And she wrestled with how to live in a homophobic environment. In the documentary film, *Beyond the Visible,* Hilma is quoted as saying, "Many players struggling in this drama have been dressed in the wrong clothing. Many a female costume conceals a man. Many male costumes conceal a woman." Was she queer? She never married. She had resided only with women. Her closest confidents were women. Only Hilma af Klint could have answered the question about her sexuality. She wrote in *Letters and Words Pertaining to Works by Hilma af Klint,* "the gleaming spiral case of chastity's endeavor lead[s] to AH," (the multi-dimensional level of higher consciousness).[34] Her art points to an expanded consciousness of human sexuality, a queer awareness. Hilma af Klint always described the situation as it was while she proclaimed the way life should be—vague, unique, undefinable, fluid, queer.[35] She had committed her life to the spiritual experience, which guided her into imagining a world her generation was not ready to embrace.

In the course of releasing her force of energy and imagination into the cosmos, Hilma af Klint created over 1,300 pieces of art and wrote 25,000 pages of explanatory text. This collection does not consider the massive amount of work she destroyed near the end of her life. Her reasons for doing so remain a mystery. Some of that material, however, may have included additional journals providing us with even deeper insight into her life. But she left more than enough for us to spend our time in awe and wonder.

MAKING ROOM FOR THE ALLY EXPERIENCE

Few of us may experience the intensity of Hilma af Klint's Ally guidance. But that doesn't mean having a similar experience isn't possible. And who's to say my sister's experience is not just as powerful as af Klint's? Each of our experiences are our own—they are real, valid, meaningful, powerful, and intense.

Your Ally might be a figure from a tarot card that you dialogue with every day. Could be a tree in your backyard who fetches you to come out and talk to her as the sun sets. Maybe your Ally is a guardian angel, or a character from a sacred text, or your great-aunt you never met, or a fifteenth-century poet, or a witch who was burned at the stake 400 years ago. Maybe your Ally is your lifelong best friend who's always got your back. And maybe your Ally is a raven. All will be well as long as you've got someone to whom you can bare your soul—your Ally, advocate, confidant, and interpreter. Are you willing to try a little experiment with us?

CHAPTER TWELVE

RITUAL WORK: NOW I MUST BURY MY LOVER

What I imagine is perhaps important for the entire world.
—Haruki Murakami

"With sad hearts, we share that our beloved fellow pilgrim, Michael Cochise Young, died yesterday," began Catherine's email to our Wisdom's Way Interfaith School participants. "She was such a kind, gentle soul with deep wisdom to share. She will be so missed." Catherine tells the story of our community losing a beloved friend.

As I wrote this November email, my mind scrolled back to the last time I saw Michael. We met at the Fair Trade Café in downtown Phoenix. She had missed our October gathering and I was catching her up on our Enneagram work.

"Oh, Catherine, you need to try this delicious Angel Tea and the banana bread is beyond scrumptious."

"Sounds wonderful. Please let me buy these for us."

"Oh, no, I must make up for my absence and for taking up your time to meet with me individually."

Once we got the Enneagram conversation out of the way. I listened to her stories of visiting her friend in Portland, Oregon, the reason she missed our gathering, and her Mrs. Penniwick tales. Mrs. Penniwick came into being one evening when Michael and her friend had retired from the dining room to the "parlour." Michael brought a cup of ginger tea in one of the delicate China cups that once belonged to her Aunt Bell, along with a saucer of half-cut black figs slathered in chevre and drizzled in balsamic syrup. There by the light of her Tiffany lamp and surrounded by her antiques, the intricate glass perfume bottles of her mother and the faded sepia images of her grandparents, they created Michael's alter ego Mrs. Penniwick. Mrs. P, as Michael fondly called her, had quite the life from that evening on. I was mesmerized by Michael's telling of Mrs. Penniwick and her life, weaving the magic of her imagination, sharing her heart and soul.

With great enthusiasm, Michael then began telling me about the children's book she was writing. She had been working on it for years. I was spellbound as she told the story of Buster the hermit crab. Buster's shell was getting too small, but he was afraid to molt and be vulnerable. She wove the fears and heart of Buster with detailed knowledge of Mother Nature's world. I was captivated. It was as if time stood still. To this day I remain humbled that I got to hear those stories from Michael. It was a ritual of tea, story-catching, and soulful listening.

Now the question became how to remember Michael at our December retreat? How do we create a ritual to allow for our feelings of loss and grief? How do we honor the brilliant gentle woman, Michael Cochise Young, while not derailing the flow of the retreat?

Here is what we created and shared:

A RITUAL FOR THE REMEMBRANCE OF MICHAEL COCHISE YOUNG

(*Everyone circles the community altar holding rose petals in their hands.*)

Leader: We have closed the circle in holy listening.

Group: In the closed circle, our lives are linked together.

Leader: We open the circle to let our souls travel to their destination.

Group: In the open circle, our lives are linked together.

A reader says:

We stand around this altar,

which represents our lives,

not all, but most of who we know ourselves to be,

or wish we were;

want to become, but not yet complete.

In this moment; we bring our "memories, reflections, dreams,"

for the altar to hold

our sorrow, our grief, our loss.

We remember, because we must;

For in the memory…our soul holds the void.

Tomorrow will come…and what was…will be.

Leader: We have closed the circle in holy listening.

Group: In the closed circle, our lives are linked together.

Leader: We open the circle to let our souls travel to their destination.

Group: In the open circle, our lives are linked together.

(*A reader shares a eulogy for Michael Cochise Young.*)

(*Rose petals are spread around the altar.*)

Leader: We have closed the circle in holy listening

Group: In the closed circle, our lives are linked together.

Leader: We open the circle to let our souls travel to their destination.

Group: In the open circle, our lives are linked together.

(*A reader shares a poem by John O'Donohue*).

Leader: We have closed the circle in holy listening

Group: In the closed circle, our lives are linked together.

Leader: We open the circle to let our souls travel to their destination.

Group: In the open circle, our lives are linked together.

As a Circle, we stood in the vibrating silence after the ritual, tears streamed down some faces, many had their heads bowed, hands palm to palm over their hearts and the profound feeling of the other world connection with Michael. She was with us in all her many forms; Mrs. Penniwick, Buster the crab, lover of literature, collector of antiques, whispering wise kind words into our hearts as we shared our love for her. Our shared experience was a warm hug swirling around us and her. The ritual offered space for hurting hearts, remembrance of a beloved, and comfort for our grief journey.

THE MAKINGS OF A RITUAL

When you hear the word ritual, what is your first thought? We asked this question of our group that had gathered for a Wisdom's Way Interfaith School retreat. The answers were as diverse as the people who were there:

• following a particular pattern or order of service

- symbolism
- routine practice
- has intent
- a specific focus like letting go or bringing in
- space for quiet and breathing
- magic flow, emptiness
- absence and presence
- body movement
- engaging ancient tools

The remembrance ceremony crafted for Michael Cochise Young is an example of creating rituals for our spiritual experiences without depending upon religious rules and expectations. Assisting our companions in creating rituals for their spiritual contemplative practices includes offering a framework for life's beginnings, endings, rites of passage and daily lives. While the spiritual but not religious might avoid religious gatherings, they often want communal ceremonies for life's milestones. In Chapter 5, we shared the practices of The Circle Way, which is itself a ritual and offers a powerful tool for connection and magic without the trappings of religious dogma.

Mara Branscombe shares some valuable wisdom about the simplicity and the depths of ritual work.

A ritual is anything that is done with intention. It can be formulaic or intuitive, elaborate or simple, personal or shared. Whether it's ritualizing your morning coffee or gathering in community to honor the solstice, a unique frequency comes alive, instilling whispers of the sacred within us. Throughout history, ritual has been at the heart of humanity. The desire to engage in ritual is primal and instinctual. When we answer the call to connect with something beyond the mundane, we generate access to infinite space.[1]

A ritual, then, requires:

- Purpose—What's the point of the ritual?
- Space—Where will it take place?
- Time—How is the time used?
- Elements—What elements are necessary to conduct the ritual?

Components of such a planned experience are intertwined, mutually affecting the interrelated choices made about the other. What words, places, things, actions, and people will express our interior thoughts, feelings, and intuitions into the exterior sensate world? Like jazz, improvisation practiced by skilled musicians, well-sculpted rituals bring freshness to our need for a shared display of those special moments in the human experience.

The writing of this book has been a ritual in and of itself—the writing of a personal myth, the imagination of a continuing narrative—a potential ritual of discovering the possible and the impossible. For a long time, this has been our secret book filled with hidden rituals, an unwritten book. This was a book we were afraid to write because someone might discover it in our library. But our Allies and spirit guides fortified us with the courage to begin. And then the book came alive and began to shape our lives and our living rituals in ways we did not expect.

Just a heads-up: This chapter includes taboo rituals. Not that we think they're out of bounds, it's that we've been told they are taboo: tattoos, tarot, talking to angels, having a spirit guide, celebrating the cycles of the moon as a divine practice, and accepting the paranormal and UFOs as real. Yes, there are rituals for all these experiences. And no, none of them are evil. All we've done here is crack open the door just a tiny bit so that you might peak inside what we've found to be a sublime world of imagination. If you decide to step through the door, you'll be invited to first cross a bridge. You can always turn around and go back.

Consider this chapter a pilgrimage of rituals. You don't have to walk down every road and you are not obligated to try every ritual. But if you're curious and interested, we've created safe yet brave ritual experiments, which have been enacted on either a literal or metaphoric labyrinth. The serpentine circle of the labyrinth will become our common language and space. We've experienced every ritual in this book. And we've suggested that others try them. We've been teaching these practices for almost ten years in our Wisdom School, on our Ireland pilgrimages, and Sacred Cauldron retreats, as well as to our numerous spiritual companions. We've created some, borrowed bits from others, and have re-worked almost every ritual you'll find in this chapter. Nothing is a first-time experiment.

The resources we've used to create these rituals may be familiar to you. Or not. You might want to practice some, discard others, but at least consider them, for none are inherently good or evil, they simply are what they are—something someone, or some group, has used or imagined using, that has enhanced our spiritual experience and expanded our conscious awareness of what is beyond us, yet is us, now and tomorrow—a perpetual oneness with the One.

THE RITUAL OF QUESTIONS

There are scientists today who are asking the "hard questions": What is consciousness? What is the mind? And what is the paranormal? Their questions are fueled by the ultimate question, "What makes a human, human?" A definition for consciousness, the mind, and the paranormal might be easier to agree upon that determining what makes the human, human.

The complex questions of "Who am I?" and "What is reality?" form a labyrinth. These are ultimately questions of spirituality. Our hunch is that you would not have picked up this book if these questions weren't on your front burner. The good news is that some researchers do care about the answer to these questions because they are confronted almost daily with answering their own question—"Does what I'm doing benefit humanity?" Or the frightening question, "Is what I'm working on propelling humanity toward its own extinction?"

Upon seeing the first atomic explosion set off in the desert of New Mexico, Robert Oppenheimer quoted the Bhagavad Gita, "Now I am become Death, the destroyer of worlds."[2] Scientists today may not be developing something as graphic as a nuclear weapon, but they may be part of a project that could someday make humans superfluous. You might think that such a notion is outlandish or the makings of science fiction. If you do, we suggest you spend some time reading historian and philosopher Yuval Noah Harari. On the final page of *Homo Deus*, he asks these three questions:

- Are organisms really just algorithms, and is life really just data processing?
- What's more valuable—intelligence or consciousness?
- What will happen to society, politics, and daily life when nonconscious but highly intelligent algorithms know us better than we know ourselves?

Contemplate Harari's complex questions for a while. Hopefully you'll arrive at your own answers or be inspired to ask your own questions. It really does matter what you think. Our questions and our answers are important because they can shape how we imagine living a healthy life in this fragile world. Meditation, contemplation, mindfulness, and inspired imagination can bring us a sense of calm, a clarity of mind, improve our health, expand our consciousness, and can help us answer the most baffling yet vital questions of life—or at least help us live with the questions, which are the foundation for the rituals we enact every day.

KEEP IT SIMPLE RITUALS

Creating rituals to mark specific milestones or experiences in our lives brings intentional power to our journeys. These rituals require more time for exploration and thoughtful planning. You may be thinking this is a bit overwhelming. How could I possibly create something truly meaningful? Where would I even begin such an endeavor? Maybe start with reflecting on something in your everyday life that could be considered a ritual. Lingering over a cup of coffee or tea at breakfast, breathing in the aroma and quieting the busy mind for a few minutes is a ritual.

> *Beginning the day with a simple greeting:* This morning I greet Mother Earth and Father Sky and the life force in all creation. This morning I greet the seen world in its beauty and the unseen world in its mystery. This morning I welcome the breath that breathes in me, the compassion that surrounds me, and the love in my heart.

> *As you get ready for bed, offering gratitude for the day:* This evening I give thanks for the gifts from Mother Earth and Father Sky and the life force in all creation. This evening I give thanks for the beauty I've seen and for the mysterious gifts from the unseen world. This evening I welcome rest and restoration for my body, the quieting of my thoughts, and wisdom from the dream world.

Practicing (W)Holy listening as a ritual is wisdom listening and can be considered a ritual of connection and compassion. Walking a labyrinth, journaling, engaging in a yoga practice, meditation, cooking a meal, coloring a mandala—almost anything you experience with intention and pause for reflection can become a ritual.

Simple rituals for beginning and ending time spent in wisdom listening with companions holds the brave safe space with compassion and meaning. Sensitivity to the companion's needs is the most important ritual practice. An open-ended question to begin the session invites the companion into full presence of your time together: "How are you arriving here?" or, "How can I hold space for you today?" If there is nervous chatter from the companion, maybe offering a suggestion like "Let's take a moment to breathe and center ourselves in this space," or "I'm going to hold silence until you are ready to begin." Closing the session relies on what feels authentic, given the depth of wisdom listening. A closing could be as simple as asking the companion how they would like to conclude your time together. Maybe it's holding silence until they offer a final word, such as "Namaste," or "May it be so", or "Thank you." You may offer a meaningful prayer for them, such as the Our Mother Prayer, or a poem or a mantra. Asking the question, "What can you imagine is your next step?" might be a way for them to visualize how to move forward on their journey. Simple opening and closing rituals bring focus and opportunities for deeper engagement for the companion pilgrimage. "May it be so."

THE RITUAL OF WATER FOR CLEANSING, HEALING, AND LETTING GO

Water may be one of the most universally prevalent components of rituals found in every religion and ancient ceremonies. Water covers the vast majority of our planet. We are born from water.

We need water to sustain life. Water is necessary for growing our food. Over time, water can smooth our stone. Yet too much water can destroy crops, collapse the well-made homes we live in, and take away our breath. And in many ancient traditions, in death, the dead were returned to the water from which they were born. For the visible (as opposed to air), nothing is more common, more powerful, and more precious than water. And this is what makes water such a rich visible symbol for use in any ritual.

We have incorporated water into rituals for cleansing the space we occupy, healing our Mindbody, and setting down the things that torment our soul, if for just a short respite. What follows is a loose framework that can be adjusted for a variety of uses. Please take this ritual and make it your own.

For a ritual of water, we suggest using a small portable table on which to place a large pitcher of water; an empty bowl that can accommodate at least half of the water in the pitcher; and four cups. Earthenware is always better to contain the water. Pottery allows the water to maintain its fresh aroma. But Earthenware is not always practical or available, so be creative and flexible in designing your ritual. We also find it nice to use some sort of decorative cloth to cover the table. And we like to place a lit candle on the table. This ritual can take place inside or out of doors. The center of a labyrinth is always a memorable place for any ritual.

The ritual of water we have created has four components: personal preparation, calling the Allies into the circle, a specific ritual of cleansing, healing, or letting go, and a concluding prayer to open the circle.

Personal preparation begins with a brief period of time to center ourselves. A few minutes of silence to calm our Mindbody. When we feel ready, then we prepare the space, gather elements and set the table. Finally, we offer thanksgiving for the table, the covering, the glassware, the candle, the matches, and the water. Something like this:

> I stand here in the presence of the earth, the air, the fire, the water, and the spirits that surround me. Here, I offer thanks for this table and its covering, for these containers, this candle, and the match that lit it. And I give thanks for water from which we were born and the water that sustains our life.

In preparation, rest in a period of silence. Following the silence, an appropriate reading can help us ready our Mindbody. The reading could be something you've written especially for the occasion. Or a poem or something from a sacred text. Now you are ready to call in your Allies.

Several traditions call their ancient allies and spirits into the ritual circle. If you are of the lineage of a tradition that honors the four directions or invites in their spirits, we would encourage you to use that practice. If not, you could write your own. We have found connections with certain Celtic traditions and use the following litany, which we have written, to call in our ancient allies. We use a drum in this ritual but a bell could work just as well.

CALLING OF THE SEVEN DIRECTIONS OF THE CELTIC ANCIENTS

> Together, as pilgrims who walk the way of wisdom, we humbly seek the presence of the ancients. We invite the ancestors of our families. They have traveled the way before us. We know some by sight, others by story, and still others by legend. The ancients populate our dreams, inspire our visions, and activate our imagination. We call them, not by demand, but by our prayers

and sweet whispers. Together, let us beckon the ancient ones.

(Strike the drum or ring the bell once.)

Please join me as we begin in the North, for it is the Realm of Air, the celebration of Imbolc. The North is home of our Ancestors, especially the crone and the sage; for they are the keeper of souls and imagination. The North witnesses the Winter Solstice, home of the Bear and a time for slowing our energy for selfcare. We invite the Spirits of the North to join us.

(Strike the drum or ring the bell once.)

Please join me as we turn our attention to the East, the Realm of Fire, the celebration of Beltaine, the season of Birth and Rebirth. The East welcomes the Spring Equinox. The East is the home of the Rooster, a time to wake-up and become a conscious person. We invite the Spirits of the East to join us.

(Strike the drum or ring the bell once.)

Please join me as we turn our attention to the South, the Realm of the Earth, the celebration of Lughnasadh, the season of Harvest. The South embraces the Summer Solstice. The South is home of the Red Deer, a time for children to play and the grapes to be gathered. We invite the Spirits of the South to join us.

(Strike the drum or ring the bell once.)

Please join me as we turn our attention to the West, the

Realm of Water, the celebration of Samhain, the season for self-reflection and dream interpretation. The West bows to the Autumn Equinox. The West is home of the Otter, a time to reimagine the next phase of our life's pilgrimage. We invite the Spirits of the West to join us.

(Strike the drum or ring the bell once.)

Please join me as we turn our attention to the Center, the grounding of the Self, the connection with what is Above and what is Below, the Union of All Seven Directions —the North, the East, the South, the West, the Center, Above, and Below. For the union of the Seven Directions is the non-space of the mystics. Here we find wholeness, grace, and maturity.

(Strike the drum or ring the bell once.)

We humbly ask you, the ancients, the Spirits of Everything intertwined within the Cosmic Consciousness, the ancestors of our many souls, to bless us with your Presence. We bow to the All.

(Strike the drum or ring the bell once.)

CALLING OF THE SPIRIT OF THE RAVEN

We (I) call upon the secret places to send the Raven into our dwelling place. The Circle is our refuge and our fortress, and the Raven is the messenger from beyond. We will be covered by the Raven's feathers. The Raven's wings will be our shield. In the Raven, we will not be afraid of the terror of the night or the arrow of the day.

No evil will befall us (me) nor plague come to our
dwelling. The Raven will call upon us (me) and I will
answer with honor and reverence. The Raven is our
guide. We seek the Raven's presence.

(*Strike the drum or ring the bell once.*)

Calling in the ancients and our spirit guides, we believe, is a
vital part of this ritual. By doing so, we are acknowledging that
we are not alone in our work and that we are a part of something bigger than ourselves. We are not making anything
happen. We are asking the spirits of those who have gone before
to engage with the Cosmic Consciousness to move energy on
behalf of those for whom we are conducting this ritual. If you
are part of a religious tradition that uses specific names for a
higher power, this is the place to offer prayers and thanksgiving
to that deity or deities.

The third component of the ritual is very specific and should
be named as such: a ritual for the cleansing of a specific space
(house, office), a ritual for healing the Mindbody of someone (or
the Earth), a ritual for letting go (of a person, or an issue). The
more specific you can name the ritual, the better the energy can
be directed toward its intended results.

The first action of this ritual begins when the person
pours water into the four cups and says: This water nourishes the Tree of Life. I drink from each cup as a reminder
of those who have gathered from each direction; those
living and the living dead.
The second action is to pour water into the bowl while
saying: I pour water into this bowl and wash my face as a
reminder that I was born from water.

(*The person washes their face.*)

I sprinkle water on my clothes as a reminder that the rain nourishes the Earth and all that grows upon it. And from the rain and the Earth, I give thanks for my nourishment.

(*The person sprinkles water on their clothes.*)

The third action is varied based upon the intent of the ritual. At this point in the ritual, we call upon our higher power as well as specific Allies to whom we seek assistance on the behalf of another or ourselves.

(*The person dips their hands into the water with each statement.*)

For cleansing: (*Standing in the center of room, flinging drops of water across the room, saying:*) We (I) seek the assistance of (Name of deity and/or ancient ally, spirit animal) for the cleansing of this space. The power of water cleanses space and drives away anything that has negative energy. Wash this place and make it clean so that healthy growth will spring forth.

(*If there is more than one room to be cleansed, move to each room with the same action and prayer.*)

For healing: (*The speaker pats the person for whom they are seeking healing with their wet hands, saying:*) (Name of deity or ancient ally) We (I) bring our (my) concerns to you. In our (my) brokenness, heal us (me). In our (my) pain, comfort us (me). In our (my) confusion, guide us (me). In our (my) frustration, sooth us (me). In our (my) uncertainty, provide us (me) a clear path.

For letting go: (*The person letting go holds a material object that represents what they are letting go of and says:*) In this moment (name of deity or Ally) I come seeking your presence, love, and affirmation of my need to let go of this relationship (the relationship is named), this hurt (the hurt is named), this unwanted feeling (the feeling is named).

(*The person places the object in the water and says:*)
I lay down what is past and look to the future.
I let go of hurt and pain and travel with hope.
I leave behind familiar paths and take new steps into the unknown.
I let go.

To conclude the ceremony, care needs to be given to four actions: disposing of excess water, cleaning the glassware, a final prayer that opens the circle, thanking the ancients for their presence, and extinguishing the candle. All excess water should be used to water plants and/or returned to the earth or a natural source of water (ocean, lake, river). The Earthenware should be cleaned and dried in silence before the ceremony concludes. A final prayer should be short and simple, for example:

(Name of deity and/or spiritual allies), we give thanks for your assistance and wise counsel in carrying out this ritual. We sought your presence; we now open the circle so that you might return from the direction from which you came. Blessings for you and your journey. Amen (or Namaste). (*Extinguish the candle, watching the smoke rise into the air.*)

Several folks we work with have taken this model and created their own rituals and written their own prayers. The actions and utensils can change based on what you have available and what seems natural to you. You might conduct the ceremony privately or invite some friends to participate. Including everyone who chooses to participate in the ceremony creates a stronger energy.

CREATING RITUAL FOR GRANDMOTHER MOON CYCLES

"Since ancient times, the moon has come to symbolically embody the realm of the unconscious, emotions, intuition, and the cycles of life and death."[3] New Moon symbolizes new beginnings, a new monthly cycle. It is a time for planting the new seeds of intentions bringing power to new projects or endeavors. The power lies in the unseen, hidden in the dark, and opening to the unconscious world of dreams.

Full Moon symbolizes something coming into culmination. It is the height of Grandmother Moon's cycle, at the peak of her energy. It is where the New Moon intentions may come to fruition with gratitude for the experiences and letting go. What needs petitioning and preparing the unconscious mind for transformation?

For a New Moon ritual, consider looking back to the last Full Moon and what was occurring.[4] What has been recorded in a journal or calendar or social media resource. Some questions to consider for this reflection might be:

- What wants to be brought to life? What wants to grow?
- What efforts will the New Moon energy fire up?
- What hopes to be harvested?
- What does the body need to feel healthy and strong? What does the mind need? The soul? The spirit?
- What is one simple action to move these intentions forward?

For a Full Moon ritual, once again look back to the last New

Moon: What was occurring then or what was being experienced?[5] Look back in a journal, calendar, or social media resource. Some questions to consider for this reflection might be:

- What was newly beginning at the New Moon time?
- What has come to fruition from New Moon intentions?
- Are any of these things coming up again? What has moved forward with any of these things? Has any growth taken place?
- What is one simple action to offer gratitude for the growth or movement since New Moon?

Once your intention is formulated for the New or Full Moon ritual, create a sacred space in your home or outside with symbolic objects to represent the intention or desire for the ritual. The objects might be rocks, feathers, crystals, cards, jewelry, photos, anything that enhances the ritual. Consider how to begin. Possibly light a candle or incense and offer a healing or empowering affirmation, something like, "I am grateful for all I experience," or "I align with Love," or "I will open my heart a little more each day."

For New Moon, what will you bring forward as an intention as Grandmother Moon begins the process of waxing toward Full? Write this intention on a piece of paper and offer these words to New Moon, asking Grandmother Moon to strengthen your intention.

For Full Moon, what will you release with gratitude? Write these words down on paper, such as, "I let go of my perfectionism," or "I let go of friends who do not support my highest good," or "I honor the work of my New Moon intentions and release them with gratitude." Offer these words in the light of the Full Moon, asking Grandmother Moon to accept your gratitude and honor the release of what you have been carrying.

Use a fireproof container to burn the paper as it curls into ashes and the smoke spirals up towards Grandmother Moon. If creating fire is a safety concern, consider burying the paper, if it's recyclable, in Mother Earth. Finally, create a symbolic closing for your ritual. Keep it simple, such as ringing a bell or extinguishing the candle, offering thanks with closing words, such as, "So may it be."

BLESSING RITUAL FOR EXPECTANT MOTHER

"We were wondering if you would be willing to help us create a Mother Blessing ritual?" began the text message from Candace and Blair to Catherine. "We would like to have the women of the West Valley Grandmothers' Circle be a part of the ritual along with some of our close women friends. Is that something you would be interested in doing?"

"Of course, I would be honored to help. What do you have in mind?"

"We've read about different Mother Blessing ideas on the internet. It would be wonderful if we could do this in person, but that won't be an option because of COVID. Do you think you could help us figure out how to do it via Zoom?"

"Sure, our Wisdom School has been meeting via Zoom and the spiritual connection is still very real."

"Okay, and it will be very important for us to include a poem to honor our becoming mothers for our adopted son."

"I'll do some internet exploring and look for options for you."

"Great!"

So began the research, several conversations, and email exchanges between us about the ritual. We talked about purpose, what needed to be included in the words and actions, how others would be involved, what the opening and closing would be, and the most challenging part—how to do this during pandemic times via Zoom. Babies don't wait for a pandemic to be over. Blair was due to have twins within a few weeks. The addition of honoring and offering blessings as newly adoptive mothers and their six-year-old son would bring all their hopes and dreams into the circle.

Candace and Blair were seeking a ritual that has its ancestral roots in the Navajo Blessingway. A Mother Blessingway was a gathering for women only where they would tell positive birth stories, give the expectant mother emotional and spiritual support, and pamper her a bit by washing her feet, putting flowers in her hair, and making her feel beautiful. Poems are read and promises to support the mother during and after the birth are made. According to the AAA Native Arts website, "The Blessingway was given to the Earth Surface People shortly after their emergence into this world. 'Blessingway' is the English translation of the name of the ceremony, but its meaning is more complex than that. The rough translation from Diné is 'continuing reoccurring long life in an environment of beauty and harmony.'"[6]

The creation of the Mother Blessing Ritual was adapted from a variety of online resources.[7] It was a collaborative process with the soon-to-be twin moms to make a meaningful, personal ritual for them. One of the adaptation challenges was the reality of not being able to conduct the ceremony in person. We were in the midst of the pandemic before vaccinations were available. Certainly, the utmost concern was the health of Blair as she was nearing the time of birth, as well as Candace, who would be her birth partner. Fortunately, all who were going to be a part of the ritual were willing and able to use Zoom as our connection vehicle.

The night of the ritual, ten women, along with Blair and

Candace, logged in. Introductions were made with friendly chatter among the women, and a few logistics were discussed.

"It's time to begin. Settle yourselves in a comfortable position and take a few deep breaths." We held silence, giving space for our minds, hearts and souls to calm.

"As you look at your screen, imagine that we are sitting in a circle of love with Blair and Candace seated in the middle. Imagine your heart pouring joy over them. Imagine your soul radiating positive energy for this Mother Blessing ritual. Now, let's begin the ritual."

Here is what we created and offered to Blair and Candace.

MOTHER BLESSING RITUAL

Leader: We gather in Circle to nurture Blair and Candace as they prepare for the arrival of the twins and transition into motherhood with their adopted son. We've adorned our hair with flowers to honor the Divine Feminine within us, bringing power to this Circle. We sit under the Grandmother New Moon, who will wax full again, carrying our intentions for Blair and Candace. We bring offerings of love, strength, and confidence. We seek to surround Blair and Candace with our encouragement and pour our joy into their hearts, minds, bodies, and souls.

Opening Reading: "For the Mother to Be Blessing" by John O'Donohue. Each of the women read one stanza of the poem. At the end of the poem, together the readers said: "Relieved, and glad in your arms."

Introduction and Sharing About Blair and Candace:
Each woman said their name into the Circle. Then they had the option to offer a succinct admiration story/anti-

dote about Blair and Candace, or a one- or two-word
piece of advice for motherhood. Everyone was encouraged to limit sharing to three minutes total for both Blair
and Candace.

Expectant Mothers' Blessing
First Reader: May your feet as they touch the Earth provide
a strong foundation, so that you have the strength to
birth your babies and raise your adopted son.

(Blair and Candace will anoint each other's feet with water.)

Second Reader: May your hands be open and gentle, so that
your body may relax as it does the job of birthing your
babies and raising your adopted son.

(Blair and Candace will anoint each other's hands with water.)

Third Reader: May your hearts be filled with tenderness,
acceptance, love, and grace. So you may give these to
yourselves and each other, while recuperating from
birthing your babies and raising your adopted son.

(Blair and Candace will anoint each other's chest with water.)

Fourth Reader: May your intuition guide you during labor
and in raising these children. You are the divine feminine.
Childbirth and motherhood are an ancient act rooted in
your DNA. May you pay attention to your natural feelings
and see things as they truly are.

(Blair and Candace will anoint each other's brow with water.)

Bedtime Blessing for Their Adopted Son

First Reader: We honor Blair and Candace for the courage, compassion and grit required for the journey of adoption. We honor their fears and triumphs. We honor the uniqueness and challenge of adoption. We honor their choice to become mothers to a child who needed a home.

Second Reader: We honor the bravery of their adopted son. We honor his fresh mind for learning how to adapt to his new family. We honor his little heart for the ordeal of trauma he has experienced. We honor his young soul for being open, loving, and wise beyond his years.

Third Reader: We honor their adopted son's birthmother for the trials she has endured. We honor all mothers who have found themselves unable to care for their children.

Fourth Reader: We honor their adopted son as he becomes the big brother. May this bedtime blessing create a ritual for him with Blair and Candace to one day share with the twins.

Leader reads Anna George's prayer for "Their Adopted Son."

Cord/Candle Commitment Ceremony
Each woman had a single cord or piece of yarn or bracelet that can fit around their wrist as well as an unlit pillar candle. Each woman tied a single cord or yarn or bracelet around the wrists to keep there until Blair was in labor. When Blair goes into labor, everyone would be informed. Then they cut the cord/yarn or remove the bracelet as a symbol of unity and light their candle holding vigil during Blair's labor until the babies are born.

Everyone takes their cord/yarn/bracelet and binds it to

their wrist. Once all the cords/yarn/bracelets are in place, everyone repeats these words as their commitment:

I commit to embracing Blair and Candace in my heart, mind, and soul as they journey towards the birth of the twins.

I commit to offering my love and strength to their journey of becoming Mothers to the twins as they hold loving space for their adopted son.

I commit to lighting a candle to hold vigil with Blair and Candace through the labor process offering my positive energy for a good birth.

I commit to supporting Blair, Candace, their adopted son, and the twins with whatever they need.

Closing Birth Blessing was read, written by Natalie Evans

Leader says: This birth belongs to you both. This birth is an opening and a beginning. Blessing to you and the birth of your twins and your adopted son.

There was an overwhelming feeling of peaceful compassion and a deep bond that had been woven among the women gathered as the ritual ended. Expressions of gratitude and joyful tears flowed from Blair and Candace. Smiles were abundant, spontaneous hearty clapping began, and euphoric jubilation was felt.

WEDDINGS

Being the officiant at a wedding carries a heavy responsibility. Everyone wants their wedding to go off without a glitch and if it doesn't, someone in the wedding party will blame the person conducting the service. With over forty years of being the wedding officiant as a Baptist pastor and Episcopal priest, Gil has done countless number of weddings.

Some have been traditional and others not. Some weddings were planned, and others were last minute affairs. Twice, the couple showed up without a license. Twice, the couple only wanted me to sign their license, saying they would do something private to "seal the deal." I didn't ask what they meant. I've done same-sex marriages before they were legal. I've conducted weddings for most all combinations of the LGBTQ rainbow. For all couples, without regard to age, previous marital status, sexuality, personality typing, financial differences, blended family issues, or any other reason you can imagine, I either did the premarital counseling or strongly suggested they receive counseling from a therapist before getting married. After the counseling, I did refuse to marry a few couples because I thought they needed more counseling. And after a few counseling sessions, a few couples told me they no longer wanted me to do the service or they simple didn't show up for any more sessions. I've done weddings in about every venue imaginable, in the church, in a living room, the backyard, standing on a diving board, an assortment of wedding halls, hotels, the zoo, botanical gardens, on a bridge, in the desert, at a State park, by a lake in Ireland, standing on a boulder that leaned out over a lake during a lightning storm, and virtually via Zoom. And the weather has often not cooperated, including windstorms and torrential rain (with and without lightening), not to mention the unpredicted cold front and unexpected heat wave. And at the very last minute, I've had family members threaten to leave the wedding, mothers scream at me about the floral arrangement (which I had nothing to do with), the best men faint during the ceremony, and grooms sob incoherently (but never a bride). I only had one person object to the wedding, not jokingly, to which I quickly responded, "Duly noted," and quickly moved on, while remembering to scratch that question from all subsequent wedding ceremonies. And thankfully, with all of the weird things that have happened I never had the bride nor groom leave the other standing at the altar. (I hope I didn't just jinx myself.) I've mentioned all that to say that weddings can be complicated at their very best and a shit show at their worse. If you still want to officiate a wedding ceremony, you have been given an appropriate heads-up.

Aside from all the warnings, the steps to planning a wedding ceremony are straight-forward: 1) set up the premarital counseling sessions; 2) meet with the couple to discuss the logistics —when and where; and 3) discuss what they want the ceremony to look like. Most couples have in mind what they think the perfect wedding will look like, but as I said above, they all don't turn out as expected. Little things like having a unity candle at an outside venue can send the wrong message when, due to a breeze, the couple can't keep the candle lit. That's just a little thing. Children, pets, and parents can all upstage the best of plans. An Arizona outdoor wedding in July at five o'clock in the afternoon—somebody is going to faint. Common sense should prevail. But remember, emotions outweigh rational decisions.

Unless you're equipped and trained to do premarital counseling, we strongly recommend that the couple find a professional who can help them sort through living life as a married couple. For every reason imaginable, no matter the maturity or experience of the couple, we all could use a little counseling.

Wedding ceremonies can be very simple. The basics of any ceremony rarely take longer than fifteen minutes. What adds time is the bridal procession, musical performances, particular religious rites, and the length of the celebrant's comments. Even then, the ceremony should not exceed thirty minutes. I've never had a wedding start on time and I've never had anyone complain it was too brief.

When meeting with the couple to prepare their ceremony, it helps to have a few templates for them to work with—working from a blank slate typically produces stories about things they've seen at other weddings: the good, the bad, and the hilarious. Once, a couple asked me to do their wedding as a stand-up comedian. They had recently been to a wedding where the celebrant was really funny and they loved it. I asked them why they didn't ask that person to do their wedding. The bride responded that her mom wanted a priest to do the ceremony. I passed on the opportunity to make a fool of myself and ruin their wedding.

Even for the most creative of magical events, couples typically want: an exchange of vows and rings, the celebrant pronouncing that they are now married, and formally being presented as a married couple to those gathered. Those three components have been at the heart of every wedding I've conducted except for the two where the couples only wanted the license to be signed.

Some couples will want to write their own vows, though few do. Most rewrite the vows from a template I offer them and make them their own. And some want traditional vows, what some might think of as standard, but of which there are many variants. Pronouncing a couple seems straight-forward, but it's never good to make assumptions about, "I now pronounce you...." Are you pronouncing them husband and wife, wife and wife, husband and husband, or a married couple, or what? And the same goes for presenting the couple. Are one or both of them changing their names, or not? Do they want to be presented as Mr. and Mrs., or Mr. and Mr., or Ms. and Ms., or as Bill and Judy, or William and Judith? Ask the couple and then you'll always get it right—don't ask and you will incur someone's wrath, usually one of the parents. For simplicity's sake, what follows is the standard template for a wedding.

- Family and friends gather.

- Parents and sometimes grandparents are seated. This is often omitted if there are issues around deceased parents, parents who are ill, parents who refuse to attend, parents who are divorced (especially if more than once).
- Groom and celebrant enter.
- Family and friends stand and the bridal party processes.
- Father presents the bride. This is becoming less of the tradition because of the symbolism that the father owns the daughter and has the right to give her to another person, which is usually a male.
- Celebrant invites family and friends to be seated.
- Celebrant says a few (emphasis on the few) words about marriage and the couple.
- Exchange of vows.
- Exchange of rings.
- Performance of songs, lighting of unity candles, hand fasting, and any religious rites can be added at this point.
- Celebrant offers a blessing for the couple.
- Pronounce the couple as now married.
- Presentation of the couple to family and friends.
- Wedding party recesses and the real party begins.

Weddings are celebrations. The ceremony is usually a centerpiece but rarely the most memorable part of the event. It's the celebrant's job to keep the focus on the couple and the flow of the ceremony moving gently along. If the celebrant can achieve those two goals, the ceremony is typically considered a success. Then everybody can go to the party and dance their heart out.

RITUALS ARE NEVER FOR RITUAL'S SAKE

Rituals never need to be for the sake of the ritual—the purpose of the ritual is the foundation of its necessity. If there's no grounding purpose for conducting a ritual, there's no reason for it take place. No one needs a wedding to get married or a funeral to be buried. You don't need to have a wedding ceremony to begin a life together. Nor does anyone need a funeral for closure because there's no such thing as closure. Grief is never-ending and always accompanies your journey. Weddings, however, are celebrations that invite our family and friends into an event that reminds every one of the powers and the fragility of love. And the same can be said for funerals—which is a celebration of life that reminds every one of the power and fragility of love and life itself. Whoever is planning and celebrating the ceremony and the ritual must know its purpose and understand its underlying foundation. At some point in the ceremony and ritual, the cele-brant must let those attending in on the secret, recognizing that the best planned rituals will reveal their purpose more often without words.

Rituals are necessary for all the obvious reasons and for those more subtle. There are many benefits for everyone who creates the ritual and for those who participate. Jessica Baron offers this:

> Researchers from business psychology to neuroscience have shown that rituals have social, psychological, and even physio-logical effects on us, making us less anxious and more resilient....Researchers from Harvard Business School found that performing a task we believe is a ritual can lower our heart rates, ease anxiety, and help us perform better.[8]

While the goal is not to enhance our performance, the benefit of soothing anxiety and offering a sense of healing for our hearts, souls, and body has much to offer to our way of being in the world.

The power of the ritual is to know that your words and actions are meaningful to you and those who may gather with you. As our Wisdom's Way companions reminded us, rituals have many diverse definitions and expressions beyond being a part of a religious ceremony. We encourage you to set an intention, choose your ritual actions with care and love, and open yourself to the power of ritual.

CHAPTER THIRTEEN

YOUR PERSONAL NARRATIVE: WRITING AS MAGIC

We create the truth by living it.
—Carl Jung

What is your personal narrative? What is the mythos that guides your life? Carl Jung said that if we're not living in our own myth, we're living in someone else's. And Hugh O'Doherty said something similar: "If you're not living in your own purpose, you're living in another person's purpose."

Our personal narrative is the story we tell ourselves about ourself. It's not our autobiography or a memoir. Our personal narrative is the story that exists behind the story we tell everyone else. The story may have been handed to us by our parents, culture, and/or religion and that narrative is probably filled with both truth and not truth. Our personal narrative might have been written on the pages of our secret journal and we have lost the journal somewhere along the way. And sometimes our myth was found on pages we've left blank because we couldn't face seeing the story in the light of day.

Writing our personal narrative is different from journaling in that journaling is meant to create a space for us to reflect. Personal narrative writing, however, is the place to imagine the future as the now we're living in. In doing the work of sorting out our lives, we can reconsider our own present purpose, which leads to determining a new potential for our future.

In speaking about the personal narrative the next sentence needs to be written in a single voice. To live my life by my personal narrative, my story must include my sacred truth, that which is simultaneously true and false. Your personal narrative is your personal narrative—not your family's, your culture's, or your religion's. If you want to include those influences, it's because you choose to do so. Your narrative, your truth is always evolving. Your truth is not permanent because paradox is the genesis of living a creative life. Conundrum is the riddle out of which genius is born. No one necessarily needs to know your backstory for you to be living out of the truth and falsity of it—but if you're not living out of your own truth, you'll be living out of someone else's.

"I'm feeling stuck."

"How so?"

"I feel like everything I do has to be perfect."

"Why do you feel that way?"

"I don't know. I guess that's the way I was raised. First child. All that stuff."

"Tell me more about how you were raised."

"I grew up in a conservative home. We went to church and were taught how to live the righteous life. Mainly because I think our parents were afraid we might do the things they were afraid we'd do: sex, drugs, and rock-and-roll. So, I guess my parents got what they wanted. We, well, I, never did any of those things. Can't speak for my siblings. But I doubt they did any of those things either."

"Did you ever want to do any of those things?"

"In college. Sex and rock-and-roll. Not the drugs. Well, not illegal drugs anyway."

"How did that work out?"

"Lots of momma guilt. So everything was experimental —once."

"How did you process all that momma guilt?"

"I started keeping a journal as a teenager. I wrote poems and stories about how life was and how I wanted it to be different than it was. Most of the things I wrote in those journals have never seen the light of day. Oddly enough, though, most of those thoughts are still informing how I live my life."

"How so?"

"The truth of what I wrote still contained the falsehoods I didn't buy into and what I wanted to escape from. Hmm. That's interesting. That's why I feel stuck. I'm still living that way. Trying to escape."

"What'd you mean?"

"I wrote to make sure I lived like my parents and church wanted me to live. But I wrote in my journal as my way to break out of that prison. Those paradoxes are scratched in my journals like a scientist's notes about the experiment of life. The institutions of family and religion created the boundaries for the first half of my life. But I'm still stuck there."

"And now. How do you want to live your life?"

"I desperately want to write a different story. I want out of the old prison cell."

"Can you imagine living the second half of your life in a borderless world where every story is simultaneously true and false? Where only some of the stories happen in what others call reality—actually, literally? While all the stories happen in *your* reality, not necessarily in other people's literal perspective. Living in the space where you can write your personal narrative and then live it out."

"How?"

"Start with a fresh journal. Pour out your dreams and visions. The more you work on the narrative, the more it will develop, mature, and evolve. Don't worry if it's true, or real, or even possible. Just write. This kind of writing is not easy work— and none of it will ever be completed. At least not in this lifetime."

BEYOND JOURNALING OUR DAILY LIFE

Writing our personal narrative has its own kind of mystique and it's more than journaling. Typically, we think of journaling as writing whatever I'm Thinking, Feeling, Sensing, Intuiting on a regular basis. I write about my experiences hoping that I can burn them before anyone ever reads them. But a personal narrative can be more than what's in the vault that contains all our deep dark secrets. Our myth can be the fertile soil for the second half of life, maybe the next life, or the potential of my future now that is unfolding in this very present moment. Writing our personal narrative is the essence of soul-making.

Artist Frida Kahlo merged her poetry and her pain into her art. *The Diary of Frida Kahlo* spans the final ten years of her life, blending her daily reflections, musing, and initial sketches of what would become masterpieces. She exposed her inner life to generate a new imaginaire. And while the story of Frida's life didn't end well, what she created has a life of its own, with her blood mingled with the words on every page.

Stephania Pandolfo's *Impasse of the Angels* and *Knot of the Soul* are two examples of what Anand Pandian and Stuart McLean describe as "experiments in ethnographic writing." In their book *Crumpled Paper Boats*,[1] they have included a chapter written by Pandolfo: "Ta'bir: Ethnography of the Imaginal." In her essay she explores the recesses of madness, poetry, dreams, all secrets we might want to bury in a deep hole. But out of the darkness she writes about, there emerges a magical potential for healing. She intertwines her own dreams and imagination into the work of revered Sufi poets; both are layered over the art and dreams of the mentally ill. Her life feels woven into the text where, at times, it's indistinguishable from those lives she's writing about. She experiments with her work, while her work works on her, reading like something more than a journal—these are the words of a person who is exploring the depths of the psyche.

Science fiction author Philip K. Dick never intended for his personal narrative to be published. Yet what emerged from the final ten years of Dick's personal notes became *The Exegesis of Philip K. Dick,*[2] the essence of his personal myth. More than 10,000 mostly handwritten pages were found on his desk after his death. He spent the final years ruminating and writing about his philosophy and ever-changing spirituality. In an effort of curiosity, respect, and love, editors Pamela Jackson and Jonathan Lethem were brought together with annotators Simon Critchley, Steve Erickson, David Gill, N. Katherine Hayles, Jeffrey J. Kripal, Gabriel Mckee, and Richard Doyle. They read, organized, and condensed the disorganized and unnumbered handwritten pages into a 944-page monograph of PKD on PKD. Evidently, historian and philosopher Jeffrey J. Kripal was so inspired by Dick's *Exegesis* that he wrote the exegesis of his own work in *Secret Body*.

Our personal narrative is the story of how we are the living embodiment of the experimental life. Our myths are our sacred texts, an ever-evolving memory scrolling into our present and potential future. Our personal narrative is the evidence of our expanding consciousness and the exploration of our Mindbody. This unique style of journaling/writing/imagining liberates the soul. The work of writing our personal myth is the "craftwork of soulwork."[3] It's when the experiment begins writing itself and that writing begins to write us—writing becomes the act of magical soul-making.

The variations on techniques used for writing our personal narrative are as numerous as the varietal of grapes used in wine-making. And as the quality of wine depends on the soil, the sun, the grower, and the maker, so the craft of writing is dependent upon a multiplicity of factors. There is no correct way to write your personal narrative—there is only your way. Writing can be both a genesis for and the integration of all our soul-making. The writing techniques with which we experiment will affect our voice in every aspect of our exegesis. What we're providing here is only a sample of techniques and experiments for your consideration.

A JOURNAL EVOLVING INTO THE PERSONAL NARRATIVE

Writing your personal narrative is the evolution of keeping a daily journal. The next level is going beyond our daily recounting of life into creating space for the imagination of the past, present, and future living into the present moment. One of the liberations of writing your personal narrative is that it doesn't need to be a linear narrative. Your personal narrative can be written in a spiral, even a series of spirals within a spiral. The beauty of the personal narrative is that we don't have to rehash or revisit the past. What we're doing is reconstructing a new potential for our imagination to play in.

Dreams, visions, and Ally conversations, sacred texts, novels, music, poetry, film all can be the grist and inspiration of our personal narrative, along with recurring dreams, dreams with common themes, and one-time epic dreams that have an overarching narrative. We can identify and follow our ancient teachers deep into the tree of life, the temple where the labyrinth leads us into other dimensions.

Writing a personal narrative is pure, spontaneous free-form

writing. It's best if written long hand without punctuation, paragraph, and spell-checking. And when words pop into our mind, we write them in our book as they appear. No need to wonder if the words fit or make sense, we simply write them on the page as they "jumped" into our mind.

AUTOMATIC WRITING

Paranormal experiences can include liminal dreams, waking visions, hearing voices of spirits and the dead. These types of experiences can produce messages of inspiration that inform our personal myth. Two examples of this type of writing and art can be found in *A Vision* by poet W.B. Yeats and *Notes and Methods* by abstract artist Hilma af Klint, who we discussed in the chapter on Ally work. Both Yeats and af Klint produced extensive troves of art and prose following extended visitations from the spirit world. While these examples might feel extreme or rare, they are not. And they cannot be excluded from the mechanics of writing our personal narrative.

One technique to use for experimentation in automatic writing is to read three books simultaneously. For example, for some time now Gil has included reading one or two pages from each of three books as the prompt for his personal narrative. Those three books have been mentioned previously: *Meditations on the Tarot*,[4] *The Exegesis of Philip K. Dick,* and *The Red Book.* The only thing these three books have in common is that the authors of the first two books had read some of Carl Jung's writings, but not *The Red Book.* All three authors were dead by the time *The Red Book* had been published. The only other thing the three books have in common is they can be classified as "weird." That has now become an official classification of literature after Erik Davis' *High Weirdness.*[5] Some days Gil begins his writing with a dream. Some days he does an exegesis on his tarot card draw. Following that writing, he reads one or two pages from each book. Most days, a word or a line from the first book catches his attention. Almost always, the second reading expounds on the first. And, typically, the third reading builds on the first two. The connection is that the readings create openings where he can focus on new interpretations related to the dream or the tarot cards—all parts of his personal myth. The point of writing our personal narrative is to create space for our unconscious to wander/wonder into our conscious, always with a little surprise.

THE PILGRIMAGE OF WRITING YOUR PERSONAL NARRATIVE

Author and critical theorist Maggie Nelson writes in a form of prose and poetry that provides a portal into the work of journal writing as personal narrative. In her books, *The Argonauts*[6] and *Bluets*, Nelson wonders about the soul muse while simultaneously condemning such a notion as naive. Much of her work is raw and unfiltered. It feels as if she copied it verbatim from her unconscious. And indeed, she may have. What we experience in her poetry and prose is Nelson experiencing her own soul work —the experiment of reflecting on her past, establishing her present purpose, and determining her potential for the future as she walks the pilgrimage of her personal narrative.

Writing our personal narrative and then living it is the pilgrimage that incorporates our exegesis of both the inner and the outer adventures in a new and yet unimagined way. It's moving beyond the narrative someone has handed us and celebrating who we really are becoming. As Jung said, if there's "no inner adventure, [there's] no outer adventure." The techniques we've shared are the tools we use for writing our own myth and the encouragement we found for living our personal narrative.

After each of the pilgrimages we've chosen to walk, and those we wish we'd never had to travel—family death, end of a career, health issues, pandemic—the same question has confronted us: "Am I feeling a hangover or experiencing an afterglow?" The combined effect of pilgrimage preparation, walking, reflection, and the rising of a new imaginaire are the soul work of myth-making. During our days, weeks, and years of charting our dreams, journaling our visions, confronting the demons of our failures, and mulling over the landscape of the simultaneous transmutation of hangover/afterglow, our personal myth continues to emerge. Some of that work—what we've came to learn and what we still have to figure out—has morphed into what you're now reading.

As Jung wrote in the *Mysterium Coniunctionis*, there's always a cost that produces the results: "Every gain for the Self, is a defeat for the ego."[7] In the Netflix original series *Sense8*, the character Capheus is a Kenyan man working as a matatu driver in Nairobi. His daily goal is to raise the money needed to provide his mother with the HIV/AIDS drugs she must have for survival. And every day, Jela, his friend and matatu conductor, is at his side through their sometimes perilous adventure. After one particularly "great day" they celebrated over a sumptuous dinner. In a moment of vulnerability, the Introvert Capheus shares his archetypal childhood dream of becoming Van Damme —the weak boy who became a martial arts hero. During an instant of unguarded self-reflection, Capheus questions the reality of what seemed to have been a foolish fantasy.

The Extroverted Jela says, "When I was a boy, my father used to tell me that if I would work hard, I could become anything in the world I wanted to be."

"And what did you want to be when you were a boy?" Capheus asks.

"The son of a rich man!" Jela laughs.

After a bit of contemplation Capheus mused, "Your father was a wise man."

The power of Jela's punch line is found in the paradox of its visible absurdity and its hidden truth. All things can be true and false at the same time—son of a father who is both poor and rich. The story of Capheus and Jela reveals much about their psychological types. And their brief conversation is abundant with symbols: the bus, the driver, the conductor, the friend, the ill mother, the son, the poor father, the rich father, the wise father, the hero, and the heroic journey are obvious; others exist below the surface. Jung said that symbols are neither allegories nor signs—"they are images" with "indefinite expressions" and "variant meanings" which are often "hidden." The meanings of symbols within myth cannot be taken literally as "external truths," but understood as life force, or essence, within themselves, often filled with paradox and contradiction. Symbols are "psychologically true" and are the "bridge to all that is best in humanity." The symbols can also be reminders of what we are not, but hope to become, or fail to see that we already are. In such stories we can discover the symbols of our own myth.

Writing our personal myth and living our life impacted by our story is about becoming our authentic self. By seeing ourselves as who we really are and living our life on our own pilgrimage, regardless of avocation, location, or sexuality, creates a new potential within us—that of soul-making. Symbolic truth far exceeds the factual currency of being the literal "son of a rich man." Capheus and Jela were writing and living their personal myths in near impossible, yet magical, circumstances. The story of *Sense8* is one of variant avocations, locations, and sexualities. Eight people who appear to be variant individuals but are at the same time a multiple-persona of the one. They are complexes of the complex—something the writers of *Sense8*, Lana and Lily Wachowski, know well. The Wachowski sisters are two transwomen who gained fame writing and directing the *Matrix* trilogy as brothers. The Wachowskis and the characters in their stories, along with other writers and artists, have provided us with some guidance for our own journey of writing and living a personal myth.

Jung insisted that life is not to be lived in isolated, detached modules, but as an integrated whole. He urged his clients to be involved simultaneously in the processes of observing the unconscious (the work found in *The Red Book*) while living in "full participation of life"—living life as a singular pilgrimage encompassing a series of pilgrimages, one as a part of the larger cosmic whole, a complex within multiple complexes.

Imagine you've traveled to Zurich perchance to visit Carl Jung. A pilgrimage if you will. You're hoping he'll be willing to see you and interpret your dream. You've taken a taxi—a thirty-minute ride down a narrow road to Bollingen. The retreat house Jung built rises two stories above a dark lake. The solitary house with two towers sits between the still water and a thick forest. Now you're standing at the front door. His wife, Emma, greets you and escorts you up the stairs to Dr. Jung's office. You shake the big thick hand of a man who looks older and more worn than you had imagined. Emma winks at you, gently touches your forearm, and then quietly excuses herself. You notice the famed psychiatrist's gold rim glasses have eased off the bridge of his nose. The room feels close, yet he's wearing a tan dress coat and a rather drab brown tie. He invites you to follow him into the extensive library, every wall lined from floor to ceiling with thick books bound in dark leather. The aroma of ancient volumes and pipe smoke lingers. There's an easel in the corner. It's holding an unfinished painting, rolled tubes of color and well used brushes at the ready. There's barely enough space for the small wooden table and two leather armchairs in the center of the room. A journal is open on the table, a sheaf of papers to the left, and a book held in place with the weight of another to the right. Other books are stacked and scattered across the table. Your attention turns to a broad window at the end of the room. Three panels of stain-glassed images cast an ethereal light across the floor where the overstuffed chairs await your presence. With one hand, Jung places his pipe on the wooden table closest to the chairs, and with the other he picks up a deck of Tarot cards.

"Please be seated," he says. He waits while you sit and then lowers himself with care into the chair next to you. "I imagine you've come to talk about a dream. Seems everyone does." He chuckles politely, but seemingly only to himself.

"I had a dream that you were my therapist."

"And so?"

"My dream was about a dream. You were in both dreams. In the first, you were interpreting my dream using Tarot. In the second, you had turned your back to me. Ignoring me, you stood in silence."

"Hmm. Tell me more."

"That's all I can remember."

He waits. You shift your weight in the chair. He hands you the cards.

"Who are you in the dream? Who am I? Who is the dream itself?"

Absentmindedly, he picks up his pipe. "Do you mind?"

You nod. He puts the pipe in his mouth and strikes a match across the table. He puffs the pipe while smoke trickles from his nostrils. The old man leans back deep into the chair that absorbs his body. You slowly sort through the tattered Marseilles deck. The colors are faded, the simple figures are marred by the hundreds of finger strokes. After a few minutes, you select three cards, placing them on the table. You carefully set the deck on two books setting askew on the edge of the table. You have a deep urge to push the books into a less precarious position, but you resist, feeling that that act would be too presumptuous. Out of the corner of your eye you see the old man breathing in rhythm with your every breath.

He waits until you look into his eyes. He speaks softly to you. "You are each of these images. Who might the first be?"

You feel a portal opening. Through a separation in the dimension, a ghostly image on the first card slips into the room. The apparition whispers a word into your ear. Your personal myth has begun once again. Always we are beginning again, spiraling, evolving, turning the page. What we write becomes our work and then it works on us and then it becomes us—and our myth is realized.

CHAPTER FOURTEEN

THE PILGRIMAGE CONTINUES: THE SACRED WAY OF WISDOM

The journey of one thousand miles begins with one step.
—Lao Tzu

Max's text read: "I'm on pilgrimage, walking the Camino, and I need to talk to you. Can we arrange a time to meet?"

Via Skype Max said, "Thanks for connecting on such short notice. Sometimes a nine-hour time difference can work to our advantage."

"How's your soul?"

"Ah, yeah. I'm on pilgrimage. That's how my soul is doing. And all kinds of stuff is coming to the surface. I've been here ten days and I've had the same dream three times."

"That's a persistent companion."

"For sure. There are two reasons I needed to talk to you about this dream. Obviously, this dream is not going to leave me alone. And two, it's about you."

"Okay. Are you sure it's about me and not about you?"

"It's about our relationship."

"Alright. Well, tell me about the dream."

"We're sitting under a tree, somewhat like that tree we would sit under at the park near the university. But this tree was much bigger and had a grand opening in the center, like a doorway. There were several people standing behind you. But they are all transparent, like they're not alive. And there was someone standing behind me. I could feel them but not see them. I knew who they were, but at the same time I wasn't sure who it was. And they told me to tell you this. But I was hesitant. Afraid. Not really afraid. I don't know."

"It's okay. You can tell me."

"I don't know. Maybe I shouldn't have reached out to you. Maybe this is nothing. It's all about me. I know. And this has nothing to do with you. I guess."

"Okay, so who do you think the people standing behind me are?"

"I'm pretty sure they're not living. They're just standing there, looking at me. They have kind faces. Encouraging faces. Like they're there to support us both."

"And the person standing behind you?"

"I think it's my mom. It feels like my mom. It sounds like my mom. Remember the first time we talked. It was about my mom."

"Your mom was talking to you and she told you to be careful. Right?"

"Yeah. But now she's telling me to tell you something."

"Being your mom has appeared three times while you've been on pilgrimage, maybe it would be okay for you to tell me what she said. Otherwise, she's probably not going to give up until you do." I chuckled.

"That's just like my mom. Dog with a bone. Guess I shouldn't say that about the dead, especially my mom."

Silence held us both.

* * *

The pilgrimage of writing a book begins with a blank page and one word keyed in at a time. Now we've arrived at the end of this particular long walk, the completion of this book. Like any intentional pilgrimage, we're feeling a bit of a hangover along with the warm feeling of afterglow. We began by laying out our roadmap for all we imagined that needed to be shared, loading up our backpacks, finding out we had packed way more than was necessary. There were many, many stops along the way to off-load unnecessary baggage. The delete key became a constant companion, leaving our egos in its wake while honing the words with greater precision (hopefully).

There were side roads needing to be explored, ramblings about searching for the next helpful road marker to show us the next turn and guiding us on wisdom's path. We've discovered that by engaging the art of (w)holy wisdom listening, our allies, our companions, our shadows, and the Divine Source have collectively exposed some excruciating revelations about our blind spots. So much we thought we knew, but in reality, so much we didn't know. Martin Buber has reminded us repeatedly, "All journeys have secret destinations of which the traveler is unaware." Writing with vulnerability, exposing our very souls, and offering our passion for walking alongside anyone who needs a fellow companion without judgment have been the yellow arrows we passed along the way. We're pretty sure we missed some of them, those hiding in the weeds and others that had fallen down.

As we said previously, we've been married for over 50 years. (That's another pilgrimage story to be told in another book.) We know a lot about each other through so many joyous experiences, deep conversations, lack of conversations, solo adventures, and agonizing heartaches. This book was our first attempt at writing something together. Our writing experiences and approach to this endeavor, not surprisingly, were not the same. (Catherine wrote best with a mango dragonfruit refresher and

Gil loved having a flat white coffee with coconut milk and two Splenda.) And we believe that our different approaches have been part of the true beauties of this book. We both intentionally open ourselves to being spiritual companions and we engage that way of being in our unique ways. We have no doubt, though, that you have been able to "see" how spiritual companioning has a common ground for all those who take up this very rewarding endeavor. It is the mystical magic that all of us invite into the companioning pilgrimage. We open our hearts, lives, and souls to shine and shimmer love into our world. That is enough. That is abundance.

Now what? We are still on the journey, integrating this exceptional opportunity into the next steps (or words) of our pilgrimage because it is our way of life. Simon Rattle reminds us, "Always the journey, never the destination." Hopefully, by reading this book, we have added some value to your journey or at least brought a chuckle or a tear or "you've got to be kidding" response.

* * *

Max continued, "I guess I need to say this, but it's not easy. The person standing behind me, my mom, I guess, wants me to tell you that I'm your spiritual director."

"You are. That's our relationship. Has been from the beginning."

"No. Like really. Not like now, mutual and all that. But like, I am your spiritual director. I guess like old school? You ask questions and I give you the answers."

"So, what do you think that means?"

"I think that means my mom doesn't know anything about being a spiritual companion."

"Jung always said the unconscious knows more than the conscious."

"Do you have a Jung quote for every scenario?"

"Sorry. I read way too much."

"Here's the really weird part. Obviously, I've been walking with this dream, hours every day, for days. Trying to figure out what this means. And then this, a poem thing, I guess started flowing out of me. I had to drop my pack and pull out my journal so I could write it down. Word for word like it came to me. Do you want to see it?"

"Yes. Of course."

"Here, I'll send you a picture of my journal entry."

A path shall appear in the desert,
   Which shall be called the sacred way.
   The arid desert shall be glad,
   The wilderness shall rejoice
   And shall blossom like a rose.

The way shall be a pilgrimage for those who seek the soul.
   While the gate is narrow,
   And the way is steep and rocky,
   The pilgrims will sing.
   And though the night's moon shall be new,
   And the day's sun eclipsed,
   The pilgrims shall behold the glory of wisdom,
   For wisdom shall be the key to the gate
   And the light of the sacred way.
   For the pilgrim, not even fools, shall go astray.

Wisdom shall lead their souls
   To discover the blue tincture of healing, which will
   Strengthen the hands of the poor;
   Make firm the tottering knees of the weak;
   Saying to the anxious of heart,
   "Be strong, fear not;

Behold the presence of wisdom is among us.

The eyes of the blind will open,
  And the deaf shall hear.
  The lame shall leap like a deer,
  And every tongue shall sing.
  For the gentle rain shall nourish the desert,
  And the streams of wilderness shall become a healing pool;
  The inhabitation of the dragons shall bloom marigolds.
  The abode of the ravens shall be the mighty cedar.
  For your pilgrimage shall crown everyone with
  their own wisdom.

Indeed, Max, you and all our companions are our spiritual directors. We offer these words of blessing for your pilgrimage of wisdom:

May you abide in lovingkindness.
May you find what you need.
May you be free from suffering.
May you be at peace.
May it be so, now and always.

NOTES

INTRODUCTION

1. Dick, Philip K., *The Exegesis of Philip K Dick*, edited by Pamela A Jackson and Jonathan Lethem, Boston: Houghton Mifflin Harcourt, 2011, 626.
2. See particularly Pew Research on America, Western Europe and Japan. Kenan Sevinc, Thomas J. Coleman III, and Ralph W. Hood, Jr. "Non-Belief: An Islamic Perspective," secularandnonreligion.org
3. Deepak Chopra
4. Diana Ali, "Safe Spaces and Brave Spaces: Historical Context and Recommendations for Student Affairs Professionals," *NASPA Policy and Practices Series*, Issue 2, October 2017, naspa.org.
5. Heraclitus quoted in Yeats, W.B., *A Vision, the Revised 1937 Edition, The Collected Works of W.B. Yeats, Volume XIV,* edited by Margaret Mills Harper and Catherine E. Paul, New York: Scribner, 2015, 145.
6. Louv, Jason, *John Dee and the Empire of Angels: Enochian magick and the occult roots of the modern world*, Rochester, VT: Inner Traditions, 2018, 112."

1. WALKING WITH THE SPIRITUAL BUT NOT RELIGIOUS

1. Kripal, Jeffrey *Secret Body: Erotic and Esoteric Currents in the History of Religion,* (Chicago: University of Chicago Press, 2017), 179, 189
2. Ibid., 179
3. Ibid., 181
4. Heline, Corrine *The Bible and the Tarot,* (Marina del Ray, CA: De Vorss & Co. Publishers, 1986), 46.
5. Nelson, Maggie *Bluets*, (Seattle, WA: Wave Books, 2009)
6. Eiesland, Nancy, *The Disabled God: Toward a Liberatory Theology of Disability,* (Nashville: Abingdon Press, 1994)
7. Ibid.
8. "Spiritual Radicals," Mallory Corbin, Kathryn Drury Wagner, Kalia Kelmenson, *Spirituality and Health*, January/February 2021, p 38-46)
9. Ibid.
10. Emily Qureshi-Hurst and Anna Pearson, *Zygon: Journal of Religion and Science,* "Quantum Mechanics, Time, and Theology: Indefinite Order and a New Approach to Salvation," July 30, 2020, https://doi.org/10.1111/zygo.12621 Wiley Online Library

11. Ibid., 669.
12. Kripal, *Secret Body*, 265.
13. Ibid., 270.
14. *Irreducible Mind: Toward a Psychology for the 21st Century*, Edward F. Kelly, Emily Williams Kelly, Adma Crabtree, Alan Gauld, Michael Corosso, Bruce Greyson, (Lanham: Rowman & Littlefield, 2007), 44-114.
15. Mogenson, Greg *A Most Accursed Religion: When a Trauma Becomes a God*, (Putnam, CT: Spring Publication, 2005).
16. Storm, Jason Amanda Josephson, *Metamoderism: The Future of Theory*, (Chicago: University of Chicago Press, 2021).
17. Brandongrahamdempsey.com

2. PILGRIMAGE: A WAY OF LIFE

1. Kripal, *Secret Body*, 292.

3. THE PILGRIMAGE OF BECOMING A SPIRITUAL COMPANION

1. Mabry, John *Noticing the Divine: An Introduction to Interfaith Spiritual Guidance*, (Morehouse, Harrisburg, PA: 2006)
2. sdicompanions.org

4. LISTENING: (W)HOLY WISDOM

1. Kay Lindahl, "Listening: A Sacred Art and a Spiritual Practice," *Presence*, December 2014
2. Kay Lindahl, illustrations by Amy Schnapper, *The Sacred Art of Listening: Forty Reflections for Cultivating a Spiritual Practice*, (Woodstock, VT: Skylight Paths Publishing, 2002).
3. Parker Palmer, *A Hidden Wholeness: The Journey Toward an Undivided Life*, (San Francisco: Jossey-Bass, 2004), 132.
4. Murphy, Kate *You're Not Listening: What You're Missing and Why It Matters*, (New York: Celadon Books, 2019), 69.
5. Kay Lindahl, TheListeningCenter@yahoo.com www:sacredlistening.com, 2020.
6. Tom Blue Wolf and Frederica Helmiere, "We're All Just Walking Each Other Home": an Interview with Native American Spiritual Guide Tom Blue Wolf with Frederica Helmiere, *Presence*, December 2021.

5. BUILDING COMMUNITY: THE CIRCLE WAY

1. Christina Baldwin and Ann Linnea, *The Circle Way: A Leader in Every Chair,* (San Francisco: Berrett-Koehler, 2010)
2. Parker Palmer and the Center for Courage and Renewal. "Circle of Trust Touchstones." http://www.m.couragerenewal.org

6. MEDITATION, CONTEMPLATION & MINDFULNESS

1. *The Bhagavad Gita,* Introduction and translation, Eknath Easwaran, (Tomales, CA: Nilgiri
   Press, 2007), 140-141
2. Anderson, Kevin *Divinity in Disguise: Nested Meditations to Delight the Mind and Awaken the Soul,* (Hagerstown, MD: CLB Press, 2003).
3. Jung, C.G. *The Red Book, Liber Novus: A Reader's Edition,* (New York: WW Norton, 2009), RB 13
4. Jung, C.G. *Collected Works,* Volume 8, "The Structure and Dynamics of the Psyche," (Princeton: Princeton University Press, 1960), 79-82.
5. Jung, C.G. *The Psychology of Kundalini Yoga,* edited by Sony Shamdasani, (Princeton:
   Princeton University Press, 1996), xix
6. Hughes Reho, James *Tantric Jesus: The Erotic Heart of Early Christianity,* Rochester, VT:
   Destiny Books, 2017).
7. Kripal, *Secret Body,* 232.
8. Hering, Karen *Writing to Wake the Soul: Opening the Sacred Conversation Within,* (New
   York: Atria Paperback, 2013).

7. PERSONALITY TYPING: DON'T PUT ME IN A BOX

1. Isabel Myers Briggs, *MBTI Manual: A Guide to the Development and Use of the Myers-Briggs Type Indicator,* (authors) Mary H. McCauley, Naomi L. Quenk, Allan L. Hammer, (Palo Alto: Consulting Psychologists Press, 1998), 22.
2. Bakhtiar, Laleh *The Sufi Enneagram: Sign of the Presence of God, Secrets of the Symbol Unveiled,* (Chicago: Institute of Traditional Psychology, 2013), xix.
3. Kripal, Jeffrey *Esalen: America and the Religion of No Religion,* (Chicago: University of Chicago Press, 2077), 7.
4. Ibid., 12-13.
5. Both Kripal and Bakhtiar make this inference in their books.
6. Wagner, Jerome, *The Enneagram Spectrum of Personality Types,* (Portland, OR:

Metamorphous Press, 1996), 75. (see also Wagner's, *Nine Lenses of the World.*)

7. Ibid., 75.
8. Jung, C.G. *Collected Works, Volume 9, Part II,* "Aion: Research Into the Phenomenology of the Self," (Princeton: Princeton University Press, 1959), 153.
9. Pike, James A., *If This Be Heresy,* (New York: Harper and Row, 1967), 122. Charges were brought against the Episcopal Bishop regarding his theological views on some traditionally held beliefs. He was also a progressive about the ordination of women and the civil rights movement. The charges had nothing to do with his participation in seances or his perspectives of life after death. Eventually the charges were dropped. Though the controversary never ceased to swirl around the outspoken Bishop of California.

8. WALKING THE LABYRINTH: THE SERPENT'S PATH

1. Vaughan-Lee, Llewellyn, *The Lover and the Serpent: Dreamwork within a Sufi Tradition,* (Longmead, Great Britain: Element Books, 1990), 59.
2. Harari, Yuval Noah, *Sapiens: A Brief History of Humankind,* (New York: Harper Perennial, 2105).

9. REIMAGINING PERSONALITY TYPING

1. *Beyond Physicalism: Toward Reconciliation of Science and Spirituality,* Edward F. Kelly, Adam Crabtree, and Paul Marshall, editors, (Lanham, MD: Rowman & Littlefield, 2015), 519.
2. Ibid., 521
3. von Franz, Marie-Louise *On Dreams and Death,* (Boston: Shambhala, 1987), 82-84.
4. Ouspensky, P.D., *In Search of the Miraculous: Fragments of an Unknown Teaching,* (San Diego: Harcourt, 1949), 294-5.
5. Yeats, W.B., *A Vision: The Revised 1937 Edition,* edited by Margaret Mills Harper and Catherine E. Paul, (New York: Scribner, 2015), 50.
6. Pike, James A. with Dianne Kennedy, *The Other Side: An Account of My Experience with Psychic Phenomena,* (New York: Doubleday, 1968), 373.
7. Ibid., 371.
8. James, William, *The Varieties of Religious Experience: A Study in Human Nature,* (New York: Penguin Books, 1982). See especially Lectures XVI and XVII, "Mysticism."
9. Kripal, Jeffrey J., *The Flip: Epiphanies of Mind and the Future of Knowledge,* (New York: Bellevue Literary Press, 2019), 11.
10. Ibid., 120.
11. Ibid., 123.

12. Ouspensky, *Search*, 278.
13. Kripal, *The Flip*, 125.
14. Jung, C.G., *The Red Book, Liber Novus: A Reader's Edition*, (New York: WW Norton, 2009), 162-63.

10. DREAM WORK: FRENCH-KISSING YOUR DEMON

1. Edinger, Edward, *The Mysterium Lectures: A Journey through C.G. Jung's "Mysterium Coniunctionis,"* (Toronto, Canada: Inner City Books, 1995), 69.
2. Jung, *The Red Book, Liber Novus*, (New York: W.W. Norton, 2009).
3. Ibid.. 162
4. Jung, *Collected Works* Vol 8, 289-90.
5. Pandolfo, Stephania, *Knot of the Soul: Madness, Psychoanalysis, Islam*, (Chicago: University of Chicago Press, 2018), 178.
6. Von Franz, *Dreams and Death*, xv

11. ALLY WORK: THE SOULMATE YOU CAN'T SEE

1. Jung, C.G., editor, *Man and His Symbols*, (New York: Dell Books, 1968), 49.
2. Ibid., 49.
3. *The Letters of Pelagius: Celtic Soul Friend*, editor Robert Van de Weyer, (Worcestershire, Great Britain: Little Giddings Books: 1995), 91.
4. *Hilma af Klint: Visionary*, Kurt Almqvist and Louise Belfrage, editors. (Stockholm, Sweden: Bokforlaget Stolpe, 2020), 37. Her great grandfather, Erik af Klint was knighted for beginning the work on the *Sweden Lake Atlas*, which his son Gustaf would later finish. The prefix 'af' signifies that the Klints belonged to nobility.
5. af Klint, *Notes and Methods, Notes and Methods*, (New York: Christine Bergin and the University of Chicago Press, 2018), 270.
6. af Klint, *Visionary*, 34.
7. Rowland, Susan, *Jungian Literary Criticism: The Essential Guide,* (London: Routledge,
     2019), 49.
8. Ryle, Jadranka, "Reinventing the Yggdrasil: Hilma af Klint and Political Aesthetics," *Information: Nordic Journal of Art and Research*, Volume 7, No 1 (2018), 246.
9. af Klint, *Visionary*, 34.
10. af Klint, *Notes and Methods*, 14.
11. Ibid., 217.
12. af Klint, *Visionary*, 34.
13. Carter, Mary Beth, "Crystalizing the Universe in Geometrical Figures: Diagrammatic Abstraction in the Creative Works of Hilma af Klint and C.G. Jung," *Jung Journal*, Summer 2020, Volume 14, Number 3, 147-167.

14. www.lifeformart.com, Lifeforms Gallery and Art Center, Hudson, NY. Quoted from an unidentified journal, November 4, 1906.
15. af Klint, *Visionary*, 42.
16. Ibid., 36.
17. Carter, "Crystalizing the Universe," 155.
18. Ryle, Jadranka, "Feminine Androgyny and Diagrammatic Abstraction: Science, Myth, and Gender in Hilma af Klint's Paintings, *The Idea of North: Myth Making and Identities*, The Birch and Star, Helsinki, 2019, www.birchand star.org. 70-87
19. Carter, "Crystalizing the Universe," 155.
20. Ibid., 155.
21. Ibid., 155.
22. af Klint, *Visionary*, 82.
23. Carter, "Crystalizing the Universe," 158-160.
24. Ibid., 165-66.
25. af Klint, *Notes and Methods*, 238.
26. Ryle, "Feminine," 88.
27. af Klint, *Visionary*, 37.
28. af Klint, *Notes and Methods*, 150.
29. From the 2020 Documentary film, "Beyond the Visible: Hilma af Klint," written and directed by Halina Dyrschka
30. af Klint, *Notes and Methods*, 264.
31. Ibid., 19-20.
32. Ryle, "Reinventing the Yggdrasil," 19
33. Ibid., 2-3.
34. af Klint, *Notes and Methods*, 270
35. Ryle, "Feminine," 71.

12. RITUAL WORK: NOW I MUST BURY MY LOVER

1. Mara Branscombe, "A Ritual-Full Life", *Spirituality and Health*, July/August 2022.
2. Cited by Yuval Noah Harari, *Sapiens: A Brief History of Humankind*, (New York: Harper Perennial, 2015), 245.
3. Alethia Luna, https://lonerwolf.com
4. Erin Bruce, https://www.theseasonalsoul.com
5. Erin Bruce, https://www.theseasonalsoul.com
6. https://www.aaanativearts.com/the-mother-blessingway-ceremony
7. Elisa Kirkpatrick, "The Blessing Way: A Complete Guide to Honoring the Mother," birthhour.com, Melissa Mapees, "Mother Blessing Ceremonies for the Birth Journey," behervillage.com, Ashleigh Hanson, "Baby Blessings," by Ashleigh, https://blessingsbyashleigh.weebly.com/expectant-mother-blessing.html.
8. "How Rituals Rewire Your Brain," *Spirituality and Health*, July/August 2022.

13. YOUR PERSONAL NARRATIVE: WRITING AS MAGIC

1. *Crumpled Paper Boat: Experiments in Ethnographic Writing,* Anand Pandian and Stuart McLean, editors, (Durham: Duke University Press, 2017) "Ta'bir: Ethnography of the Imaginal," Stephania Pandolfo, 94-115.
2. Dick, Philip K. *The Exegesis of Philip K. Dick,* (Boston: Houghton Mifflin Harcourt, 2011).
3. This term is borrowed from Gaymon Bennett, professor of Religion, Science, and Technology at Arizona State University and creator of the project "Craftwork as Soulwork: Sanctifying Science among Genetics Researchers" and recipient of a Templeton Foundation grant for the same project.
4. *Meditations on the Tarot: A Journey into Christian Hermeticism,* author is anonymous, (New York: Penguin Putnam, 1985).
5. Davis, Erik, *High Weirdness: Drugs, Esoterica, and Visionary Experience in the Seventies,* (Cambridge: MIT Press, 2019).
6. Nelson, Maggie, *The Argonauts,* (Minneapolis: Greywolf Press, 2015).
7. Jung, C.G., *Mysterium Coniunctionis: An Inquiry into the Separation and Synthesis of Psychic Opposites in Alchemy,* (Princeton: Princeton Press, 1963), 546.

ABOUT THE AUTHORS

CATHERINE STAFFORD, EdD, is a seeker of Sophia Wisdom and a pilgrim of compassionate presence. Her journey has included being an educator for thirty-eight years as an elementary teacher, college professor, and finally a public-school superintendent. In 2012, she stepped off the public-school trail onto a new path, which lead her into the forests, fields, waterways, and sometimes deserts of interfaith spiritual exploration and companioning. All along these trails and paths wisdom listening has been her practice.

GIL STAFFORD, PhD, DMin, Episcopal priest and former Canon Theologian for the Episcopal Diocese of Arizona Stafford was the President of Grand Canyon University, previously the university's baseball coach. He is the author of *Wisdom Walking: Pilgrimage as a Way of Life* and *When Leadership and Spiritual Direction Meet: Reflections and Stories for Congregational Life*. And *Meditations on Blue Jesus: Listening to the Disabled God*. Life is a pilgrimage and Stafford has taken many, including walking Ireland coast-to-coast.